Macroeconomics and Financial Crises

Macroeconomics and Financial Crises

BOUND TOGETHER BY INFORMATION DYNAMICS

GARY B. GORTON AND
GUILLERMO L. ORDOÑEZ

PRINCETON UNIVERSITY PRESS
PRINCETON & OXFORD

Published by Princeton University Press
41 William Street, Princeton, New Jersey 08540
99 Banbury Road, Oxford OX2 6JX

press.princeton.edu

Library of Congress Cataloging-in-Publication Data

Names: Gorton, Gary B., 1951– author. | Ordoñez, Guillermo L. (Guillermo Luis), 1975– author.
Title: Macroeconomics and financial crises : bound together by information dynamics / Gary B. Gorton and Guillermo L. Ordoñez.
Description: 1st Edition. | Princeton: Princeton University Press, [2023] | Includes bibliographical references and index.
Identifiers: LCCN 2022058216 (print) | LCCN 2022058217 (ebook) | ISBN 9780691227016 (hardback) | ISBN 9780691227023 (ebook)
Subjects: LCSH: Macroeconomics. | Finance, Public. | Financial crises. | BISAC: BUSINESS & ECONOMICS / Economics / Macroeconomics | BUSINESS & ECONOMICS / Public Finance
Classification: LCC HB172.5 .G676 2023 (print) | LCC HB172.5 (ebook) | DDC 332—dc23/eng/20221208
LC record available at https://lccn.loc.gov/2022058216
LC ebook record available at https://lccn.loc.gov/2022058217

British Library Cataloging-in-Publication Data is available

Editorial: Joe Jackson, Josh Drake, and Whitney Rauenhorst
Production Editorial: Nathan Carr
Jacket/Cover design: Wanda España
Production: Danielle Amatucci
Publicity: William Pagdatoon

This book has been composed in Arno and Sans

Printed on acid-free paper. ∞

Printed in the United States of America

10 9 8 7 6 5 4 3 2 1

For Lori, Nicole, and Danielle

For Kathy and Diego

It is scarcely a matter of surprise ... that every ... crisis occurring in this country is promptly followed by a literature ... discussing the phenomena of their supposed causes.... One feature these productions have in common: they deal with proximate causes only ... each crisis appearing to be the result of its own separate accident, — usually some event lying on the surface of commercial history. (Mills 1868)

CONTENTS

LIST OF FIGURES

LIST OF TABLES

PREFACE

We met at Yale in late 2009, becoming new colleagues at the end of the Panic of 2007–2008. At that time, it was clear that macroeconomics was in shock. No one had taken the possibility of a financial crisis seriously. Indeed, it was a common belief that that problem was "solved." Financial crises had simply been assumed away, or just modeled as "large negative shocks," so macro models did not bother including a financial sector or credit dynamics explicitly. And while post-crisis macroeconomists have worked to patch up their models, adding time-varying credit constraints for example, it seemed clear that macroeconomics needed a more involved and deeper renovation. Macro would have to be rebuilt brick by brick, starting with thinking seriously about the interactions of financial markets with the rest of the economy and defining exactly what financial crises are, what their recurrent properties are and how they relate to the rest of macroeconomic variables. This we set out to do. This book is based on work we did starting in the Spring of 2010.

The spirit of this book is to bring theoretical clarity on thinking about financial crises as an intrinsic component of macroeconomics. We do not articulate a complete macro model that could be calibrated yet, but we identify two critical elements that have to be included in that new paradigm: *information* and *credit*. These two elements have to be included in the standard macro toolbox if there is any hope of making financial crises an inherent macroeconomic phenomenon, as it is. From our point of view, this work must be done in the future. However, throughout the book we provide empirical evidence and tests to suggest that we are on the right track, and that both information and credit depend on and affect macroeconomic outcomes. We have found evidence both that information is a critical element in understanding financial changes and that credit booms and financial crises are intimately related, and shape, macroeconomic fluctuations.

Conversations with many others (too many to thank without being unfair to some) were instrumental for our work. We want to single out, however, Tri Vi Dang and Bengt Holmström, with whom we worked on related topics and discussed many of these ideas, for helping us think about these issues. Chapter 5 and material in Chapter 4 come from papers that we wrote jointly with Kyriakos Chousakos. We thank Kyriakos. We also thank our many PhD students during this decade-long effort, who were test subjects for many of the ideas in this book and who provided constant motivation and challenges. Finally, thanks to Diego Ordoñez for help with the cover art.

Some of the material we include appeared in academic journals. We thank the American Economic Association and the European Economic Association for permission to include content from articles published in their journals, though in different form and structure. This list includes:

INTRODUCTION

A financial crisis is a devastating event for people and for firms. Without swift action a financial crisis leads to a collapse of the financial system, dragging down the real economy. Firms fail. People lose their jobs and their homes. There is no bigger disruption in the functioning of economies. Indeed macroeconomics was motivated, and founded as a discipline, by the sudden, and puzzling, Great Depression. Keynes and his contemporaries put a lot of emphasis on the role of financial markets in explaining that damaging event. We saw this again in the Financial Crisis of 2007–2008, when macroeconomics, now a more mature discipline, was taken by surprise.

Even more surprising was that the recent financial crisis, as well as crises in other countries and other times, was rationalized as an unexpected unique event. But financial crises occur in all economies, over and over again, and will occur again in the future. It is important then that macroeconomics treat financial crises as an inherent and structural element in the functioning of market economies, incorporating them explicitly. In this book we ask questions that will lay the groundwork to do that. How can macroeconomic models accommodate financial crises? Financial crises are usually preceded by credit booms. Does the model need to explain credit booms? What is a "credit boom"? How do booms start? Do they always end in crises? How should the model relate booms and crises to technology and productivity? Are cycles exogenous or determined by the linkages between technology and finance? All these questions should be at the forefront of efforts to understand fluctuations in an economy.

Here we identify and expand on common elements that are present in all financial crises: *short-term debt, collateral, and information*. Short-term debt is a critical element needed for market economies to function. It is needed to store value over short periods of time without fear of loss, and as such it becomes important to sustain transactions. As documented by Gorton (2010), Gorton, Laarits, and Metrick (2020), Gorton and Metrick (2012), Covitz, Liang, and Suarez (2013), and Gorton, Laarits, and Metrick (2020), *short-term debt* was at the heart of the Great Depression and the Financial Crisis of 2007–2008. Short-term debt is, however, a promise and must be backed by collateral. The basic problem in a growing market economy is, however, a lack of good collateral, which, as discussed in Gorton, Lewellen, and Metrick (2010) and Krishnamurthy and Vissing-Jorgensen (2012), is not necessarily provided by the government (see Planck 1968).

To be more concrete, and using a painful recent example, the Panic of 2007–2008 was a bank run in the sale and repurchase market (the "repo" market; see Gorton and Metrick

2012 and Gorton, Laarits, and Metrick 2020). Repo is a form of short-term debt. Institutional investors lend to banks for short periods. Banks also lend to other banks for short periods, usually overnight. These loans are collateralized with bonds and other securities. A lender may lend, for example, $500 million overnight, and receive collateral in the form of bonds with a market value of $500 million. The loan might even be over-collateralized, so the lender might receive $550 million worth of bonds, for instance. Every morning trillions of dollars of repo loans are "rolled," that is, the lender agrees to lend for another twenty-four hours. This implies that trillions of dollars in collateral are needed.

If credit risk analysis was required for such a volume of collateral every time that short-term debt was renewed, the market would simply not be feasible. If the lender said that it would take a week to study the proposed collateral, overnight loans would not be possible. This is where information enters into the picture. The operation of this market is only possible when nobody is informed. Is it a mistake, or a miscalculation, that a trillion-dollar market operates every day with *opacity* and without due diligence? The answer is no. In fact, what happens is that the collateral is designed so that it pays no party to investigate the collateral, and all parties know this. So, this market is possible not only when nobody is informed but also when everybody knows that. In other words, it is beneficial that collateral is *information insensitive*. If the collateral is accepted without questions, then repo can work as a short-term store of value. The next morning the lender can receive the cash back if needed, no questions asked.

All short-term debt works this way: it is backed by collateral and sustained by opacity. Bank debt, such as demand deposits, is backed by portfolios of loans and the deposits are over-collateralized to the extent that the bank has equity. Other forms of privately produced short-term debt, such as private banknotes and asset-backed commercial paper, are also backed by portfolios of collateral. Similar to repo, if you need cash in the morning you go to an ATM and get money from your checking account. And just like the collateral that backs repo contracts, banks' portfolios are complex and opaque, that is, they are information insensitive. (See Dang et al. 2017.)

A *financial crisis* occurs when holders of short-term debt rationally come to suspect that the backing collateral is insufficient to protect that debt. This suspicion usually arises from a public signal that is interpreted to mean this. In that case the debt becomes *information sensitive*, which means that agents produce information about the backing collateral or suspect that other agents are secretly producing this information. Then agents run on the repo contracts, not renewing the loans, or run to the banks and demand to "see the cash." The switch from not producing information to producing information is an economy-wide event. Why? Because by the construction of opacity no agent knows which are the weak assets and they have to examine them all. But under what conditions is there a switch from an information-insensitive regime to an information-sensitive regime?

The well-oiled functioning of short-term debt markets sometimes leads to rapid credit growth. These *credit booms* tend to precede financial crises. As a credit boom advances there is an endogenous depreciation of information and an endogenous reduction of productivity and the return on financed investments. More and more firms and households get loans because their collateral appears to be good enough. When the quality of investments remaining is low enough, a crisis occurs when short-term debt turns information sensitive. The crisis comes from an endogenous increase in systemic risk, and it is a function of the length of the credit boom: the longer the preceding boom, the larger the crisis will be.

Our conception of a financial crisis is very different from the view that a crisis is a manifestation of multiple equilibria. Such theories do not explain how or why there is a switch from one equilibrium to another. This standard view is based on the idea that runs on short-term debt are coordination failures among depositors (due to an assumed sequential service constraint where depositors must line up to withdraw at the bank). What creates the coordination friction is that all depositors have rights to a portion of the portfolio but no right to a specific portion. In other words, each depositor has a claim on a common pool of assets. The weakness of this view was revealed in the recent financial crisis. Repo contracts do not face a common pool problem. Instead, each investor has a claim on a contractually specified amount of collateral that the lender gets possession of. The sunspot coordination failure view cannot explain the recent crisis.

Our informational view of crises can, however, accommodate both standard bank runs and the recent run on repo. If lenders have suspicions about the backing collateral, they will not roll over bank deposits or repo loans. Even though with repos short-term debt is not contractually backed by a portfolio pool, all collateral is "informationally pooled" as there is no information about which collateral is of good quality and which is not. When there is a run on banks or on repo, throughout the banking system, the economy is on the verge of a systemic collapse of the financial system. But even taking this into account the debt is still an optimal arrangement. When there is such a crisis, the central bank must act *to restore information insensitivity to the entire banking system.*

Financial crises occur in all market economies, those with and without central banks, with and without deposit insurance. All have common fundamental elements. And studying financial crises requires studying the forces that are bound up with crises. These forces include credit booms, technological change, and information dynamics. In particular, the amount of information in the economy varies depending on the state of the macroeconomy. It is not only the sudden shift of information-insensitive debt to information-sensitive debt, which is a volcanic eruption of information production. The stock market is always information sensitive, producing information about individual companies. We will see that information in the stock market can affect the behavior of lenders in the credit market. There will be a dynamic interaction between these two markets. As we will show, information from the stock market may be able to prevent a financial crisis from happening, but it may also choke up credit markets and growth.

One might reasonably ask why traditional macroeconomics did not include financial crises and credit booms prior to the Panic of 2007. In 1977 Lucas laid out the post-Keynesian macro research program, including the idea that business cycles are deviations from trend. The deviations were taken to be caused by "shocks." But this created a difficulty. Was the Great Depression a deviation from trend? A big "negative shock"?

The answer provided by Prescott (1983) was that the Great Depression could safely be excluded from thinking about aggregate dynamics. It seemed like an extraordinary event. The previous history of financial crises was deemed irrelevant because they were in the "past." Financial crises in emerging economies were deemed irrelevant because they happened in "immature" economies. In this book we bring back past crises and crises in all countries, and combine them with modern crises. We will see that they all have a common structure, namely short-term debt.

When compared to financial crises in the previous century, one problem in studying modern financial crises is the confusion that expectations about potential central bank or government actions create. Gorton (1988) claimed that without a central bank, there would have been panics starting in June 1920 and December 1929. There was no panic in 1920 because banks had availed themselves of the Federal Reserve discount window. But because of the introduction of stigma by the Fed, banks did not borrow from the discount window in 1929 and 1930. Depositors thought that the banks had gone to the window, but the banks knew that they had not. The banks "ran on themselves" by shrinking, cutting off credit, and ramping up U.S. Treasuries. The economy shrank, although the bank runs only came later when depositors saw large banks fail. (See Gorton, Laarits, and Muir 2020.) Indeed, the Great Depression was different from the earlier panics in the pre-Fed era. The mistake of not understanding the Great Depression meant that macroeconomics developed without considering the possibility of financial crises. This was then apparently confirmed when deposit insurance eliminated bank runs, reinforcing the theoretical view of runs as coordination failures. It also seemed to rule out the idea that other forms of short-term debt are also subject to runs. Indeed, deposit insurance did not, and could not, prevent bank runs on modern repos.

The Financial Crisis of 2007–2008 highlighted the need to broaden macroeconomics to include financial crises as one of the fundamental factors behind macroeconomic fluctuations. That is why we wrote this book.

Road Map

We start with data. Chapter 1 is devoted to laying out a set of stylized facts that a macro model must address when accommodating credit booms and financial crises. These are the facts that we will address with the subsequent models. This chapter highlights in particular macro facts associated with financial markets that have not been noticed or explored to date. First and foremost we discuss little-known regularities surrounding financial crises. They are not rare. Just looking at the U.S. post–World War II period, it would seem that financial crises are no longer a threat, or are a phenomenon of the past. This is inaccurate. While they do not necessarily happen at regular intervals, financial crises are an inherent feature of market economies, both developed and emerging.

After documenting how frequent and prevalent financial (and in particular banking) crises are, we study the relation between the movements of technology and productivity with credit booms. We show that booms tend to be triggered by positive technological improvements and can end suddenly and dramatically in a financial crisis if the productivity boost is not large enough or gets exhausted (a bad boom), but it may persist or end without a crisis when accompanied by productivity growth (a good boom).

Chapter 2 lays out a static benchmark model that demonstrates the importance of information about collateral on the credit that firms can raise through debt. We show that debt is designed to be *information insensitive*: the benefit of producing private information about a security's payoff outweighs the cost; otherwise, the security is information sensitive.

In the book (except for Chapter 6) we abstract from including financial intermediaries explicitly, and instead we have households lending directly to firms. The debt we have in mind is short-term debt like repurchase agreements ("repo") or other money market instruments. In these cases, the collateral is either a specific bond or a portfolio of bonds and loans. Here we have called the collateral "land," but realistically we have in mind a mortgage-backed security (MBS) or asset-backed security (ABS), both of which are hard to value. This type of security does not trade in centralized markets where prices are observable.

Chapter 3 takes the model of Chapter 2 and turns it into a dynamic model. We show how a rational credit boom can occur and, while the boom evolves, systemic risk—the risk and size of a financial crisis—builds up. The credit boom happens because agents do not find it optimal to produce information about the collateral backing loans. But as this happens, information in the economy depreciates, tossing more and more collateral into an "informational pool." In this chapter we discuss how a small negative shock in the average quality of collateral can induce information acquisition. The longer the boom, the more collateral there is in the informational pool and the larger the crisis. Take a mortgage-backed security, for example. Such securities are complicated and investors cannot value them. They rely on ratings. The model shows that even a small "shock" can trigger a crisis. But we also show that the social planner likes credit booms because output and consumption go up. But the social planner does not want the boom to go on as long as private agents do.

What we call a shock that triggers the "financial crisis" is the arrival of public information, making a financial crisis an *aggregate information event* that triggers the fear of *idiosyncratic information acquisition*. It is triggered by some public news that induces debt holders (depositors and/or lenders) to run on all or many banks and/or repo contracts demanding to convert their (short-term) debt claims into cash to such an extent that this demand for cash cannot be met. The run is rational. The debt holders have reason to suspect the collateral backing the debt (which could be a portfolio of loans or a single bond), and the information about it by the rest, and this suspicion results in runs on both good and bad collateral, as by construction nobody knows what is what.

This chapter highlights a key factor driving macroeconomic variables and financial crises in particular: the amount of information about collateral in the economy. It also highlights that a crisis is an informational event in which the system travels from an information-insensitive to an information-sensitive regime. But there is no multiple equilibrium. The crisis is a sudden burst of information production (or incentives to produce information). In the credit models we study here there is always symmetry, either symmetric information (everyone knows everything) or symmetric ignorance (no one knows anything). There is never asymmetric information and adverse selection. What drives moving from symmetric ignorance to symmetric information (a crisis), however, is the fear of adverse selection.

Chapter 4 adds technological change, both exogenous and endogenous, to the picture. We show that a credit boom starts with a positive technology shock. Booms can be good booms, which do not end in a crisis, or bad booms, which do end in a crisis, depending on the contemporaneous endogenous evolution of productivity in the economy. There are no "shocks" in the model of this chapter and still there can be financial crises. The dynamics are driven by technological change and happen at a lower frequency than what is usually studied. The difference between a good boom and a bad boom lies in the rate of growth of technological change. If the growth dies off rapidly during the boom, it will result in a bad boom. Otherwise, it will be a good boom. Importantly, crises are not the result of exogenous shocks, as in Chapter 3, but instead the result of an endogenous buildup of fragility due to an endogenous depreciation of information about collateral. The amounts of good and bad collateral are fixed, but the perceptions of which collateral is good and which bad evolve with total credit, changing productivity and consequently the incentives to examine the collateral that sustains credit.

Both Chapters 3 and 4, considered together, show that financial crises may be generated by negative contemporaneous shocks, but this is not necessary. The seeds of a financial crisis can also be planted many years before the actual event, and the crisis is just an endogenous reaction to the endogenous evolution of productivity. In this sense, economic fluctuations depend on the evolution of productivity, but such productivity has exogenous components (as in standard macroeconomic models) and endogenous components (as credit determines the marginal quality of projects that are financed). Different patterns of productivity growth affect the likelihood and size of credit booms and crises. The business cycle depends on the trend.

Chapter 5 adds a stock market to the model of Chapter 4. This is because credit markets are not the only market for which information (or lack thereof) is a critical input. There is another one that works completely differently: the stock market. In stock markets agents produce information about firms' values, which is then impounded in prices, improving the allocation of resources in the economy. While the nature of stock prices is to be information sensitive, credit markets, particularly collateralized credit markets, work better when information about collateral is *not* produced—when debt is information insensitive. But the incentives to learn about collateral are determined partly by what lenders learn about firms, and they tend to learn that from stock prices. On the flip side, the incentives to learn about firms are also determined partly by what lenders learn about collateral and the availability of credit.

Ignorance in credit markets is the opposite of information-revealing prices in stock markets. These two systems, one an information-sensitive system (the stock market), where the price responds, and the other an information-insensitive system (credit markets), where quantities respond, interact. And it is the dynamics of this interaction that is of primary importance for understanding the macroeconomy. Information in stock markets affects information in credit markets, hence booms and busts, and vice versa. The information in both markets depends, and shapes, other macroeconomic variables, such as productivity.

In the model of this chapter, information revealed in the stock market can identify firms with low productivity. Since they are more likely to default on their loans, lenders, having observed the stock price, may decide to investigate the collateral of these firms. If this happens to a sufficient extent, then lenders to the remaining firms do not find it optimal to produce information about their collateral. So, the stock market can act as an endogenous macroprudential mechanism in the sense that it slows down the depreciation of information about collateral, preventing financial crises. Information in stock markets, however, is not exogenous but also depends on the amount of credit in the economy, as credit affects productivity endogenously. This generates interesting dynamics depending on the technological state of the economy. The technological trend affects the information intensity in both stock and credit markets, and then the cyclical properties of economic activity.

In Chapter 6 we study central bank policy when a financial crisis is already happening. What should be done? What actions should a central bank take when such a crisis is informationally generated? In this chapter we explicitly introduce banks. When there is a bank run, the central bank wants to intervene, exchanging safe assets (government bonds) for private assets in their portfolio that are under suspicion and then under risk of examination (toxic assets). We show, importantly, that these programs should be conducted in secret, not revealing which banks have participated. What happens is this: A bank, knowing that it has a bad asset, can take it to the central bank and exchange it for a government bond. If this is kept secret, it creates an information externality by raising the average quality of assets in the whole banking system. Then, the program does not need to replace all assets under suspicion, which after a long credit boom is basically the assets of all banks. Increasing the expected quality of assets in the banking system mitigates the desire of depositors to examine all banks' assets, thereby avoiding a withdrawal of funds from those banks that are found to have less than average asset quality.

But if having government bonds in the portfolio is so effective to avoid runs, a bank that now has a government bond might want to reveal its participation in the program to depositors. If this were to happen, the information externality would be destroyed. What keeps a bank from doing this is "stigma." Stigma is the negative inference made about a bank's quality from its need to borrow from the government. Stigma then is the means that allows opacity to be maintained in the system, in clear opposition to the literature that considers opacity of the program as a means to prevent stigma.

Chapter 7 is not only the conclusion but also a road map for future endeavors in creating macroeconomic models that embrace financial markets and information dynamics as inherent elements of macroeconomic fluctuations. As we hope to make clear in this chapter, much more work is needed to connect these elements. This book is a first step.

Most proofs and empirical results are contained in the text, but some are reserved for the Appendix A.

1

Crises, Credit, and Macro Facts

1.1 Chapter Overview

In this chapter we provide some evidence about aspects of the macroeconomy and its relation to credit and financial crises that motivate the subsequent models. These are facts about credit and productivity that any macro model must take into account. Later, when contrasting the testable implications of our proposed models with data, we document how information measures interact with credit and productivity. The goal of this chapter is to highlight important properties of credit booms and busts, and their cyclical relation with macroeconomic variables (notably productivity), that should be incorporated in a macro model with credit that captures crises.

1.2 Financial Crises Are Not Rare

Financial crises occur in all market economies, in emerging market economies as well as in developed economies. Reinhart and Rogoff (2013) show that the incidence of crises is the same in high- and middle-income countries. They occur in economies with and without a central bank, with and without deposit insurance. Countries have had heterogeneous experiences with respect to financial crises. Some countries have crises more frequently than others. Some countries go for long periods with no crisis. Nevertheless, it is clear that financial crises plague all market economies. This point has been made by, for example, Kindleberger (1978, 1993), Reinhart and Rogoff (2009) and Cassis (2011)—crises occur over and over. Reinhart and Rogoff (2013, 4559), note that "for the advanced economies . . . the picture that emerges is one of serial banking crises." Countries do not seem to develop to a point where they do not experience financial crises anymore. Crises are not only common, prevalent, and recurrent, but they seem to be an inherent feature of market economies and an intrinsic shortcoming of financial markets and their benefits.

Laeven and Valencia (2012) count 151 systemic banking crises since 1970. They also report that 62 percent of the crises in their modern era sample had bank runs. Modern crises appear chaotic and their common element is not so clear. For this modern era, Laeven and Valencia define a financial crisis as an event where two conditions are satisfied:

- Significant signs of financial distress in the banking system (i.e., significant bank runs, losses in the banking system, and/or bank liquidations).
- Significant banking policy interventions in response to significant losses in the banking system. These interventions include deposit freezes, bank holidays, bank nationalizations, extensive liquidity support, and debt guarantees.

In the modern era, dating the start and end of a crisis is typically based on observing government actions. This makes it difficult to precisely date crises. (See Boyd, De Nicolo, and Loukoianova 2011.) The Federal Reserve was founded in 1914, so in the U.S. National Banking Era (1863–1914) financial crises occurred whenever agents received information that a leading indicator of recession had exceeded a threshold. This was the start of the crisis. (See Gorton 1988). Because there was no central bank during this period, we can get a clear picture of crises: a bank run was the start of the crisis. (See Gorton and Tallman 2018.)

The fundamental point that bank runs occur in all market economies has been obscured by modern crises that take place in the presence of a central bank. When a central bank exists agents expect it to act when there is the possibility of a run. Households in the economy wait. But the intervention by the central bank may be late, and the run may come later in the midst of chaotic events. The run may be latent or quiet—that is, deposits are withdrawn slowly but in significant amounts. There may be no run, often because of a blanket guarantee by the government, nationalization of banks, or bailouts. But, although crises may appear different, at root they are the same. That should be comforting because when economists see something occurring over and over again, it is sensible to suspect that there is a common explanation, a single root cause. This chapter aims to identify common elements that we can then incorporate into a comprehensive model that accommodates common movements of macroeconomic variables around financial crises.

Notice the implications of this. Explanations that rely on governmental behavior, such as the moral hazard risk of "too-big-to-fail," are inconsistent with the idea that crises are bank runs on short-term debt. Even without a central bank, in the United States large banks bailed out other large banks (see Gorton and Tallman 2018). Historically, the backing for the short-term debt has been a variety of types of long-term debt. This is not always about mortgages either. During the U.S. National Banking Era, banks were not allowed to hold mortgages, and yet there were systemic bank runs.

The dates that researchers choose to identify as the onset of modern crises are based on observed public events, such as the failure of one or more large banks, the announcement of a blanket guarantee of bank debt, bank nationalization, or a bailout. But such announcements respond to some underlying events, which outside observers do not see. Boyd and colleagues (2011) studied the four leading crisis classification schemes and the dating of modern crisis events from 1970 to 2017. They show that extreme drops in loans can predict the start dates of modern crises and that the true start date is prior to the date listed in crisis databases. In other words, the crisis had already begun and banks knew it, so they cut lending. Depositors appear to wait to see what the government will do, but banks are proactive and reduce lending. Gorton, Laarits, and Muir (2020) show that this logic explains the curious first year of the U.S. Great Depression.

Financial crises are an intrinsic part of macroeconomic movements. Crises do not happen at random times but typically occur following credit booms and near the peak of the business cycle. Gorton (1988) studied the U.S. National Banking Era, a period during which banking panics regularly occurred, and shows that the arrival of news forecasting a recession resulted in a panic when the news variable exceeded a threshold. The news arrived near business cycle peaks. Dimsdale and Hotson (2014) summarize the U.K. experience since 1825: "The general pattern is one in which financial crises occur close to business cycle peaks, and are followed by a downturn in the wider economy" (2014, 26).

Historically recessions and depressions have been largely coincident with financial crises. But this apparent link appears to have been broken by expectations of central bank and government action. In fact, the link has not been broken, but the timing has changed.

1.3   Credit Booms Are Not Rare Either

A "credit boom" is a period of sustained growth in credit relative to GDP. Financial crises are usually preceded by a credit boom. But not all credit booms end in a financial crisis. Why do some booms end in a crisis while others do not? We address this question later. Below we first define and identify "credit booms" in the data and then analyze the aggregate-level relations between credit, total factor productivity (TFP) and labor productivity (LP) growth, and the occurrence of financial crises. To do this we follow the empirical strategy in Gorton and Ordoñez 2020b.

1.3.1   Data

To empirically focus on financial crises requires facing a trade-off between breadth of countries and length of the time series, as developed countries have better data and longer time series but fewer events of financial crisis. We study a cross section that includes emerging countries at some cost of time series length, as do Gourinchas, Valdes, and Landerretche (2001), Mendoza and Terrones (2008), and Herrera, Ordoñez, and Trebesch (2020). More specifically, we analyze a sample of 34 countries (17 advanced countries and 17 emerging markets) over a fifty-year time span, 1960–2010. A list of these countries is in Table B.1 in Appendix B. Schularick and Taylor (2012) study 14 developed countries over the period 1870–2008, almost 140 years, which is the other alternative.

For credit we use domestic credit to the private sector over GDP, from the World Bank Macro Dataset.[1] This variable is defined as loans, purchases of non-equity securities, trade credit, and other account receivables that establish a claim for repayment. Gourinchas and colleagues (2001) and Mendoza and Terrones (2008) measure credit as claims on the non-banking private sector from banking institutions. We choose domestic credit to the private sector because of its breadth—it includes not only bank credit but also corporate bonds and trade credit. Details about the definition of the variables and about the data sources are provided in Table B.2 in Appendix B.

For total factor productivity, we obtain measured aggregate TFP constructed by Mendoza and Terrones (2008) through Solow residuals. Mendoza and Terrones back out the capital stock from investment flows using the perpetual inventory method and use hours-adjusted employment as the labor measure. For labor productivity we use the hours-adjusted output-labor ratio from the Total Economy Database (TED).

1.3.2 Definition and Classification of Credit Booms

There is now a rich body of evidence showing that credit *growth* predicts crises, where credit growth is typically defined as the previous three years or five years of cumulative growth.[2] But, with regard to credit *booms*, there is no consensus in the literature as to what constitutes a "credit boom."

What is a credit boom? There are only a few publications that venture to put forth a definition to capture it empirically. Examples include Gourinchas, Valdes, and Landerretche 2001, Dell'Ariccia et al. 2016, Mendoza and Terrones 2008 and Richter, Schularick, and Wachtel 2021. These authors are interested in the relationship between credit booms and crises. Gourinchas and colleagues "define a lending boom episode as a deviation of the ratio between nominal private credit and nominal GDP from a rolling, backward-looking, country-specific stochastic trend" (2001, 52). They require that the deviation be larger than a given threshold. Gourinchas and colleagues use a definition close to that of Gourinchas and colleagues (2001) but use a backward-looking country-specific cubic trend. Mendoza and Terrones (2008) use real credit per capita and detrend with the Hodrick-Prescott (HP) filter (see Hodrick and Prescott 1997). Richter and colleagues also use a version of the Hodrick-Prescott filter.

Does the definition matter? By construction different detrending procedures capture different phases of credit booms and then impose preconceptions on the evolution of related macro variables.[3] Dell'Ariccia et al. (2016) show that pairwise correlations across boom definitions are all above 50%, not too high.

We want to impose as few preconceptions as possible so we propose a definition of a "credit boom" that is very simple with regard to trends. We only detrend implicitly using the ratio of credit to the private sector divided by GDP. This means that credit has to grow faster than GDP to possibly be part of a credit boom. Such "detrending" is country-specific but we do not further detrend this ratio. We then define a credit boom as starting whenever a country experiences three consecutive years of positive credit growth (as a fraction of GDP) that average more than x^s. The boom ends whenever a country experiences at least two years of credit growth (also as a fraction of GDP) not higher than x^e. In our

Table 1.1. Financial Crises in the Sample

Number of crises occurring at the end of a boom	34
Number of crises occurring not at the end of a boom	8
Number of crises not associated with booms	5
Total number of crises in the sample	47

baseline experiments we choose $x^s = 5\%$ and $x^e = 0\%$. The choice of thresholds is based on the average credit growth in the sample. Changes in thresholds do not alter the results qualitatively. We find 87 booms based on this definition, which are listed in Table B.3 in Appendix B.

There are several reasons for our approach. First, we do not want to implicitly set an upper bound on the length of the boom by further detrending the ratio of credit to GDP. Using deviations from a trend implies that a boom has predetermined maximum length, as a protracted boom would be included in the trend component. We want to avoid this so the data inform us as to whether crises are associated with longer or shorter booms. Second, as Aguiar and Gopinath (2007) argue, shocks to the trend may be the source of cyclical behavior rather than transitory shocks around a trend. To allow for this possibility we do not want to detrend twice. Third, the data on credit exhibit very large heterogeneity across countries. Sometimes there are strong increases in credit that appear as structural breaks, sometimes credit grows slowly, while at other times there are large, sudden movements. We do not take a stand on which of these events are more relevant for studying "credit booms."

Once we have identified the credit booms, we can classify them as *bad* or *good* depending on whether they end with a financial crisis in the neighborhood of three years of the end of the boom, or not, respectively. Our results are not significantly altered, however, if for example we look for crises within two years of the end of the boom. In our sample there are 47 crises identified by Laeven and Valencia (2012). Table 1.1 shows that 34 of those crises happened at the end of one of the 87 booms we have identified (hence we have 34 bad booms in the sample). There were 8 crises that did not occur at the end of a boom (but occurred during a boom), and there were 5 crises that were not associated with any boom. So, there are good booms and bad booms, but also crises unrelated to the end of booms, or with no booms at all.

1.4   Properties of Good Booms and Bad Booms

In Table 1.2 we present summary statistics for a number of variables over different periods, which include total credit as a fraction of GDP, credit to households and to the corporate sector, TFP, patents, real GDP, investment, and labor productivity. Consistent with the technological change discussed in the Introduction, the average length of a boom is about eleven years.

The table also provides an overview of boom periods compared to non-boom periods and it compares booms that end with a crisis with booms that do not end in a crisis.[4] The

Table 1.2. Descriptive Statistics

	Whole Sample	Non-Booms	Booms	t-Stat for Means	Booms with a Crisis	Booms without a Crisis	t-Stat for Means
Avg. Credit growth (%)	3.83	−2.41	8.96	15.02	9.84	8.30	1.27
Avg. Total Cr'd growth (%)	8.09	1.59	13.43	14.34	13.95	13.03	0.70
Avg. H'd Cr'd growth (%)	6.07	3.93	7.55	1.07	6.71	8.47	−1.64
Avg. C't Cr'd growth (%)	1.76	−0.83	3.58	6.39	3.57	3.59	−0.04
Avg. TFP growth (%)	0.83	0.78	0.87	0.62	0.47	1.17	−3.57
Avg. Pt Gnt'd growth (%)	3.87	3.72	3.99	0.10	2.33	5.48	−0.90
Avg. rGDP growth (%)	2.56	2.29	2.78	3.08	2.40	3.07	−3.28
Avg. INV growth (%)	1.48	1.08	1.79	2.19	1.67	1.88	−0.49
Avg. LP growth (%)	2.52	2.45	2.57	0.72	2.06	2.96	−4.29
Avg. Duration (years)			10.68		11.76	9.98	0.93
Avg. Time spent in boom			27.32		11.76	15.56	
Number of booms			87		34	53	
Sample size (years)	1,695	766	929		400	529	

variable "Credit" is our main measure of credit (granted to the private sector as a fraction of GDP) from the World Bank Macro Dataset; "Total Cr'd" is the growth in total credit (the numerator on "Credit"). "H'd Cr'd" refers to credit to the household sector from the BIS data; "C't Cr'd" is credit granted to the corporate sector, also from BIS.[5]

Comparing boom periods to non-boom periods, what stands out is that all measures of credit (the first four rows) are significantly larger during booms. The average change in capital expenditures (the variable "INV growth") is significantly higher during booms compared to non-booms, consistent with investment booms coinciding with credit booms. Real GDP growth (rGDP) is also higher during booms as is credit both to the corporate sector and to households. Turning now to comparing good booms and bad booms, we see that the average growth in TFP and LP is significantly higher in good booms as compared to bad booms. Real GDP growth is also higher in good booms, but not investment nor credit.

Figure 1.1 shows the evolution of the average growth rates for TFP, LP, real GDP, and capital formation, around the initial stages of both good booms and bad booms. The figure shows that both types of credit booms start with a positive shock to productivity but then the paths of growth rates subsequently differ for good booms and bad booms. At the onset of credit booms (date 0 in the figure), TFP grows at 1.5% compared to an average of 1% in the previous three years for good booms and 1% versus an average of 0.2% for bad booms. For LP these differences are 3% versus an average of 2.05% for good booms and 1.7% versus an average of 1.6% for bad booms.

In bad booms, however, the productivity growth rates remain lower and die off faster than in good booms (as do the growth rates for real GDP and capital formation). Panel (b)

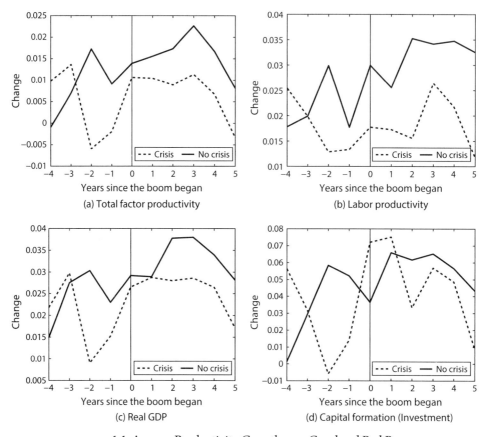

FIGURE 1.1. Average Productivity Growth over Good and Bad Booms

makes the point dramatically for labor productivity, which is measured with less error. In good booms LP growth is high and flat, while in bad booms it nosedives by the fourth year after the boom starts.

These figures are stylized so next we confirm more systematically that the different patterns between good booms and bad booms suggested in panels (a) and (b) of Figure 1.1 are statistically significant.

We ask whether the changes in TFP and LP predict the type of boom, good or bad, by running the following regression.

$$Pr(BadBoom_{j,t}|Boom_{j,t}) = F_L\left(\alpha + \beta \Delta X_{j,t}\right),\qquad(1.1)$$

where F_L is the cumulative logistic function, $F_L(z) = \frac{1}{1+e^{-z}}$, $BadBoom_{j,t}$ represents a boom in country j at period t that has been identified as bad, and $\Delta X = \{\Delta TFP, \Delta LP\}$ is the change in the respective measure of productivity in country j between periods $t-1$ and period t.

If the change in TFP, for example, is on average declining over the boom, then the coefficient on the prediction of bad booms should be negative, that is, a positive change in TFP

Table 1.3. Productivity Growth as an Indicator of Bad Booms

	TFP			Labor Productivity		
	LOGIT	LPM		LOGIT	LPM	
α	−0.23	0.44		−0.02	0.49	
t-Statistic	−3.39	26.91		−0.15	21.19	
β	−7.09	−1.70	−1.41	−9.86	−2.31	−3.02
t-Statistic	−3.72	−3.82	−4.29	−4.05	−4.18	−7.06
Marginal	−0.06	−0.06	−0.05	−0.08	−0.07	−0.10
R^2		0.01	0.48		0.02	0.49
N	929	929	929	761	761	761
FE	No	No	Yes	No	No	Yes

is making the boom less likely to be a bad boom.[6] We see exactly this pattern in Table 1.3, for both of our measures of productivity change.[7]

The marginal effect in the table shows the change in the probability of being in a bad boom given a change of one standard deviation in the relevant productivity growth variable. The first column of Table 1.3, for example, shows that, conditional on being in a boom, an increase of one standard deviation in TFP reduces the probability of being in a bad boom (a boom that will end in a crisis) by 6%.[8]

1.4.1   How Do Booms Start?

How do credit booms start? The data suggest that there is a positive technology shock that triggers the start of a credit boom. Panels (a) and (b) in Figure 1.1 are also suggestive as they show that the changes in TFP and LP for the five years prior to the start of the boom are positive. We investigate this further by asking whether changes in TFP and LP predict the start of a boom, by running the following regression.

$$Pr(Boom_{j,t}) = F_L\left(\alpha + \beta \Delta X_{j,t}\right), \tag{1.2}$$

where F_L is the cumulative logistic function, $F_L(z) = \frac{1}{1+e^{-z}}$, $Boom_{j,t}$ is an indicator variable for the year of the start of a boom in country j at period t, and $\Delta X = \{\Delta TFP, \Delta LP\}$ is the change in the respective measure of productivity in country j at period t. Table 1.4 shows that lagged changes of TFP are significant predictors of the start of a credit boom, on total credit but not on credit to households. This is not the case for labor productivity.[9]

That positive productivity shock occurs at the start of a boom has been noted by economic historians and growth economists. Indeed, in the long term, technology such as the steam locomotive, telegraph, electricity, or IT has played a central role in understanding growth (see Kendrick 1961; Abramovitz 1956; Gordon 2010; and Shackleton 2013).

Table 1.4. An Increase in TFP Predicts Credit Booms

	TFP		LP	
	Credit	HHCredit	Credit	HHCredit
α	−2.97	−2.99	−3.00	−2.86
t-Statistic	−25.24	−18.31	−14.90	−12.37
β	5.27	2.50	11.81	−1.51
t-Statistic	1.75	0.67	1.80	−0.22
Marginal	0.01	0.01	0.02	−0.00
N	1,695	1,367	610	610

Field, studying the period 1890–2004 in the United States, argues that TFP growth rates are "consistent with a view that the arrival of economically important innovations may be quite discontinuous and cluster in particular epochs" (2010, 329).

1.4.2   The Effect of Productivity Growth on Crises

Now that we have characterized what happens at the onset of and during these two types of booms, we turn to examining directly the effects of TFP and LP growth on the likelihood of a financial crisis. Studies such as Jorda, Schularick, and Taylor 2011 have converged on the growth in credit as the key predictor of financial crises. We first verify that this is also true in our sample by examining how lagged measures of credit growth predict financial crises with a Logit model

$$Pr(Crisis_{j,t}) = F_L\left(\alpha + \beta \Delta Cred_{j,t-1}\right),$$

where $Pr(Crisis_{j,t})$ is the probability of a crisis at period t in country j.

We follow the literature and examine two measures of lagged credit growth, the change in credit over the previous five years (5Ychange) and the lagged five-year moving average of credit growth (5YchangeMA). The results, with and without country fixed effects, are shown in Table 1.5. Consistent with previous literature, the table shows that both measures of credit growth are significant predictors of the likelihood of a financial crisis and that country fixed effects are not a critical determinant in this relation. The marginal effect in the table shows the change in the probability of a crisis given a change of one standard deviation in the credit. The first column, for example, shows that an increase of one standard deviation in the volume of lagged credit increases the probability of a crisis by 1%. This is an economically significant effect as well when considering that the unconditional probability of a crisis in the sample is 2.7% (46 crises in a sample of 34 countries over 50 years).

We now turn to asking whether changes in TFP and LP during the boom, measured by the lagged five-year change and the lagged five-year moving average, reduce the likelihood

Table 1.5. Credit as Crisis Predictor

	5Ychange			5YchangeMA		
	LOGIT	LPM		LOGIT	LPM	
α	−4.05	0.01		−3.93	0.02	
t-Statistic	−20.11	3.59		−19.28	3.78	
β	0.78	0.03	0.04	0.89	0.04	0.04
t-Statistic	4.04	4.48	4.63	3.25	3.42	3.59
Marginal	0.01	0.02	0.02	0.01	0.01	0.02
R^2		0.01	0.02		0.01	0.02
N	1,525	1,525	1,525	1,389	1,389	1,389
FE	No	No	Yes	No	No	Yes

of the boom ending in a financial crisis, as suggested by Figure 1.1.

$$Pr(Crisis_{j,t}) = F_L \left(\alpha + \beta \Delta Cred_{j,t-1} + \gamma \Delta X_{j,t-1} \right),$$

where $\Delta X = \{\Delta TFP, \Delta LP\}$. The results are shown in Table 1.6. Growth in TFP and LP both mitigate the likelihood of a crisis, while credit growth remains statistically important. To put this result in context, even though an increase of one standard deviation in credit over GDP increases the probability of a crisis by roughly 1%, if this increase is accompanied by a contemporaneous increase of one standard deviation in productivity the probability of a crisis also declines by roughly 1%, making the increase in credit relatively innocuous.

1.4.3   Types of Credit Granted during a Boom

What type of credit is being granted during a credit boom? Some have argued that housing credit, in particular mortgages, is the important component of credit booms that end in crises. (See, e.g., Leamer 2007; Schularick and Taylor 2012; Jorda, Schularick, and Taylor 2014, 2015; Mian and Sufi 2014; Mian, Sufi, and Verner 2016.) We saw in Table 1.2 that investment booms (capital formation) tend to accompany credit booms so it seems that more is going on than just mortgage lending. Gourinchas and colleagues (2001), for example, also point out that lending booms are associated with domestic investment booms. In this section we explore this further.[10]

The Bank for International Settlements (BIS) "Total Credit Statistics" provides data on credit to households and credit to corporations. This panel data is not as complete as our series "credit to the private sector" from the World Bank. In fact, it is quite sparse. Of our 34 countries only 23 have observations in this data set. Only one of the countries has data starting in 1960 only four have data that starts prior to 1970; and only eight countries have data starting prior to 1980. Table B.4 in Appendix B shows the coverage of the data sets.

Table 1.6. Credit and Productivity Growth as Crises Predictors

	TFP			Labor Productivity		
	LOGIT	LPM		LOGIT	LPM	
α	−3.93	0.02		−3.68	0.03	
t-Statistic	−21.51	5.58		−17.80	5.29	
β	1.11	0.05	0.05	1.02	0.05	0.05
t-Statistic	2.19	2.43	2.49	1.93	2.18	2.23
Marginal	0.00	0.01	0.01	0.00	0.01	0.01
γ	−9.27	−0.22	−0.23	−11.74	−0.29	−0.34
t-Statistic	−2.42	−2.43	−2.51	−2.46	−2.48	−2.71
Marginal	−0.01	−0.01	−0.01	−0.01	−0.01	−0.014
R^2		0.01	0.02		0.01	0.02
N	1,661	1,661	1,661	1,337	1,337	1,337
FE	No	No	Yes	No	No	Yes

Table 1.7. Correlation of Credit with Its Components (Levels and Changes)

	CorpCredit	HHCredit	Credit
CorpCredit	1.000		
HHCredit	0.596***	1.000	
Credit	0.712***	0.830***	1.000

	$\Delta CorpCredit$	$\Delta HHCredit$	$\Delta Credit$
$\Delta CorpCredit$	1.000		
$\Delta HHCredit$	0.018	1.000	
$\Delta Credit$	0.203***	0.063	1.000

$^{+}p < 0.10, {}^{*}p < 0.05, {}^{**}p < 0.01, {}^{***}p < 0.001$

Table 1.7 shows the correlations of the levels and changes. In the table "Credit" refers to credit to the private sector divided by GDP. Credit to the household sector (HHCredit) has a significant correlation of 0.83 with Credit and credit to corporations (CorpCredit) has a correlation of 0.71 with Credit (not surprisingly then the credit to households and corporations are also positively and significantly correlated). In other words, countries with a large fraction of credit to GDP have this credit flowing to both households and corporations. The table also shows these correlations for changes in credit. Even though all correlations are positive, the only statistically significant case is the correlation between Credit and CorpCredit, suggesting that it is the credit to corporations that commoves more strongly with total credit.

Table 1.8. Credit to Households and Corporations

	Household	Corporate	t-Statistic for Means
Credit - Good Booms	38.780	64.760	−9.44
Credit Change - Good Booms	0.085	0.036	4.38
Credit - Bad Booms	60.803	88.980	−8.99
Credit Change - Bad Booms	0.067	0.036	4.48

Table 1.9. Descriptive Statistics Using Credit to Households

	Whole Sample	Non-Booms	Booms	t-Stat for Means	Booms with a Crisis	Booms without a Crisis	t-Stat for Means
Avg. H'd Cr'd growth (%)	6.07	3.13	7.99	1.40	6.99	9.62	−2.30
Avg. TFP growth (%)	0.53	0.29	0.69	1.82	0.41	1.15	−2.65
Avg. Pt Gnt'd growth (%)	−0.81	−2.14	−0.00	0.72	2.76	−4.84	1.72
Avg. rGDP growth (%)	2.28	1.83	2.58	3.16	2.23	3.16	−2.91
Avg. INV growth (%)	1.87	1.60	2.04	0.89	1.92	2.24	−0.47
Avg. LP growth (%)	2.13	2.07	2.17	0.47	1.95	2.54	−2.09
Avg. Duration (years)			11.53		13.41	9.40	1.61
Avg. Time spent in boom			18.45		11.40	7.05	
Number of booms			32		17	15	
Sample size (years)	610	241	369		228	141	

Looking just at the two BIS series, Table 1.8 shows the mean difference between the amount of credit granted to households and credit granted (as a percent of GDP) to corporations during good and bad booms as well as the differences in changes in credit over the two types of booms. While credit to corporations is always greater in levels than credit to households, in both types of booms, the increase in credit to households is larger than the increase in credit to corporations in both types of booms. This is consistent with investment booms occurring during both types of booms, as households have more access to credit to consume and corporations have more access to credit to invest and produce to cover the larger demand.

To get at this further, and to focus on credit to households, in Table 1.9 we repeat the analysis of the previous section using only HHCredit, in which case we get 32 booms, 17 of which ended in a crisis, compared to 87 booms in the full data set using total credit, of which 34 ended in a crisis. Of the 32 booms based on credit to households, 28 begin within two years of the start of the booms defined previously.

During a credit boom, credit to households is highly correlated with other types of credit. Household credit does not seem to be divorced from the positive technology shock that starts the credit boom. Instead, household credit seems to be part of the overall phenomenon, which responds to the technology shock and results in an investment boom. For our purposes it is not necessary, however, to take a strong stand on the possible separate role of household credit.

1.5   Summary

We have shown that credit booms and financial crises are common events in the economy. Credit booms are a decade long on average, so the average country spends half its time in a boom, hence happening at a lower frequency than macroeconomics usually studies. Financial crises are large, systemic, and common events.

Credit booms and financial crises are related, but that relation is qualified by underlying macroeconomic variables, most notably productivity. Credit booms start with a positive technology shock. If the technological growth is not sustained, the boom ends in a financial crisis.

These regularities call for a model that connects credit booms and financial crises first, and then qualifies such relation with the evolution of productivity. In the next chapter we will maintain productivity fixed and explore the connection between credit booms and financial crises in a single period. We will propose an informational linkage, which not only provides a rationale for the connection between credit booms and financial crises but also is consistent with a property that has been well-documented and is common for macroeconomic variables. Cycles are asymmetric: credit booms are slow while financial crises are sudden and large. Later, we will show that several information measures behave consistently with the proposed model.

2

Collateral and Information

2.1 Chapter Overview

In this chapter we lay out a model of collateralized credit relations between a lender (a household) and a borrower (a firm) in *a single period* and study the *informational implications* for the collateral. As this is a single period, our goal is not to connect credit booms and financial crises yet, which is inherently a dynamic connection. Instead, our goal is to highlight the informational property of debt relations. We start by studying a single credit relation and then show how to aggregate into total credit and output when there is a continuum of lenders and borrowers with heterogeneous collateral.

Our focus is on identifying the incentives that a lender has to privately examine the collateral that backs a loan. Based on these incentives, we can identify the conditions under which a loan is information sensitive (the collateral is examined) or information insensitive (the collateral is not examined). This analysis constitutes a building block that we embed into a dynamic setting in the next chapter, showing that information production or not is behind both the increase of credit and its demise.

In this chapter we also use these insights to discuss how borrowers would like to structure collateral in a security to reduce the likelihood of examination of collateral and in the process increase the credit that can be obtained in the market. This design of a security involves pooling collateral of different expected quality, tranching a unit of collateral into different layers to manage the expected quality of the pool, and engineering the structure to be more complex so as to discourage information acquisition and examination.

2.2 A Collateralized Credit Market

Here we start to lay out the basic forces that affect information in credit markets in a single-period setting. As credit booms are intrinsically a dynamic concept, in the next chapter the setting is extended to many periods to discuss how collateral gets transferred across periods and how their quality and perception about quality evolve dynamically.

2.2.1   Setting

Agents, Goods, and Preferences.   There are two types of agents in the economy, each with mass 1—firms and households—and two types of goods—*numeraire* and *"land."* Agents are risk neutral and derive utility from consuming numeraire at the end of the period. While numeraire is productive and reproducible—it can be used to produce more numeraire—land is not. Since numeraire is also used as *"capital"* we denote it by K.

Technology.   Only firms have access to an inelastic fixed supply of non-transferable managerial skills, which we denote by L^*. These skills can be combined with numeraire in a stochastic Leontief technology to produce more numeraire, K'.

$$K' = \begin{cases} A \, min\{K, L^*\} & \text{with prob. } q \\ 0 & \text{with prob. } (1-q). \end{cases} \quad (2.1)$$

We assume production is efficient, $qA > 1$. Then, the optimal scale of numeraire in production is simply $K^* = L^*$. The assumption of a Leontief technology is useful to characterize very cleanly the optimal scale of production, but the important element is that there is an optimal scale of production. While assuming that the production function is stochastic is critical to talk about credit frictions, the binary representation of success and failure with no output is just useful to simplify the notation, as we will highlight when solving the optimal credit contract.

Credit and Benchmarks.   Households and firms differ not only in their managerial skills but also in their initial endowments of numeraire. Only households are born with an endowment of numeraire $\bar{K} > K^*$, enough to sustain optimal production in the economy. This assumption implies that resources are in the wrong hands. Only households have numeraire while firms only have managerial skills, but production requires that both inputs be in the same hands. The extreme that firms do not have any numeraire (or no net worth in the standard language of financial frictions) is just a normalization, as the important constraint is that firms have less numeraire than needed to operate at optimal scale. They need external financing.

We can now define two extreme benchmarks, one in which there are no frictions in credit markets and the other in which frictions prevent any credit from being granted. Since production is efficient, if output were observable and verifiable in a court of law, then it would be possible for firms to borrow the optimal amount of numeraire K^* by issuing state-contingent claims. This complete contract (without strategic default) would specify that the firm can promise to pay K^*/q if the project succeeds (which is feasible because $AK^* > K^*/q$ by definition of positive NPV project) and nothing in case of default, and make the households indifferent between lending or not. In this benchmark efficient projects are always financed at optimal scale. An advantage of our simple set of assumptions is to characterize very transparently the unconstrained (no financial frictions) first best: all firms produce at scale K^*.

The other polar extreme is also very easy to characterize. Assume numeraire is not verifiable in court. This implies a very extreme form of financial friction, as now default is also strategic. Indeed the firms would never repay as they would always claim that the project failed. Foreseeing this reaction, households would never lend. In this other extreme the output is also very transparent: no firm would produce at all.

Most literature has departed from the first benchmark by assuming some sort of financial friction (low contract enforcement, lack of output verifiability, moral hazard that affects q, monitoring, costly state verification, etc.). Similarly, the second benchmark tends not to be so extreme, and the literature has studied how financial intermediation and optimal contracting can improve credit allocation in the presence of those frictions. In what follows we will explore a particular solution: the use of collateral, and a particular potential constraint to its use: costly information acquisition about the quality of collateral.

Relation with Literature on Inefficient Credit Booms.   Our assumption that all projects have positive net present value (and that the opportunity cost of funds is fixed) implies that all credit is beneficial in our setting. This is why the first best is characterized by the financing of all firms in the economy, which not only clarifies and simplifies the exposition but also allows us to isolate our efforts in studying the role of information in the buildup of credit booms, the generation of crises, and the speed of recoveries.

There is a rich literature on inefficient credit booms, in which there are externalities or excessive risk-taking behavior that leads to the financing of projects with negative net present value. Examples include Lorenzoni (2008), which opens the door to justify the implementation of macroprudential policies, such as Bianchi and Mendoza (2018). Even though we abstract from these forces in our setting, with the intention of focusing on the role of information dynamics on credit and macroeconomics, it is possible to introduce these frictions and create an interesting discussion of the role of information design to curb inefficiencies in the provision of credit in the economy.

2.2.2   Collateral

We have assumed that firms need numeraire but they do not have numeraire. We assume now, however, that they are endowed with land (one unit of land per firm). Even though land is non-productive (it does not enter into the production function), it potentially has an intrinsic value. If land is "*good*," it delivers $C > K^*$ units of numeraire at the end of the period. If land is "*bad*," it does not deliver any numeraire at the end of the period. We assume a fraction $\hat{p}$ of land is good. Firms can commit to transfer a fraction of land to households if they do not repay the promised numeraire, which relaxes the financial constraint imposed by the non-verifiability of output. Land will serve as collateral, and then will relax the financial friction and allow for credit. Its quality heterogeneity implies that not all land is useful in relaxing the friction, but the extent of this heterogeneity will depend on the amount of information about land that is endogenously produced in the economy.

To capture the role of heterogeneity and information we assume that at the beginning of the period, the unit of land of each firm i will have a given prior probability of being good. We denote these perceptions p_i. For now we assume these are exogenously given and when we extend the model to dynamics we will discuss how these perceptions depend on information accumulated about the unit of land in the past. We also assume that each p_i is common across all agents in the economy, that is there is no asymmetric information about land at the beginning of the period.

Even though all agents share the same perception about a given unit of land being good, we will endow the households with a technology to learn privately whether the unit of land is indeed good or not at a cost γ in terms of numeraire.[1] This is perhaps the main element in our research. Even though the starting point is common information, or lack thereof, about collateral, there is the possibility of asymmetric information sneaking into the credit market if the lender secretly exercises his option to acquire information. This information can be thought as acquiring a credible certificate. While acquiring the certificate is a private activity (nobody knows the lender has the certificate unless he decides to show it), its result is not contestable as it cannot be forged. While having the certificate or not is private information during the period, we assume its result becomes public at the end of the period, unless lenders decide to disclose it earlier. This implies that asymmetric information can potentially exist during the period but not at the end. This assumption will be relevant once we introduce dynamics as we avoid well-known complications from dispersed information and higher-order beliefs.

To fix ideas it is useful to think of an example. Assume oil is the intrinsic value of land. Land is good if it has oil underground, which can be exchanged for C units of numeraire at the end of the period. Land is bad if it does not have any oil underground. Oil is non-observable at first sight, but there is a common perception about the probability each unit of land has oil underground. It is possible to confirm this perception by drilling the land at a cost γ units of numeraire.

To talk about collateral and model it as land deserves some discussion. Of course, the use of land as collateral is not meant to be taken literally. For the model's purposes, we need to be as concrete as possible about the asset we discuss and its characteristics so the model is internally consistent. When mapped to reality we intend to capture the role of several assets that, with differing levels of complexity, serve as collateral and are heterogeneous in quality such that information can be acquired. Examples include mortgage and other asset-backed securities, houses in mortgages, cars in car loans, machinery in industry, and so forth.

The perception about the quality of collateral is critical in facilitating the granting of credit. Good land is able to sustain credit for the optimal scale of production. Bad land is not able to sustain any credit (which is just a normalization). But how much can a firm with a piece of land that is good with probability p borrow? Is information about the true value of land produced or not? We study these questions next: How useful is land as collateral and does it depends on the perception about its quality?

Relation with Literature on Collateral-Based Credit.   There is a large and rich literature in which credit to finance projects is based on collateral. A seminal study in this spirit is Kiyotaki and Moore (1997). In their work, as in most of the subsequent scholarship, firms buy capital to produce, using that same capital used in production to collateralize the loan. Then, the value of collateral is connected to the productivity of capital. This generates an interesting dynamic feedback, in which a negative productivity shock reduces both the gains from financing the project and the value of collateral.

In our setting we take a completely different route. We decouple collateral from production. We assume that land is useful as collateral but does not enter directly into production. This allows us to focus on the informational dimension of collateral and not on its relation with productivity. We focus on information about the value of collateral and not the determinants of the value of collateral.

Our approach is more natural when studying financial assets as collateral, as that collateral does not directly enter into the projects the loan is financing. A large fraction of collateral in the economy, particularly the collateral that suffered during the recent financial crisis, is of the type we highlight in this book.

While Kiyotaki and Moore (1997) study how collateral constraints magnify and extend business cycles generated by productivity shocks, they cannot capture the asymmetry of large and sudden crises that may follow long booms (not without resorting to large and sudden negative productivity shocks). Brunnermeier and Sannikov (2014) introduce nonlinearities in a continuous time version of Kiyotaki and Moore (1997). In contrast, our informational approach generates crises from a quite natural asymmetric evolution of information about collateral.

A more recent literature, such as Quadrini (2000) and Mendoza, Quadrini, and Ríos-Rull (2009), studies the effect of a direct shock to collateral constraints (an exogenous decline in the pledgeability of collateral, for instance) resulting in a dramatic reduction of credit (a crisis) and the recovery of the economy. Our approach endogenizes the sudden increase in collateral constraints during a crisis, once information about collateral is generated at large scale. In this sense, we do not resort to an exogenous shock to generate a crisis, and it is not a result of a decline in the value of collateral but of its perception.

Remark on the Absence of Banks.   In the model there are no explicit banks nor any financial collateral. These are simplifications. Financial intermediaries and financial collateral can be introduced at the cost of more model structure, but this is not necessary for our insights. Here's how to think about such an extended model. Assume firms need intermediaries (banks) to borrow from households and that debt must be collateralized because households cannot verifiably monitor the bank. The household only knows what firm the bank has loaned to, but the household cannot see the firm's output realization. The bank can verifiably monitor the firm, determining the output, which is the bank's monitoring function. The bank takes the money deposited by households and lends it to the firm. This is essentially what we have modeled.

In this extension there is an intermediary and the debt could be a repurchase agreement ("repo") or other money market instruments and the collateral, which we have called "land," could be either a specific bond, a portfolio of bonds and loans, or a mortgage-backed security if the borrower were another household. Other than the specifics of these contracts, what is important is that, as "land," collateral does not trade in centralized markets where prices can reveal the information that has been produced.

2.2.3   Information and Credit

We start by studying the optimal collateralized debt for a single firm, considering the possibility that households may want to produce information about the land posted as collateral. Since we're interested in the characteristics of the contract, we will dispense from considerations about competition for loans. As such, we assume that each firm is randomly matched with a single household and the firm has the negotiation power in determining the loan conditions. In this section then we will talk about a firm with collateral of perceived probability of being good p and a household.

The firm understands that the lender has the option to learn about the collateral quality. Then, the firm can request a loan that is "conditional" on the presentation of "the certificate." We call debt that triggers information acquisition about the collateral *information-sensitive debt* and debt that does not, *information-insensitive debt*. Information-sensitive debt is costly because it raises the cost of borrowing to compensate for the monitoring cost γ. However, information-insensitive debt may also be costly because it may imply less borrowing to discourage the household from producing information in secret (and then face asymmetric information). This trade-off determines the information sensitiveness of the debt and, ultimately, the volume and dynamics of information in the economy.

2.2.3.1 INFORMATION-SENSITIVE DEBT.   Under this contract, the lender learns the true value of the borrower's land by paying an amount γ of numeraire, and loan terms are then conditional on the resulting information (the certificate's evaluation of the land's quality). Since by assumption lenders are risk neutral and break even,

$$p(qR_{IS} + (1-q)x_{IS}C - K) = \gamma, \qquad (2.2)$$

where K is the size of the loan, R_{IS} is the face value of the debt, and x_{IS} is the fraction of land posted by the firm as collateral.

The firm will pay the same in case of success or failure. If $R_{IS} > x_{IS}C$, the firm would always default, handing over the collateral rather than repaying the debt. In contrast, if $R_{IS} < x_{IS}C$ the firm would always obtain the numeraire C directly from the land at the end of the period and repay the lender R_{IS}. Information-sensitive debt is then risk free, which renders the results under risk neutrality to hold without loss of generality. This condition pins down the fraction of collateral that a firm posts as a function of p,

$$R_{IS} = x_{IS}C \qquad \Rightarrow \qquad x_{IS} = \frac{pK + \gamma}{pC} \le 1.$$

It is feasible for firms to borrow the optimal scale K^* only if $\frac{pK^* + \gamma}{pC} \le 1$, or if $p \ge \frac{\gamma}{C - K^*}$. If this is not the case, firms can only borrow $K = \frac{pC - \gamma}{p} < K^*$ when posting the whole unit of good land as collateral. Finally, it is not feasible to borrow with an information-sensitive debt if $pC < \gamma$.

What are the expected profits for the firm, net of the land value pC (i.e., the profit that the project generates), from information-sensitive debt? These are given by the expected output from the project minus the expected payment of the loan,

$$E(\pi \,|\, p, IS) = p(qAK - x_{IS}C),$$

and using x_{IS} from above,

$$E(\pi \,|\, p, IS) = pK^*(qA - 1) - \gamma. \tag{2.3}$$

Intuitively, with probability p collateral is good and sustains expected production of $K^*(qA - 1)$ of numeraire and with probability $(1 - p)$ collateral is bad and does not sustain any loan or production. However, the firm always has to compensate in expectation for the monitoring costs, γ.

Naturally, it is profitable for firms to borrow at the optimal scale when $E(\pi \,|\, p, IS) \ge 0$, or $p \ge \frac{\gamma}{K^*(qA-1)}$. Combining the profitability and feasibility conditions, if $\frac{\gamma}{K^*(qA-1)} > \frac{\gamma}{C-K^*}$ (or $qA < C/K^*$), whenever the firm wants to borrow, it is feasible to borrow the optimal scale K^* if the land is found to be good. Simply to minimize the kinks in the firm's profit function, we assume this condition holds

$$E(\pi \,|\, p, IS) = \begin{cases} pK^*(qA - 1) - \gamma & \text{if} \quad p \ge \frac{\gamma}{K^*(qA-1)} \\ 0 & \text{if} \quad p < \frac{\gamma}{K^*(qA-1)}. \end{cases} \tag{2.4}$$

2.2.3.2 INFORMATION-INSENSITIVE DEBT.   Another possibility is for firms to borrow under the presumption that no information about collateral would be produced. For this to be possible the contract should have specifications that do not induce the household to acquire information. Again, since by assumption lenders are risk neutral and break even:

$$qR_{II} + (1 - q)px_{II}C = K, \tag{2.5}$$

subject to debt being risk free, $R_{II} = x_{II}pC$ for the same reasons as above. Then

$$x_{II} = \frac{K}{pC} \leq 1.$$

For this contract to be information insensitive, borrowers should be confident that lenders do not have incentives to deviate, secretly checking the value of collateral and lending only if the collateral is good, pretending that they do not know the collateral value. Lenders do not want to deviate if the expected gains from acquiring information, evaluated at x_{II} and R_{II}, are less than its costs, γ. Formally,

$$p(qR_{II} + (1-q)x_{II}C - K) < \gamma \qquad \Rightarrow \qquad (1-p)(1-q)K < \gamma.$$

Intuitively, by acquiring information the lender only lends if the collateral is good, which happens with probability p. If there is default, which occurs with probability $(1-q)$, the lender can enjoy fraction $x_{II}C$ of the collateral that was effectively purchased at $K = px_{II}C$, making a net gain of $(1-p)x_{II}C = (1-p)\frac{K}{p}$.

It is clear from the previous condition that the firm can discourage information acquisition by reducing borrowing. If the condition does not bind when evaluated at $K = K^*$, there are no incentives for lenders to produce information. In contrast, if the condition binds, the firm will borrow as much as possible given the restriction of not triggering information acquisition:

$$K = \frac{\gamma}{(1-p)(1-q)}. \tag{2.6}$$

Even though the technology is linear, the constraint on borrowing has p in the denominator, which induces convexity in expected profits.

Information-insensitive borrowing is then characterized by the following debt size:

$$K(p|II) = \min\left\{K^*, \frac{\gamma}{(1-p)(1-q)}, pC\right\}. \tag{2.7}$$

That is, borrowing is constrained either technologically (there are no credit constraints but firms do not need to borrow more than K^*), informationally (there are credit constraints and firms cannot borrow more than $\frac{\gamma}{(1-p)(1-q)}$ without triggering information production), or by low collateral value (the unit of land is not worth more than pC).

Expected profits net of the land value pC for information-insensitive debt are:

$$E(\pi|p,II) = qAK - x_{II}pC,$$

and using x_{II}

$$E(\pi|p,II) = K(p|II)(qA - 1). \tag{2.8}$$

Considering the kinks explicitly, these profits are:

$$E(\pi \,|\, p, II)$$

$$= \begin{cases} K^*(qA - 1) & \text{if } K^* \le \frac{\gamma}{(1-p)(1-q)} & \text{(no credit constraint)} \\ \frac{\gamma}{(1-p)(1-q)}(qA - 1) & \text{if } K^* > \frac{\gamma}{(1-p)(1-q)} & \text{(credit constraint)} \\ pC(qA - 1) & \text{if } pC < \frac{\gamma}{(1-p)(1-q)} & \text{(low collateral value).} \end{cases}$$

The first kink is generated by the point at which the constraint to avoid information production is binding when evaluated at the optimal loan size K^*; this occurs when financial constraints start binding more than technological constraints. The second kink is generated by the constraint $x_{II} \le 1$, under which the firm is not constrained by the threat of information acquisition, but it is directly constrained by the low expected value of the collateral, pC.

2.2.3.3 INFORMATION-SENSITIVE DEBT OR INFORMATION-INSENSITIVE DEBT?   Depending on the belief p about its collateral, a firm compares equations (2.3) and (2.8) to choose between issuing information-insensitive debt (II) or information-sensitive debt (IS). The next proposition comes from this comparison.

Proposition 1 (Information (In)Sensitive Debt).   Firms borrow with a contract that induces information acquisition if

$$\frac{\gamma}{qA - 1} < pK^* - K(p|II), \tag{2.9}$$

and without inducing information acquisition otherwise.

Figure 2.1 shows the ex ante expected profits, net of the expected value of land, under the two information regimes, for each possible p.

The cutoffs highlighted in Figure 2.1 are determined in the following way:

1. The cutoff p^H is the belief that generates the first kink of information-insensitive profits, below which firms have to reduce borrowing to prevent information acquisition:

$$p^H = 1 - \frac{\gamma}{K^*(1 - q)}. \tag{2.10}$$

2. The cutoff p_{II}^L comes from the second kink of information-insensitive profits:[2]

$$p_{II}^L = \frac{1}{2} - \sqrt{\frac{1}{4} - \frac{\gamma}{C(1 - q)}}. \tag{2.11}$$

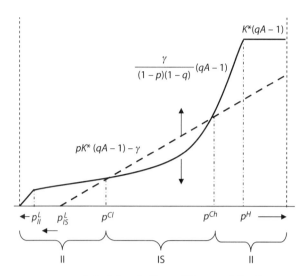

FIGURE 2.1. A Single-Period Expected Profits

3. The cutoff p_{IS}^{L} comes from the kink of information-sensitive profits:

$$p_{IS}^{L} = \frac{\gamma}{K^*(qA - 1)}. \tag{2.12}$$

4. Cutoffs p^{Ch} and p^{Cl} are obtained from equalizing the profit functions under information-sensitive and information-insensitive debt, and solving the quadratic equation:

$$\gamma = \left[pK^* - \frac{\gamma}{(1-p)(1-q)} \right] (qA - 1). \tag{2.13}$$

Information-insensitive loans are chosen for collateral with high and low beliefs p. Information-sensitive loans are chosen for collateral with intermediate values of p. The first regime generates symmetric ignorance about the value of collateral. The second regime generates symmetric information about the value of collateral.

Then, conditional on γ, borrowing for each possible belief p follows the schedule,

$$K(p) = \begin{cases} K^* & \text{if } p^H < p \\ \frac{\gamma}{(1-p)(1-q)} & \text{if } p^{Ch} < p < p^H \\ pK^* - \frac{\gamma}{(qA-1)} & \text{if } p^{Cl} < p < p^{Ch} \\ \frac{\gamma}{(1-p)(1-q)} & \text{if } p_{II}^{L} < p < p^{Cl} \\ pC & \text{if } p < p_{II}^{L}. \end{cases} \tag{2.14}$$

2.2.4   Information Costs and the Choice of Collateral

How do these regions depend on information costs? The five arrows in Figure 2.1 show how the cutoffs and functions move as we reduce γ. If information is free ($\gamma = 0$), all collateral is information sensitive (i.e., the IS region is $p \in [0, 1]$). As γ increases, the two cutoffs p^{Ch} and p^{Cl} converge and the IS region shrinks until it disappears when γ is large enough (i.e., the II region is $p \in [0, 1]$ when $\gamma > \frac{K^*}{C}(C - K^*)$).

Following these comparative statics, and examining Figure 2.1, one could ask what is the combination of p and γ that allows for the largest loans. In other words, if a firm could choose between land with a given probability of being good and a given cost of examination, which one would it choose?

Fixing the information costs γ, borrowing always increases in p, and then it is clear (and quite intuitive) that as long as collateral relaxes credit, it is always better to have land with a higher probability of being good, a higher p. Fixing p, however, borrowing does not depend on γ so monotonically. While credit decreases in γ in the information-sensitive region, it increases in γ in the information-insensitive region (unless credit is constrained by pC, in which case γ does not impact credit).

The result is intuitive: conditional on γ it is weakly preferred to have a better collateral quality. Conditional on p, however, the cost of information increases credit when collateral is information insensitive because it relaxes the incentives to deviate and allows firms to obtain more credit without inducing lenders to examine collateral, but it decreases credit and output when collateral is information sensitive, as the firm has to compensate lenders to produce such information.

The next proposition summarizes the answer, which comes from the analysis of Figure 2.1.

Proposition 2 (Effects of p and γ on Borrowing).   Consider collateral characterized by the pair (p, γ). The reaction of borrowers to these variables depends on financial constraints and information sensitiveness.

1. Fix γ.
    a) No financial constraint: Borrowing is independent of p.
    b) Information-sensitive regime: Borrowing is increasing in p.
    c) Information-insensitive regime: Borrowing is increasing in p.
2. Fix p.
    a) No financial constraint: Borrowing is independent of γ.
    b) Information-sensitive regime: Borrowing is decreasing in γ.
    c) Information-insensitive regime: Borrowing is increasing in γ if higher than pC and independent of γ if pC.

Figure 2.2 shows the borrowing possibilities for all combinations (p, γ). The amount K^* refers to the loan without financial constraints, $pK^* - \frac{\gamma}{(qA-1)}$ to the loan in the *IS*

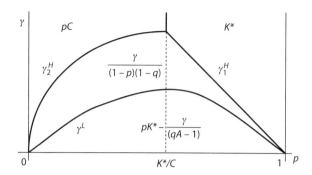

FIGURE 2.2. Borrowing for Different Types of Collateral

regime, while $\frac{\gamma}{(1-p)(1-q)}$ and pC are the loans in the II regime. The thresholds γ_1^H and γ_2^H on information costs refer to points above which firms can obtain the optimal loan size K^* and below which they face a credit crunch. The threshold γ^L on information costs refers to points below which loans become information sensitive.

If it were possible for borrowers to choose the lenders' difficulty level in monitoring collateral with belief p, then they would set $\gamma > \gamma_1^H(p)$ for that p, such that $p > p^H(\gamma)$ and the borrowing is K^*, without information acquisition.

This analysis suggests that, endogenously, an economy would be biased toward using collateral with relatively high p and relatively high γ. Agents in an economy will first use collateral that is perceived to be of high quality. As the needs for collateral increase, agents start relying on collateral of worse and worse quality. In the next section we entertain the possibility that firms can combine and manage collateral units to design a security that creates even better collateral.

2.2.5   Collateral Design

In the previous section we discussed which unit of land firms prefer. Here we expand this discussion and consider whether designing a new piece of collateral (a security) that combines multiple units of land can increase the amount of credit granted and thereby increase expected output in the economy. We discuss the benefits of *pooling* units of land of different expected quality and of *tranching* securities to have new parts that can be used to generate additional securities, and finally we consider making the securities more and more *complex*. This process is known as securitization.

Instead of presenting a full model of security design, we will highlight the main roles of these strategies assuming just two firms, each with a unit of land and a project as described above. Each firm knows that its unit of collateral can be either $\bar{p} = 1$ (a unit of known good land) or $\underline{p} < p^{Ch}$. We ask, can each firm enter ex ante (before knowing the quality of the land) into a contract arrangement that specifies a combination of these units of land (a security), for example, use half the security as collateral instead of an ex ante unknown unit of land as collateral?

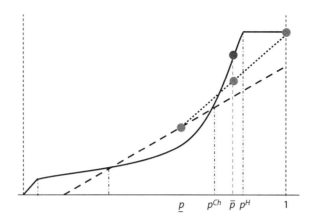

FIGURE 2.3. Gains from Pooling and Tranching

Pooling.   As we have assumed that the firm can have either one unit of land that is known to be good and then obtain credit for K^* or a unit of land with expected quality $\underline{p}$ that triggers information acquisition and then the firm obtains the optimal loan size with probability $\underline{p}$ (and no waste of information cost), the ex ante expected credit size is $\frac{1}{2}K^* + \frac{1}{2}\left[\underline{p}K^* - \frac{\gamma}{qA-1}\right]$. This ex ante expected credit is depicted in Figure 2.3 by the convex combination of the two possible loan sizes.

Now, we consider the possibility of pooling the two units of land to generate a security backed by those assets. The expected quality of the security is then $\bar{p} = \frac{1}{2}1 + \frac{1}{2}\underline{p}$. As is clear from the dot on the solid line in Figure 2.3, as the security does not induce information acquisition, the expected credit from the security (the dark dot) is higher than the expected credit of using land individually as collateral (the light dot in the convex combination).

The gain from pooling comes from a sort of insurance, which goes beyond the standard diversification logic highlighted in much of the literature about securitization and that relies on risk aversion (our firms are risk neutral). Intuitively, pooling assets allows for the relatively low-quality land to be confused with high-quality assets. The increase in its expected quality discourages information acquisition and wasting resources in information costs.

Even though this is an illustration, the logic is quite general, and with a rich heterogeneity and availability of units of land it is possible to combine them so that the average quality of the security is not below p^H. But what if the availability of land is constrained, as in our example, and it is not possible to increase further the average quality of the security with the available characteristics of the individual units of collateral? In what follows we discuss two possibilities to "reach to the peak" given by p^H. One is to tranche assets to complete the diversity of heterogeneity of p. The other is to *increase* information costs (the security's complexity) and reduce p^H.

Tranching.   In the case where there is a scarcity of good enough land, or there is an abundance of relatively bad land, one possibility is to "carve out" a senior tranche from several

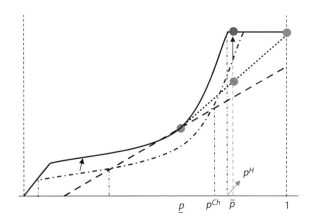

FIGURE 2.4. Gains from Increasing Complexity

low-quality units of land. If this is possible, these better-quality tranches can be used to fill the security with enough good-quality pieces that increases $\bar{p}$ enough so as to reach p^H and then the kink that allows for borrowing K^* with the security. Tranching is a way to carve out quality from remaining assets and to complete the set of beliefs p in the economy, and then fine-tune the average quality of securities. If this strategic design is successful, it is possible to create as many securities as possible, all with expected quality $\bar{p} = p^H$, and max- imize total credit in the economy. As we will see in the next chapter, this security design also maximizes fragility.

Complexity.   An alternative to achieving the expected quality of the security $\bar{p}$ so as to reach the kink given by p^H is not by increasing $\bar{p}$ (with pooling and tranching) but rather by reducing p^H. This can be achieved by designing the security in a way that makes it too complex to examine privately, identifying the quality of underlying collateral and the correlation between their qualities. From the standpoint of the model this is isomorphic to an increase of γ. This possibility is depicted in Figure 2.4.

As previously discussed, increasing γ relaxes lenders' incentives to acquire information and then allows firms to obtain higher loan sizes per expected quality of the security. This reduces p^H and then improves the credit that is obtained with a designed information- insensitive security.

This way to rationalize pooling, tranching, and complexity is useful to understand the increase in securitization as credit increases. As credit needs rise, good-quality underlying collateral becomes scarce. This can be initially compensated for by pooling the relatively bad collateral with the best collateral around. As there is more and more bad collateral, one possibility is to tranche it to carve out some "good portions" and maintain the rel- atively high quality of the securities. As this process continues, another possibility is to structure securities in more and more complex ways to allow worse-quality securities to remain information insensitive.[3]

2.2.6   Aggregation

In the previous discussion we characterized the loan for a match between a household and a firm with land that is good with probability p. For a single match, the expected consumption of the household is $\overline{K} - K(p) + E(repay|p)$ and the expected consumption of the firm is $E(K'|p) - E(repay|p)$. As there is a mass 1 of replications of these matches, aggregate consumption from production (net of initial endowments and the numeraire that comes from land) is the sum of the consumption of all households and all firms in the economy. Since $E(K'|p) = qAK(p)$,

$$W = \overline{K} + \int_0^1 K(p)(qA - 1)f(p)dp, \qquad (2.15)$$

where $f(p)$ is the distribution of beliefs about collateral types in the economy and $K(p)$ is monotonically increasing in p, as is clear from equation (2.14).

We can recover our two extreme benchmarks. If all firms have good land (this is $p = 1$ for all firms), there is no information acquisition and all loans would be of size K^*. In this case the financial friction would be overcome completely by the existence of high-quality collateral, implementing the unconstrained first best that would exist if there were no financial frictions (verifiable output, for example). We denote the unconstrained first-best aggregate consumption from

$$W^* = K^*(qA - 1).$$

The other extreme occurs when all firms have bad land (this is $p = 0$ for all firms) and then there is no valuable collateral in the economy to relax the financial friction. Then no firm would get credit, $W = 0$, and there is no extra consumption coming from production.

Since collateral with relatively low p is not able to sustain loans of K^*, the deviation of consumption from the unconstrained first best critically depends on the distribution of beliefs p in the economy. When this distribution is biased toward low perceptions about collateral values, financial constraints hinder total production. The distribution of beliefs introduces heterogeneity in production, purely given by heterogeneity in collateral and financial constraints, not by heterogeneity in technological possibilities.

2.3   Summary

This chapter has developed a static model of collateralized lending in which lenders can privately acquire information about collateral. This gives the conditions under which credit displays information about collateral (information-sensitive loan) or not (information-insensitive loan). Based on this setting we discussed how collateral is designed and structured to reduce incentives for information production, which allows firms to obtain credit unconditional on the collateral quality and without loss from information acquisition. We also showed how this economy aggregates to obtain total credit and output.

In the next chapter we extend this setting to be dynamic to capture credit booms and busts. We will introduce *idiosyncratic shocks to collateral*, which will generate a credit boom when the environment is in an information-insensitive regime, as those shocks will generate information depreciation in the economy, with more and more firms obtaining loans. We also introduce *aggregate shocks to collateral*, which may generate a financial crisis when the economy moves from the information-insensitive regime to an information-sensitive one.

3

Credit Booms and Financial Crises

3.1 Chapter Overview

In this chapter we add dynamics and study the implications of information in credit markets in a dynamic setting. Lack of information about collateral leads to credit booms (as idiosyncratic shocks to collateral make information depreciate). But it also leads to financial fragility, where a small aggregate shock can sometimes result in a financial crisis characterized by sudden information acquisition. In short, "tail risk" is endogenous. In subsequent chapters we extend and enrich this model to bring in other elements, such as technology and stock markets, that also affect information acquisition, and then booms and busts in credit markets.

That a small shock can cause a crisis is important to understand the fragility of credit markets. Claiming that the 2007–2008 crisis, for instance, was caused by a "large shock" is a not an explanation since empirically there was no clearly identifiable "large" shock. For example, the realized losses on AAA/Aaa subprime bonds were very small. Park (2011) calculates the realized principal losses on the $1.9 trillion of AAA/Aaa-rated subprime bonds issued between 2004 and 2007 to be 17 basis points as of February 2011. More recently, Ospina and Uhlig found that AAA residential mortgage-backed securities (RMBS) "did ok: on average, their total cumulated losses up to 2013 are 2.3 percent" (2018, 11). But the principal-weighted loss rates on AAA-rated subprime securities were on average 42 basis points. As Ospina and Uhlig say: "the subprime AAA-rated RMBS did particularly well" (2018, 11).

The key dynamic in the model concerns how the perceived quality of the collateral backing short-term debt evolves if (costly) information about its quality is not produced. Collateral is subject to mean-reverting idiosyncratic shocks so that over time, without information production, information depreciates and all collateral looks more and more alike: some collateral is known to be bad, but it is not known which specific collateral is bad.

When information is not produced and the perceived average quality of collateral is high enough, firms with good collateral can borrow (as they could also with information), but in addition some firms with bad collateral can borrow (and they could not with information production). In fact, if the projects to be financed are independent of the collateral quality and are efficient, consumption is highest if there is never information production about collateral, because then all firms can borrow, regardless of their true collateral quality. The resulting credit boom occurs as information about collateral depreciates in the economy, resulting in increased consumption because more and more firms receive financing and produce output.

In our setting opacity dominates transparency and the economy can enjoy a blissful ignorance. If there has been information-insensitive lending for a long time, that is, information has not been produced for a long time, there is a significant decay of information in the economy—all is gray, there is no black and white, good or bad—and only a small fraction of true collateral is of known quality, sustaining large volumes of credit.

In this setting aggregate shocks may decrease the perceived average value of collateral in the economy. If the shock happens after a long credit boom, in which more and more firms were borrowing with debt backed by collateral of unknown type (but with high perceived quality), a larger fraction of collateral is under examination than if the same aggregate shock happened when the credit boom was shorter or if there was a lot of collateral of known quality.

A negative aggregate shock, however, does not always trigger a crisis, with sudden information acquisition. If the shock is not so large, then borrowers may prefer to cut back on the amount of the loan to avoid costly information production. The reason is that the firm may prefer to have the certainty of a smaller loan than face a lottery in which credit dries up if the collateral is found to be bad. We denote this situation as a "credit crunch." The crisis corresponds to the case where information is produced and only good collateral can be used once it has been identified. In either case, output declines when the economy moves from a regime without fear of asymmetric information to a regime where asymmetric information is a real possibility. The extent of this decline, and whether the economy faces a credit crunch or a credit crisis, depends on the size of the shock and the length of the preceding boom.

3.2   Dynamics

Credit booms and busts are dynamic concepts, so now we extend the single period's insights into a dynamic model. We nest the previous analysis for a single period in an overlapping generations economy. The purpose is to study the evolution of the distribution of collateral beliefs that determines the level of production in the economy in each period. The choice of an overlapping generations structure is particularly useful in that it allows us to focus on the evolution of information and of beliefs about collateral and to bypass valuation considerations of land when taking into account future conditions.

We assume that each unit of land changes quality over time, mean reverting toward the average quality in the economy, and we study how endogenous information acquisition shapes the distribution of beliefs over time. First, we study the case without aggregate shocks to land, in which the average quality of collateral in the economy does not change, and discuss the effects of endogenous information production on the dynamics of credit.

Then, we introduce aggregate shocks that reduce the average quality of land in the economy and study the effects of endogenous information acquisition on the size of crises and the speed of recoveries.

3.2.1 Extended Setting

The overlapping generations structure is as follows. Every period is populated by two cohorts of individuals who are risk neutral and live for two periods. These individuals are born as households (when "*young*"), with a numeraire endowment of $\overline{K}$ but no managerial skills, and then become firms when "*old*," with managerial skills L^*, but no numeraire to use in production. We assume the numeraire is non-storable and land is storable until the moment its intrinsic value (either C or 0) is extracted, after which the land disappears. This implies that as long as land is transferred, its potential value as collateral remains.

As in the single-period model, we still assume there is random matching between a firm and a household (a young and an old agent) in every period. The timing is as follows:

- At the beginning of the period land that is good with probability p_{-1} may suffer idiosyncratic or aggregate shocks that move this probability to p.
- After the shocks, each member of the "young" generation (households) matches with a member of the "old" generation (firms) with land that is good with probability p. The household determines the conditions of a loan (pairs $(R_{II}; x_{II})$ and $(R_{IS}; x_{IS})$) that make him indifferent between lending or not (conditions 2.2 and 2.5). The firm then chooses a lending contract that maximizes profits, selecting the maximum between $E(\pi|p, IS)$ and $E(\pi|p, II)$ (equations 2.3 and 2.8), and begins production. Depending on whether there is information acquisition or not beliefs are updated to 0 (bad land) or 1 (good land) or remain at p respectively.
- At the end of the period, the firm can choose to sell its unit of land (or the remaining land after default) to the household at a price $Q(p)$ or to extract and consume its intrinsic value.

The Market for Land.   The optimal loan contract follows the characterization described in the single-period model above. The market for land is new. Land can be transferred across generations and agents want to buy land when young to use it as collateral to borrow productive numeraire when old. This is reminiscent of the role of fiat money in overlapping generations, with the critical differences being that land is intrinsically valuable and is subject to imperfect information about its quality. Still, as in those models, we have multiple equilibria based on multiple paths of rational expectations about land prices that incorporate the use of land as collateral.

However, here we are not interested in credit booms, bubbles, or crises arising from transitions across multiple equilibria, which are typical features of some other models. So, we impose restrictions to select the equilibrium in which the land price just reflects the expected intrinsic value of land when it can be used as collateral (that is, the price of a unit of land with belief p is just $Q(p) = pC$). Choosing this particular equilibrium has the advantage of isolating the dynamics generated by information acquisition.[1]

The first restriction is that information can only be produced at the beginning of the period, not at the end. This assumption means that firms prefer to post land as collateral rather than sell land with the risk of information production. The second restriction is that buyers (households) make take-it-or-leave-it offers for the land of their matched firm at the end of the period; households have all the bargaining power. This implies that sellers will be indifferent between selling the unit of land at pC or consuming pC in expectation.[2]

Under these assumptions, the single-period analysis from the previous section just repeats over time. The only changing state variable linking periods is the distribution of beliefs about collateral. How much information about collateral is generated in one period affects not only credit in that period but also the distribution of beliefs and credit in later periods. We can now define the equilibrium formally.

Definition 1 (Equilibrium Definition).   In each period and for each match of a household and a firm of type p, an equilibrium is given by:

- A pair of debt face values $(R_{II}$ and $R_{IS})$ and a pair of fractions of land to be collected in case of default $(x_{II}$ and $x_{IS})$ such that lenders are indifferent; and a profit-maximizing choice of information-sensitive debt or information-insensitive debt.
- A land price $Q(p)$ is determined by a take-it-or-leave-it offer by the household.
- Beliefs are updated after information or shocks using Bayes rule.

Next we study the interaction between shocks to collateral and information acquisition to study the dynamics of production in the economy. First we impose a simple mean-reverting process on idiosyncratic shocks and show that information may vanish over time, generating a credit boom sustained by increased symmetric ignorance in the economy. Then, we allow for an unexpected aggregate shock that may introduce the threat of information acquisition and generate a crisis.

This is the main advantage of focusing on the equilibrium in which the price of collateral just reflects its intrinsic value, and not the future value of collateral. First, credit booms do not arise from bubbles in the price of each unit of collateral but from an increase in the volume of land that can be used as collateral. Second, credit crises are not generated by shifting from a good to a bad equilibrium but by shifting from the information-insensitive to the information-sensitive regimes that coexist in a unique equilibrium.

Relation with Literature on Bubbles and Credit.   A recent literature has highlighted a positive role of bubbles in improving credit in the economy, which as in our case is efficient. Among these, papers, Martin and Ventura (2012) and Asriyan, Laeven, and Martin (2019) stand out. When the collateral constraint depends on the value of the asset posted as collateral, the higher the price at which the lender will be able to sell the asset in case of default, the easier it is to get credit, regardless whether such higher price is fundamental or the result of a bubble.

By making assumptions that guarantee that the price of land is the fundamental value pC, we purposefully abstract from the effect of bubbles on credit. These two lines of research are indeed complementary. While the bubbles and credit literature shows how bubbles can increase the credit sustained by each unit of asset used as collateral, our setting shows how lack of information can increase credit by expanding the units of assets that can be successfully used as collateral.

3.2.2   No Aggregate Shocks

First we study the role of idiosyncratic shocks (by assuming no aggregate shocks) on dynamics. We impose a specific process of idiosyncratic mean-reverting shocks that are useful in characterizing analytically the dynamic effects of information production on aggregate consumption. First, we assume that the idiosyncratic shocks are observable, but their realization is not observable, unless information is produced. Second, we assume that the probability that a unit of land faces an idiosyncratic shock is independent of land type. Finally, we assume that the probability that a unit of land becomes good, conditional on having an idiosyncratic shock, is also independent of its type.

These three assumptions are very useful in simplifying the exposition. The reason is that there is no uncertainty about which unit of land suffers the idiosyncratic shock, restricting the changes in perception about quality over time only to land that suffers the shock. The assumption that the shock and the result of the shock are independent of the quality type is also useful to restrict beliefs about all land in three categories, land known to be good, land known to be bad, and land of uncertain quality. The main results, in terms of booms and busts, are robust to richer stochastic properties (with shocks and realization conditional on the type, with persistence, etc.) as long as there is mean reversion of collateral in the economy.

Formally, in each period either the true quality of each unit of land remains unchanged with probability λ or there is an idiosyncratic shock that changes its type with probability $(1 - \lambda)$. In this last case, land becomes good with a probability $\hat{p}$, independent of its current type. Even when the shock is observable, its realization is not, unless a certain amount of the numeraire good γ is used to learn about it.[3]

Remark on the Interpretation of the Idiosyncratic Shock Process.   The idiosyncratic shock process is realistic. Here's an example. Imagine that the collateral is a mortgage-backed security (MBS) with a portfolio of 20,000 mortgages in the portfolio backing the MBS. There is a large number of such MBS in the economy. Some of the MBS are good, meaning that the homeowners are more likely to make their payments compared to the bad MBS. In either case, at any moment the mortgages in a single MBS may become delinquent, that is, the homeowners are behind in their payments, but such delinquencies may be cured if they make up the payments that are in arrears. An "idiosyncratic shock" that is observable means that something observable happened to an individual MBS. Suppose, for example, that it is announced that a particular MBS has changed its servicer (independent of the MBS type), the company collecting the payments from the borrowers. Some servicers are better than others at "curing" delinquencies, that is, getting homeowners to make up their delinquent payments. But investors do not know if the new servicer is good or bad without producing private information.

In this simple stochastic process for idiosyncratic shocks, and in the absence of aggregate shocks to $\hat{p}$, land falls into one of three categories, and then this distribution has a three-point support: $0, \hat{p}$, and 1. The reason this is convenient is that the aggregate production in steady state is the same as the expected production of a firm with land of expected quality $\hat{p}$, and then whether $\hat{p}$ is located in the information-sensitive or in the information-insensitive region. The aggregate consumption from production in steady state is then simply

$$W_t = K(p)(qA - 1),$$

where $K(p)$ is given by equation (2.14).

To understand the transition toward such a steady state, assume that we start from a situation in which there is perfect information about land qualities. If $\hat{p}$ is in the information-sensitive region, consumption is constant over time and is lower than the unconstrained first best: this is the steady state.

If $\hat{p}$ is in the information-insensitive region, consumption grows over time as more and more units of land accumulate in the category of "unknown quality," with belief $\hat{p}$. Assume, for instance, that $\hat{p} = p^H$ in Figure 2.1. In the initial period the aggregate production is characterized by the dotted line, and as time passes production grows toward the black line (the unconstrained first best in this case), which is the steady state. When $\hat{p}$ is high enough (higher than p^H), the economy has enough good collateral to sustain production at the optimal scale. As information vanishes over time good collateral implicitly subsidizes bad collateral, as firms with good collateral have more collateral than needed while firms with bad collateral have more needs than collateral. After enough periods virtually all firms are able to produce at the optimal scale, not just those with good collateral.

3.2.3   Aggregate Shocks

Now we introduce negative aggregate shocks that transform a fraction $(1 - \eta)$ of good collateral into bad collateral, reducing the average fraction $\hat{p}$ of good collateral in the economy. As with idiosyncratic shocks, the aggregate shock is observable, but which good collateral changes type is not. When the shock hits, there is a downward revision of beliefs about all collateral. That is, after the shock, collateral with belief $p = 1$ gets revised downward to $p' = \eta$ and collateral with belief $p = \hat{p}$ gets revised downward to $p' = \eta\hat{p}$.

Based on the discussion about the endogenous choice of collateral, which justifies that collateral would be constructed to maximize borrowing and prevent information acquisition, we focus on the case where, prior to the negative aggregate shock, the average quality of collateral is good enough such that there are no financial constraints (that is, $\hat{p} > p^H$). In the next chapter, once we introduce a double-sided information acquisition, in which we also allow borrowers to privately examine the collateral, we show that only collateral of relatively high p can sustain information-insensitive loans.

In the next proposition we show that the longer the economy does not face a negative aggregate shock, the larger the consumption loss when such a shock does occur.

Proposition 3 (Information and Crises).   Assume $\hat{p} > p^H$ and a negative aggregate shock η hits after t periods of no aggregate shocks and transition toward the information-insensitive steady state. The reduction in consumption $\Delta(t|\eta) \equiv W_t - W_{t|\eta}$ is non-decreasing in the size of the shock η and non-decreasing in the time t elapsed previously without a shock.

The intuition for this proposition is the following. Pooling implies that bad collateral is confused with good collateral. This allows for a credit boom because firms with bad collateral get credit that they would not otherwise obtain. Firms with good collateral effectively subsidize firms with bad collateral since good collateral still gets the optimal leverage, while bad collateral is able to leverage more.

However, pooling also implies that good collateral is confused with bad collateral. This puts good collateral in a weaker position in the event of negative aggregate shocks. Without pooling, a negative shock reduces the belief that collateral is good from $p = 1$ to $p' = \eta$. With pooling, a negative shock reduces the belief that collateral is good from $p = \hat{p}$ to $p' = \eta\hat{p}$. Good collateral gets the same credit regardless of having belief $p = 1$ or $p = \hat{p}$. However, credit may be very different when $p = \eta$ and $p = \eta\hat{p}$. In particular, after a negative shock to collateral, credit may decline since either a high amount of the numeraire needs to be used to produce information or borrowing needs to be excessively constrained to avoid such information production.

If we define "*fragility*" as the probability that aggregate consumption declines more than a certain value, then the next corollary immediately follows from Proposition 3.

Corollary 1.   Given a negative aggregate shock, the *fragility* of an economy *increases* with the number of periods the debt in the economy has been informationally insensitive, and hence *increases* with the fraction of collateral that is of unknown quality.

Information deterioration may induce credit booms, while the threat of information acquisition may induce crises. What happens after a crisis? How does information production affect the speed of recovery?

Proposition 4 (Information and Recoveries).   Assume $\hat{p} > p^H$ and that a negative aggregate shock η generates a crisis in period t. The recovery from the crisis is faster if information is generated after the shock when $\eta\hat{p} < \overline{\eta\hat{p}} \equiv \frac{1}{2} + \sqrt{\frac{1}{4} - \frac{\gamma}{K^*(1-q)}}$, where $p^{Ch} < \overline{\eta\hat{p}} < p^H$. That is, $W_{t+1}^{IS} > W_{t+1}^{II}$ for all $\eta\hat{p} < \overline{\eta\hat{p}}$ and $W_{t+1}^{IS} \leq W_{t+1}^{II}$ otherwise.

The intuition for this proposition is the following. When information is acquired after a negative shock, not only are a lot of resources being spent in acquiring information but also only a fraction $\eta\hat{p}$ of collateral can sustain the maximum borrowing K^*. When information is not acquired after a negative shock, collateral that remains with belief $\eta\hat{p}$ will restrict credit in the following periods, until mean reversion moves beliefs back to $\hat{p}$. This is equivalent to restricting credit proportional to monitoring costs in subsequent periods. Not producing information causes a kind of *lack of information overhang* going forward. The proposition generates the following corollary.

Corollary 2. There exists a range of negative aggregate shocks (η such that $\eta\hat{p} \in [p^{Ch}, \overline{\eta\hat{p}}]$) in which agents do not acquire information, but recovery would be faster if they did.

Relation with Literature Linking Information and Crises. There is also a rich, and more recent, literature that considers the conceptual link between information production and economic booms and busts, such as Veldkamp (2005), Van Nieuwerburgh and Veldkamp (2006), Straub and Ulbricht (2017), Fajgelbaum, Schall, and Taschereau-Dumouchel (2017), and Farboodi and Kondor (2019). Perhaps the closest to the setting here is the work by Asriyan, Laeven, and Martin (2019), who study a setting in which credit can be backed either by collateral (with perfect information) or by the costly screening of projects, with this mix affecting macroeconomic dynamics and the probability and recovery from crises. Our setting considers both information about projects for trading in stock markets and information about collateral in credit markets, the effect of their interaction for macroeconomic dynamics, the likelihood of crises, and the optimal cost of information acquisition in both markets.

3.2.4   Dispersion of Beliefs

An important element in our analysis is the cross-sectional dispersion of beliefs about collateral quality in credit markets. This statistic is directly related to the amount of information in the economy.

If there is full information about the quality of all land in the economy, the belief distribution is $f(0) = 1 - \hat{p}$ and $f(1) = \hat{p}$ and the variance of beliefs is

$$Var(p) = \hat{p}^2(1-\hat{p}) + (1-\hat{p})^2\hat{p} = \hat{p}(1-\hat{p}).$$

During a credit boom, as there is depreciation of information in the economy, a fraction of land becomes of unknown type. Assume that a fraction Λ of land is of unknown quality, with belief $\hat{p}$. The belief distribution then is $f(0) = (1-\Lambda)(1-\hat{p}), f(\hat{p}) = \Lambda$, and $f(1) = (1-\Lambda)\hat{p}$. Then, the variance of beliefs is

$$Var(p|\Lambda > 0) = (1-\Lambda)[\hat{p}^2(1-\hat{p}) + (1-\hat{p})^2\hat{p}] = (1-\Lambda)\hat{p}(1-\hat{p}).$$

Notice that the variance of beliefs about collateral is directly related to information about collateral. The larger the fraction of collateral of unknown quality (i.e., the larger Λ is), the lower the cross-sectional standard deviation of beliefs.

This very trivial and natural result in our setting, given the three-point distribution of beliefs, is a much more general property of any distribution that is mean reverting. As long as the depreciation of information reduces the difference between the belief of a unit of land and the average belief, the standard deviation of beliefs declines as information depreciates.

The next proposition follows trivially from the previous discussion.

Proposition 5 (Information and Belief Dispersion).   A proxy for information about collateral in credit markets is the standard deviation of beliefs about collateral quality.

Given the direct mapping between the belief about a unit of land and its price (and there is a weakly direct mapping between the belief about collateral and the amount of credit backed by such collateral), the next corollary follows trivially from the previous proposition.

Corollary 3.   A proxy for information about collateral in credit markets is the standard deviation of collateral prices and of loan sizes.

As we discuss in later chapters, this is an important result. As our model relies on dynamic collateral information to explain credit booms and busts, we can use measures of the amount of information from cross-sectional standard deviations of various economic variables to validate our results. These measures can also be used to assess the amount of information (or lack thereof) existing in credit markets, and then about the fragility in the system when combined with other macroeconomic variables.

The next proposition describes the evolution of the standard deviation of beliefs in the economy during credit booms and credit crises.

Proposition 6 (Dispersion of Beliefs during Booms and Crises).   During a credit boom, the standard deviation of beliefs declines. During a credit crisis, if the aggregate shock η triggers information production about collateral with belief $\eta\hat{p}$, the standard deviation of beliefs increases. This increase is larger the longer the preceding boom.

Intuitively, credit booms are generated by vanishing information. Since over that process beliefs increasingly center on the average quality $\hat{p}$, the dispersion of the belief distribution about collateral declines. If this process develops long enough, an aggregate shock that triggers information reveals the true type of most land, and beliefs return to $p = 0$ and $p = 1$, increasing the dispersion of the belief distribution. This effect is stronger the longer the preceding boom that accumulated collateral with beliefs $\hat{p}$.

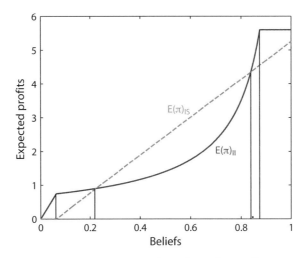

FIGURE 3.1. Expected Profits and Cutoffs

3.2.5 Numerical Illustration

Now we illustrate, with a numerical example, the dynamic reactions to aggregate shocks. We assume idiosyncratic shocks happen with probability $(1 - \lambda) = 0.1$, in which case the collateral becomes good with probability $\hat{p} = 0.92$. Other parameters are $q = 0.6$, $A = 3$ (investment is efficient and generates a return of 80% in expectation), $\overline{K} = 20$, $L^* = K^* = 7$, $C = 15$ (the endowment is large enough to provide a loan for the optimal scale of production and to buy the most expensive unit of land), and $\gamma = 0.35$ (information costs are 5% of the optimal loan). These parameters are clearly not disciplined quantitatively but are useful to show graphically the propositions above.

Given these parameters, the relevant cutoffs are $p^H = 0.88$, $p_{II}^L = 0.06$, and the information-sensitive region of beliefs is $p \in [0.22, 0.84]$. Figure 3.1 plots the ex ante expected profits with information-sensitive (dotted line) and information-insensitive (solid line) debt, and these cutoffs.

We simulate the model for 100 periods, assuming there is perfect information about all land in the economy at period 0. In periods 5 and 50 we perturb the economy by introducing negative aggregate shocks that transform a fraction $(1 - \eta)$ of good collateral into bad collateral. We consider shocks of different size ($\eta = 0.97$, $\eta = 0.91$, and $\eta = 0.90$) and compute the dynamic reaction of aggregate production to them. We choose the size of these shocks to guarantee that $\eta\hat{p}$ is above p^H when $\eta = 0.97$, is between p^{Ch} and p^H when $\eta = 0.91$, and is less than p^{Ch} when $\eta = 0.90$.

Figure 3.2 shows the evolution of the average quality of collateral for the three negative aggregate shocks. Since mean reversion guarantees that average quality converges back to $\hat{p} = 0.92$ after the shocks, their effects are only temporary.

Figure 3.3 shows the evolution of aggregate production for the three negative aggregate shocks. A couple of features are worth noting. First, if $\eta = 0.97$, the aggregate shock is so

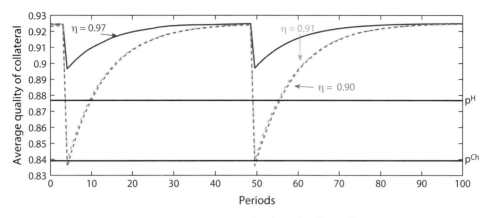

FIGURE 3.2. Average Quality of Collateral

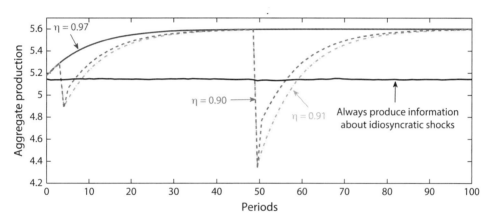

FIGURE 3.3. Aggregate Production

small that it never constrains borrowing or modifies the evolution of production. Second, as proved in Proposition 3, if $\eta = 0.91$ or $\eta = 0.90$, aggregate production drops more in period 50, when the credit boom is mature and information is scarce, than in period 5. In the former a lot of information has already depreciated in the economy, while in the latter there is still a large volume of information about collateral. Critically, the crisis is larger in period 50, not only because it finishes a large boom but also because credit drops to a lower level. Indeed, aggregate production in period 50 is lower than in period 5 because credit dries up for a larger fraction of collateral when information is scarcer.

As proved in Proposition 4, a shock $\eta = 0.91$ does not trigger information production, but a shock $\eta = 0.90$ does. Even when these two shocks generate production drops of similar magnitude, recovery is faster when the shock is slightly larger and information is replenished.

Figure 3.4 shows the evolution of the beliefs' dispersion, a measure of information availability. As proved in Proposition 6, a credit boom is correlated with a decline in the dispersion of beliefs and, given that after many periods without a shock most collateral

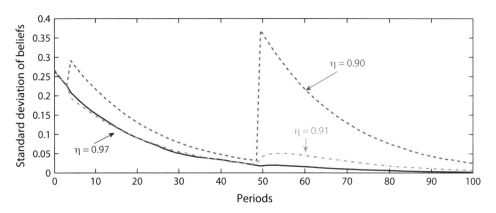

FIGURE 3.4. Standard Deviation of Distribution of Beliefs

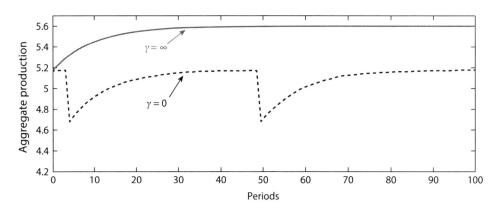

FIGURE 3.5. Extreme Information Costs

looks the same, the information acquisition triggered by a shock $\eta = 0.90$ generates a larger increase in dispersion in period 50.

Finally, to illustrate the negative side of information, Figure 3.5 shows the evolution of production under two very extreme cases: information acquisition is free $(\gamma = 0)$ and it is impossible $(\gamma = \infty)$. Aggregate production is lower and more volatile when information is free. It is lower because only firms with good collateral get loans. It is more volatile because the volume of good collateral is subject to aggregate shocks. When information acquisition is free, the reaction of credit is independent of the length of the preceding boom and only depends on the size of the shock. In contrast, when information acquisition is impossible, over time all land is used as collateral and shocks do not introduce any fear that someone will acquire information and leads to a credit decline.

3.3   Policy Implications

An overlapping generations model implies a sort of myopia of agents; as they survive for just two periods, their information production decisions affect future agents' opportunities. How would a planner that cares about future generations' production modify information acquisition? We assume the planner faces the same information restrictions and costs as households and firms. More specifically, welfare is measured by

$$U_t = E_t \sum_{\tau=t}^{\infty} \beta^{\tau-t} W_t. \tag{3.1}$$

The planner chooses an endowment transfer (loan size) from households to firms and decides whether to generate information about firms' collateral or not, facing two types of constraints. First, *collateral constraints* prevent the planner from lending a firm more endowment than the expected value of the firm's collateral. This is

$$K(p) \leq \min\left\{K^*, pC\right\}. \tag{3.2}$$

Second, *information constraints* prevent the planner from lending to a firm without acquiring information, if the loan would have triggered information acquisition by private agents in a decentralized economy. This implies that the planner cannot lend a firm more than the amount in equation (2.6) without acquiring costly information. Then, if

$$K(p) > \frac{\gamma}{(1-p)(1-q)}, \tag{3.3}$$

the planner has to acquire costly information. Assuming the planner faces the same exogenous shocks as private agents, if the planner acquires information it is subject to collateral constraints based on the new information. We now define the constrained planner's problem.

Definition 2 (Constrained Planner's Problem). For each firm with collateral p, a planner chooses the loan size $K(p)$ for production and decides whether or not to acquire information about the firm's collateral to maximize welfare (3.1), subject to collateral constraints (3.2) and information constraints (3.3).

It is intuitively clear that, without collateral and information constraints, the planner would optimally lend $K(p) = K^*$ to each firm, since it is efficient to finance all projects at optimal scale. This is what we referred to above as *unconstrained first best*. It is also intuitively clear, from Figure 3.5, that without information constraints it is optimal for the planner to always avoid information acquisition.

In what follows we first study the economy without aggregate shocks and show that a planner would like to produce information for a wider range of collateral p than short-lived agents. Then, we study the economy with negative aggregate shocks and show that it may still be optimal for the planner to avoid information production, riding the credit boom even when facing the possibility of collapse.

3.3.1   No Aggregate Shocks

The next proposition shows that, when $\beta > 0$, the planner wants to acquire information for a wider range of beliefs p. Given that the planner is constrained by both collateral and information considerations, the only source of inefficiency arises from the myopic behavior of all agents, who only consider the benefits of information for one period and not its potential future costs.

Proposition 7 (Planner's Optimal Information with No Aggregate Shocks).   The planner's optimal range of information-sensitive beliefs is wider than the decentralized range of information-sensitive beliefs from equation (2.9). Specifically, the planner produces information if

$$(1 - \beta\lambda)\frac{\gamma}{qA - 1} < pK^* - K(p|II), \tag{3.4}$$

and does not produce information otherwise.

Comparing this condition with equation (2.9), it is clear that the cost of information production is effectively lower for the planner. The planner expects to relax collateral constraints if finding out the collateral is good and give a loan to such collateral of K^* in all future periods until a new idiosyncratic shock hits. Decentralized agents, however, do not internalize these future gains when deciding whether to trigger information acquisition or not, since they are myopic and do not weigh the information impact on future generations. This difference widens with the planner discounting (β) and with the probability that the collateral remains unchanged (λ).

The planner can align incentives easily by subsidizing information production by a fraction $\beta\lambda$ of information acquisition, possibly using lump sum taxes on individuals. In this way, after the subsidy, the cost of information production that agents face is effectively $\gamma(1 - \beta\lambda)$. Figure 3.6 illustrates this efficiently wider range of information-sensitive beliefs p.

We denote by $\widetilde{K}(p)$ the net effective loan a planner can give a firm with collateral p, considering the effects on future loans and obtained by the upper contour of the solid curve and the upper dashed line of Figure 3.6.

$$\widetilde{K}(p) = \max\left\{ K(p|II), pK^* - \frac{\gamma(1 - \beta\lambda)}{qA - 1} \right\},$$

where $K(p|II)$ is given in equation (2.7) and the function follows the same schedule as $K(p)$ in equation (2.14), but using instead the effective information cost $\gamma(1 - \beta\lambda)$ and the cutoffs $\widetilde{p}^{Ch}$ and $\widetilde{p}^{Cl}$ depicted in Figure 3.6.

3.3.2   Aggregate Shocks

In this section we assume that the planner assigns a probability μ per period that a negative shock η will occur at some point in the future. The next proposition shows that there

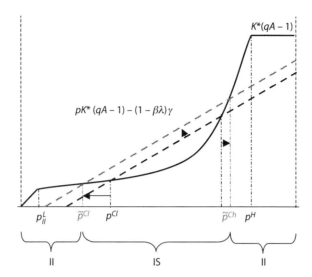

$$K^*(qA - 1)$$

$$pK^*(qA - 1) - (1 - \beta\lambda)\gamma$$

$$p_{II}^L \quad \widetilde{p}^{Cl} \quad p^{Cl} \qquad \widetilde{p}^{Ch} \quad p^H$$

II   IS   II

FIGURE 3.6. Information Acquisition by the Planner

are levels of p for which, even in the presence of the potential future shock, the planner prefers not to produce information, maintaining a high level of current output rather than avoiding a potential reduction in future output. This insight is consistent with the findings of Ranciere, Tonell, and Westermann, who show that *"high growth paths are associated with the undertaking of systemic risk and with the occurrence of occasional crises"* (2008, 360).

Proposition 8 (Planner's Optimal Information with Aggregate Shocks). The possibility of a future negative aggregate shock does not necessarily justify acquiring information, reducing current output to avoid potential future crises. In the presence of possible future negative aggregate shocks, the planner produces information if

$$(1 - \beta\lambda)\frac{\gamma}{qA - 1} > \frac{(1 - \beta\lambda)}{(1 - \beta\lambda) + \beta\lambda\mu}[pK^* - K(p|II)]$$

$$+ \frac{\beta\lambda\mu}{(1 - \beta\lambda) + \beta\lambda\mu}[p\widetilde{K}(\eta) - \widetilde{K}(\eta p)], \qquad (3.5)$$

and does not produce information otherwise.

The *IS* range of beliefs widens if $[pK^* - K(p|II)] < [p\widetilde{K}(\eta) - \widetilde{K}(\eta p)]$. Furthermore, the effect of future shocks η on the *IS* range of beliefs increases with their probability μ.

To build intuition, assume the aggregate shock is not large enough to make $\widetilde{K}(\eta) < K^*$ but is large enough to make $\widetilde{K}(\eta p) < K(p|II)$ (for example, $\eta > p^H$ and $p = p^H$). In this case, the aggregate shock, regardless of its probability, does not affect the expected discounted consumption of acquiring information (since even with the shock, a firm with a unit of good land is able to borrow K^*), but the shock reduces the expected discounted consumption of not acquiring information (since with the shock, the loan size declines

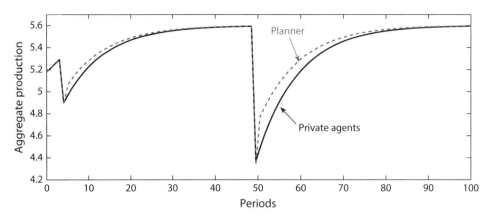

FIGURE 3.7. Dynamics with an Aggregate Shock $\eta = 0.91$

from $K(p|II)$ to $\widetilde{K}(\eta p)$. In this example, producing information relaxes the potential borrowing constraint in the case of a future negative shock. Hence, when that shock is more likely, there are more incentives to acquire information.

Now assume larger shocks. Take, as an example, the extreme case $\eta = 0$, such that all collateral becomes bad. In this case, condition (3.5) simply becomes

$$(1 - \beta\lambda + \beta\lambda\mu)\frac{\gamma}{qA - 1} < pK^* - K(p|II),$$

increasing effective information costs, and hence reducing the incentives to acquire information. In this extreme case the planner wants to acquire less information than in the the absence of shocks (condition 3.4) but still wants to acquire more information than decentralized agents (condition 2.9).

Discussion of Dynamics.   There are aggregate shocks that induce the same dynamics in the planning and decentralized economies. For example, if $\hat{p} > p_H$ and aggregate shocks are small, then both dynamics are identical to the solid curve in Figure 3.5. In essence the shock does not induce information production in either of the two economies.

There are, however, aggregate shocks that may induce different dynamics between planning and decentralized economies. As an illustration, consider the numerical example in Section 3.2.5. If $\beta = 0.9$, then the planner's range for information acquisition is $[0.16, 0.85]$, wider than the decentralized case depicted in Figure 3.1.

Figure 3.7 shows dynamics when aggregate shocks of size $\eta = 0.91$ hit in periods 5 and 50. In this case decentralized agents do not acquire information when the shock hits but the planner does, inducing different dynamics.

The solid curve is identical to the lower dashed curve in Figure 3.3 for the decentralized economy. The dashed curve shows that the planner induces less production in the period of the shock, when acquiring information, but induces a faster recovery afterward. Since private agents do not value the future, they prefer to produce more in the year of the crisis, not internalizing the costs in terms of a slower recovery. Agents are myopic and do not take into account the effect of their decisions on crises for future generations. This inefficiency is the direct result of our overlapping generations environment and naturally disappears in a dynastic model in which agents value the consumption of future generations.

3.4   Summary

It has been difficult to explain financial crises and how they are linked to credit booms. "Large shocks" or multiple equilibria do not incorporate credit booms and are not convincing explanations of financial crises. Further, they do not lead to policy recommendations. Explaining a financial crisis requires the modeling discipline of fixing the shock size and showing how that shock can sometimes have no effect and sometimes lead to a crisis. The explanation given in this chapter is based on the endogenous dynamics of information in credit markets about collateral, which creates fragility as a rational credit boom develops. Confidence is lost when a long-lasting credit boom is tipped by a potentially small shock and the fear of asymmetric information filters into the system. This constitutes a departure from models that explain crises based on a change in asymmetric information. In our setting, endogenously there is always symmetry, either symmetric information or symmetric ignorance. What creates a crisis is not more asymmetric information but instead a reaction to avoid it.

An important lesson of this chapter is that the amount of information in an economy is time-varying. It is not optimal for lenders to produce information every period about the borrowers because it is costly. Hence, information about collateral may degrade over time; a kind of (optimal) amnesia sets in. Instead of knowing which borrowers have good collateral and which have bad collateral, all collateral starts to look alike. These dynamics of information result in a credit boom in which firms with bad collateral can borrow. During the credit boom, output and consumption rise, but the economy becomes increasingly fragile. The economy becomes more susceptible to small shocks. If information production becomes a credible threat, all collateral with depreciated information can borrow less, *a credit crunch*. Alternatively, if information is effectively produced after such a shock, firms with bad collateral cannot access credit, *a financial crisis*.

A credit boom results in output and consumption rising, but it also increases systemic fragility. Consequently, a credit boom presents a delicate problem for regulators and the central bank. We showed that a social planner would produce more information than private agents but would not always want to eliminate fragility.

In this chapter we have only allowed idiosyncratic and aggregate shocks to collateral, which drive both booms and busts. We have, however, documented in Chapter 1 a close relation between productivity growth and how a boom ends. In the next chapter we will maintain idiosyncratic shocks to collateral that bring to life credit booms but will dispense with aggregate shocks to collateral that tip them into crises. Instead, we allow for the possibility of productivity shocks and for an endogenous evolution of productivity as a function of credit. We will show that under these assumptions we can generate financial crises also as a response to negative contemporaneous shocks to productivity. This is the closest result to standard real business cycles assumptions, but with a well-modeled credit market that triggers a recession with a financial crisis. Perhaps the most interesting result, however, is that a positive shock to productivity may induce the start of a credit boom. If productivity decays as credit increases, then a financial crisis may ensue, not because of any shock in the economy but instead as a result of an exhausted credit boom.

4

Technology and Financial Crises

4.1 Chapter Overview

In this chapter we add the endogenous evolution of productivity. In the previous two chapters we studied changes in the incentives to produce information in credit markets, in isolation from other macroeconomic variables. But credit is used to finance production, and by affecting the results of production, it can in principle affect the operation of credit markets and in particular incentives to acquire information about collateral.

In Chapter 2 we indeed showed that credit booms, productivity growth, and financial crises are closely related. We showed that credit booms are not rare, they are low frequency events, and some end in a financial crisis (*bad booms*) and others do not (*good booms*). Credit booms start with a *positive shock* to productivity growth, but in bad booms productivity growth tends to die off quickly while this is not the case for good booms.

In this chapter we extend the model of the previous chapter so that we can understand how *positive productivity shocks* can lead to credit booms that sometimes end with a financial crash and sometimes do not, and perhaps even more important, how the deterministic process of productivity can create endogenous cycles with crises *in the absence of any shock, to either productivity or collateral.*

We extend the model along two dimensions. First, unlike the static model in Chapter 2, where only lenders could produce information about collateral, here we allow two-sided information production: both borrowers and lenders can acquire information. With a single-sided information production, in the previous chapter we showed that, as information pressures mount, the economy moves smoothly from a credit crunch (a reduction in the amount of credit) to a crisis (a sudden sorting out of good and bad collateral). With two-sided information, in contrast, there is a discontinuous collapse in credit once information incentives surpass a critical threshold, a sudden and dramatic crisis with information acquisition.

The second extension is dynamic. Unlike the dynamic model in Chapter 3, where only collateral beliefs evolve, here we introduce decreasing marginal returns and changes to the set of technological opportunities. High-quality projects are scarce, so as more firms operate in the economy increasingly lower-quality projects become active. As a credit boom evolves two forces move in tandem. First, there is a depreciation of information about collateral (as in the previous chapter). Second, the average productivity in the economy endogenously declines as more firms obtain credit and operate, in which case lenders increasingly have incentives to acquire information about the collateral backing a loan.

If at some point the average productivity of the economy declines enough—*a bad boom*—there is a change of the information regime in credit markets that leads to the examination of the collateral that is used to obtain credit. As a result, some firms that used to obtain loans cannot obtain loans anymore and output goes down—*a crisis*. Immediately after the crash fewer firms operate, average productivity improves, and the process restarts—*a sequence of bad booms*. We characterize the set of parameters under which the economy experiences this credit cycle in steady state, which is a purely endogenous deterministic cycle in steady state, not triggered by any contemporaneous exogenous shock. Interestingly, it is the endogenous evolution of productivity that determines the cyclical properties of the economy. If the technology is good enough, as the credit boom evolves, the endogenous decline in average productivity may not be enough to trigger a change of the information regime. If this is the case, the credit boom ends, but not in a crisis—*a good boom*.

We show that exogenous movements in technology still matter. Transitory negative shocks to productivity can induce crises and speed up the cycle. A trend of technological improvement can move the economy from a steady state characterized by an endogenous sequence of bad booms and crises to a steady state with a long good boom without crises.

In summary, combining decreasing returns to the probability of success of projects with two-sided information acquisition of collateral generates a cyclical steady state that is symmetric—a smooth expansion that ends with a sudden and dramatic crisis. We also introduce an exogenous evolution of technology that is able to move the economy across steady states with and without crises.

Given that in this chapter we introduce explicitly more standard macroeconomic elements, we examine growth accounting to decompose the growth rate of output between the growth of credit and productivity during the credit boom. We also show that our setting is not unique to financing firms but also applies to financing housing with mortgages. Finally, our setting generates testable implications linking the real economy and credit. We test those predictions in the data to offer more evidence of the plausibility of the linkages we highlight.

4.2   The Model

4.2.1   The Extended Setting

We extend the dynamic economy described in the previous two chapters in two important ways. In this chapter the stochastic production function described in equation (2.1) does not have a fixed probability of success, q, but one that declines with the level of economic activity.

To be more precise, we assume that there is a limited supply of projects in the economy per period, also with mass 1. There are two types of projects that are available: A fraction ψ has *high* probability of success, q_H, and the rest have a *low* probability of success, q_L.

We assume all projects are efficient, that is, $q_H A > q_L A > 1$, which implies that it is optimal that households use all their labor in the project, $L = L^*$, and so $K^* = L^*$ is the optimal scale of numeraire for all projects, independent of their *quality* $q \in \{q_L, q_H\}$. We refer to the fraction of high-quality projects, ψ, as *technology*.

We say a firm is *active* if it can obtain a loan in the credit market. We denote by η the *mass of active firms*, which we will show later is endogenous to available credit in the economy. We assume that active firms are randomly assigned to a queue to choose their project. When a firm has its turn to choose its project according to its position in the queue, an active firm naturally picks the project with the highest q among those remaining in the pool. This protocol induces an average productivity of projects among active firms, which we denote by $\widehat{q}(\eta)$, that is given by

$$\widehat{q}(\eta|\psi) = \begin{cases} q_H & \text{if } \eta < \psi \\ \frac{\psi}{\eta} q_H + \left(1 - \frac{\psi}{\eta}\right) q_L & \text{if } \eta \geq \psi. \end{cases} \tag{4.1}$$

The average quality of projects in the economy depends on two factors: an exogenous fraction of good projects in the economy, ψ, and the endogenous fraction of firms operating projects, η.

Notice that the concept of productivity has two components: the probability that a project succeeds, q, and the productivity conditional on success, A. Empirically, productivity is usually measured as a residual, such as total factor productivity (TFP), but as we will see these two components have different implications for the generation of crises. The component that induces information acquisition about collateral in credit markets is the one that drives the probability that projects succeed, as this determines the probability that firms default and that lenders end up owning the collateral. The second component determines the surplus for the firms conditional on success and does not affect lenders' incentives to acquire information about collateral; consequently it does not affect the likelihood of a crisis.

As in the previous setting, we assume land is non-productive (it is not an input into the project) but may have an intrinsic value, so that it is useful as collateral. Still we will assume that a fraction $\widehat{p}$ land is "*good*" (delivers C units of numeraire, but only once) and the rest "*bad*" (does not deliver anything). In this chapter, the model will generate purely endogenous crises, so we assume there are no aggregate shocks to the expected value of land (no shocks to $\widehat{p}$). We keep assuming that $C > K^*$ so that land that is known to be good can sustain the optimal loan and that land that is known to be bad is not able to sustain any loan. Then we refer to firms that have land with a positive probability of being good ($p > 0$) as *active firms*, our parameter η, since in contrast to firms that are known to hold bad land, they can actively raise funds to start their projects.[1]

In this chapter there is two-sided information acquisition. More specifically, the land type can be privately observed (and certified) at the beginning of the period, at a cost γ_l in units of numeraire by households (diverting its use from consumption) and/or at a cost γ_b in units of labor by firms (diverting its use from production). Again, we assume information (the certification) is private immediately after being obtained and becomes public at the end of the period. Still, the agent can credibly disclose his private information (the certificate) immediately if it is beneficial to do so.

As a summary, while in the previous chapter the quality of the projects, q, was constant and crises were generated by exogenous shocks that reduced the average quality of collateral, $\widehat{p}$, here we keep the average quality of collateral fixed while the average quality of projects, $\widehat{q}\,(\eta|\psi)$, changes endogenously with changes in η or exogenously with changes in ψ. Therefore, in contrast to the previous model, the source of the shock that may induce a crisis here is in the production sector and it has an endogenous component that evolves with credit.

Notice that this model nests the setting in the previous chapter by assuming $\psi = 1$ (so all projects have a fixed $q = q_H$) and $\gamma_b = \infty$ (so only lenders can obtain information at a cost $\gamma = \gamma_l$).

Timing and Equilibrium.   We maintain the timing within a period t, which starts with a *market for loans* in which an old and a young individual randomly match and determine the loan size and information about collateral. Both the lender and borrower share the belief p about land and, while the borrower knows the quality of its project q, the lender only knows $\widehat{q}\,(\eta|\psi)$. After production and contracts are settled, an old and a young also randomly match in a *market for land* and trade land at the fundamental price pC. As before, between periods land is subject to idiosyncratic shocks, as described in the previous chapter. The equilibrium is also defined in the same way as in the previous chapter, with the only addition that the borrower also optimally chooses whether to acquire information or not, privately, depending on the loan contract.

4.2.2   *Information and Credit*

As we analyzed in detail in Chapter 3, we first characterize the optimal short-term collateralized debt contract for a single firm with a project that has a probability of success q, with a unit of land that is good with probability p, and when there is a total mass of active firms η. Loans that trigger information production (information-sensitive debt) are costly—borrowers either acquire information at a cost γ_b or have to compensate lenders for their information cost γ_l. Loans that do not trigger information production (information-insensitive debt), however, may not be feasible as they introduce a fear from asymmetric information—they introduce incentives for either the borrower or the lender to deviate and acquire information privately to take advantage of its counterparty. The magnitude of this fear determines the level of debt that can be information insensitive and, ultimately, the volume and dynamics of information in the economy. As in Chapter 2 we will study these two possibilities separately.

4.2.2.1 INFORMATION-SENSITIVE DEBT.   In the extended model, when the contract specifies information acquisition, there are two possibilities: either the lender or the borrower acquires the information.

When the lender acquires the information (the case that we denote by IS^l), the break-even condition for the lender is the same as in equation (2.2), but replacing q with $\widehat{q}\,(\eta)$, as now the lender makes the choice based on the project's expected success probability that depends on the mass of active firms η, and replacing γ with γ_l as now we specify the cost of information is incurred by the lender. That is, the break-even condition in this case is

$$p[\widehat{q}\,(\eta)R_{IS^l} + (1 - \widehat{q}\,(\eta))x_{IS^l}C - K_{IS^l}] = \gamma_l.$$

Following the same solution of the contract as the one leading to equation (2.4), *expected net profits* (net of the land value pC from the first term) from information-sensitive debt, conditional on lenders acquiring information, are simply

$$E(\pi\,|p, q, IS^l) = \max\{pK^*(qA - 1) - \gamma_l, 0\}.$$

Intuitively, with probability p collateral is good and sustains $K^*(qA - 1)$ numeraire in expectation and with probability $(1 - p)$ collateral is bad and does not sustain any borrowing. The firm always has to compensate lenders for not consuming γ_l.

The two-sided information-acquisition extension forces us to distinguish the previous case from the one in which the borrower acquires the information (the case that we denote by IS^b). In this case borrowers need to use γ_b of labor (the only endowment available to them before credit), leaving only $L^* - \gamma_b$ to be used in the project, which would generate $A\min\{K, L^* - \gamma_b\}$ in case of success (with probability q) and 0 otherwise. A lender's participation constraint binds when

$$\widehat{q}\,(\eta)R_{IS^b} + (1 - \widehat{q}\,(\eta))x_{IS^b}C - K_{IS^b} = 0.$$

Regardless of what the borrower finds, the firm will only have $L^* - \gamma_b$ labor remaining for use in the project. If the borrower finds out that the land is good he will then just borrow $K_{IS^b} = K^* - \gamma_b$ to operate at the (now lower), optimal scale. The truth-telling constraint is $R_{IS^b} = x_{IS^b}C$ and $x_{IS^b} = \frac{K^* - \gamma_b}{C}$. Ex ante expected total consumption for the borrower is $pC + p(qA(K^* - \gamma_b) - x_{IS^b}C)$. Substituting x_{IS^b} in equilibrium, *expected net profits* (again net of the land value pC) are

$$E(\pi\,|p, q, IS^b) = \max\{p(K^* - \gamma_b)(qA - 1), 0\}.$$

Putting these two possibilities together, expected profits from information-sensitive debt effectively are

$$E(\pi\,|p, q, IS) = \max\left\{pK^*(qA - 1) - \gamma, 0\right\} \tag{4.2}$$

as in equation (2.4) but with $\gamma \equiv \min\{\gamma_l, \gamma_b p(qA - 1)\}$, the minimum between the cost of information for lenders and for borrowers, both expressed in terms of numeraire.

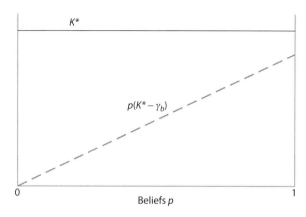

FIGURE 4.1. Expected Loan Size with Information-Sensitive Debt

In the case of using an information-sensitive loan, firms choose to produce information if $\gamma_b p(qA - 1) < \gamma_l$, and prefer that lenders produce information otherwise. When lenders produce information, borrowers compensate them for not consuming γ_l. When borrowers produce information, they divert resources away from the project, which is costly, only if they find out the land is good (with probability p) and cannot use γ_b managerial skills for production.

In Figure 4.1 we show the expected information-sensitive loan for the case in which $\gamma_b p(qA - 1) < \gamma_l$ for all p. As can be seen, the expected loan is increasing in p as the project is less likely to be financed when the collateral is less likely to be good, and it is always below the optimal loan size, K^*, as labor is inefficiently wasted in monitoring the quality of land.[2]

4.2.2.2 INFORMATION-INSENSITIVE DEBT.   Another possibility for firms is to borrow such that there is no information acquisition. As in Chapter 2, equation (2.5), lenders' participation constraint binds when

$$\widehat{q}(\eta)R_{II} + (1 - \widehat{q}(\eta))px_{II}C = K,$$

which imposing truth telling implies, $R_{II} = x_{II}pC$ and, $x_{II} = \frac{K}{pC} \leq 1$.

For this contract to be information insensitive (II), we have to guarantee that neither lenders nor borrowers have incentives to deviate and check the value of collateral privately. Lenders want to deviate because they can lend at beneficial contract provisions if the collateral is good and not lend at all if the collateral is bad. Borrowers want to deviate because they can borrow at beneficial contract provisions if the collateral is bad and renegotiate even better conditions if the collateral is good.

As in Chapter 3, following the derivation of equation (2.7), lenders do not have incentives to deviate as long as

$$K < K^l(p|\widehat{q}(\eta), II) \equiv \min\left\{K^*, \frac{\gamma_l}{(1-p)(1-\widehat{q}(\eta))}, pC\right\}. \tag{4.3}$$

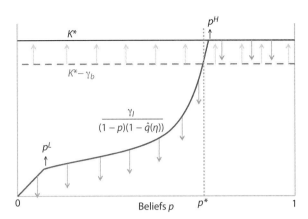

FIGURE 4.2. Expected Loan Size with Information-Insensitive Debt

As depicted in Figure 4.2, the region of information-insensitive debt that does not induce lenders to privately deviate and acquire information is the one under the solid curve.

Given the two-sided information-acquisition extension in this chapter, we need to additionally guarantee that borrowers do not want to deviate from the contract by acquiring information. Borrowers want to deviate if the expected gains from acquiring information, evaluated at x_{II} and R_{II}, are greater than the losses γ_b from acquiring information. Specifically, if borrowers acquire information, their expected benefits are $p(K^* - \gamma_b)(qA - 1) + (1 - p)\min\{K, K^* - \gamma_b\}(qA - 1)$. With probability p land is good and the firm borrows $K^* - \gamma_b$ as there are only $L^* - \gamma_b$ managerial skills remaining. With probability $1 - p$ land is bad and the firm borrows the minimum between the original contract K or the optimum conditional on having used managerial skills to acquire information, $K^* - \gamma_b$. If borrowers do not acquire information, their benefits are $K(qA - 1)$. Hence borrowers do not acquire information if

$$p(K^* - \gamma_b)(qA - 1) + (1 - p)\min\{K, K^* - \gamma_b\}(qA - 1) < K(qA - 1).$$

The condition that guarantees that borrowers do not want to produce information under information-insensitive debt can also be expressed in terms of the loan size,

$$K > K^b(p|\widehat{q}(\eta), II) \equiv K^* - \gamma_b. \tag{4.4}$$

As depicted in Figure 4.2, the region of information-insensitive debt that does not induce borrowers to privately deviate and acquire information is the one above the horizontal dotted line.

Combining conditions (4.3) and (4.4), information-insensitive debt is feasible only when the loan is both above the dotted line in Figure 4.2 (to avoid information acquisition by borrowers) and below the solid line (to avoid information acquisition by lenders). In other words, information-insensitive debt is feasible only for relatively high beliefs $p > p^*$,

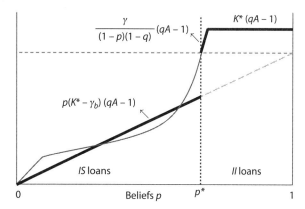

FIGURE 4.3. Expected Profits in Equilibrium

where the threshold p^* is given by the point in which $K^l(p^*) = K^b(p^*)$ from equations (4.3) and (4.4). Then

$$p^* = \max\left\{1 - \frac{\gamma_l}{(K^* - \gamma_b)(1 - \widehat{q}(\eta))}, \frac{K^* - \gamma_b}{C}\right\}. \tag{4.5}$$

It is clear from inspecting equation (4.5) that the information-insensitive debt region widens with information costs (p^* decreases with γ_b and γ_l) and shrinks with the mass of active firms (p^* increases with η since η reduces $\widehat{q}$). This is summarized in the next lemma.

Lemma 1. *The cutoff p^* is monotonically decreasing in γ_b and γ_l and increasing in η.*

The optimal loan K^* is feasible under information-insensitive debt when $p > p^H$, where the threshold p^H is given by the point in which $\frac{\gamma_l}{(1-p^H)(1-\widehat{q}(\eta))} = K^*$ from equation (4.3). Then

$$p^H = 1 - \frac{\gamma_l}{K^*(1 - \widehat{q}(\eta))}. \tag{4.6}$$

Finally, and just for completeness, the threshold p_L is given by the point in which $\frac{\gamma_l}{(1-p^L)(1-\widehat{q}(\eta))} = p^L C$ from equation (4.3). Then[3]

$$p^L = \frac{1}{2} - \sqrt{\frac{1}{4} - \frac{\gamma_l}{C(1 - \widehat{q}(\eta))}}. \tag{4.7}$$

4.2.2.3 LOANS WITH OR WITHOUT INFORMATION PRODUCTION?   Figure 4.3 shows the ex ante expected profits in both regimes (information-sensitive and information-insensitive debt) for a firm with private information about its own probability of success q, net of the expected value of land assuming $\gamma_b(q_H A - 1) \le \gamma_l$ (i.e., even firms with $p = 1$ and $q = q_H$ acquire information at a lower cost than lenders).[4]

We can summarize the expected loan sizes for different beliefs p, graphically represented with a wide black discontinuous function in Figure 4.3, by

$$K(p|\widehat{q}(\eta)) = \begin{cases} K^* & \text{if } p^H < p \\ \dfrac{\gamma_l}{(1-p)(1-\widehat{q}(\eta))} & \text{if } p^* < p < p^H \\ p(K^* - \gamma_b) & \text{if } p < p^*. \end{cases} \qquad (4.8)$$

We can see here the implication of the two-sided information-acquisition extension when comparing Figure 4.3 with Figure 2.1. With two-sided information acquisition a crisis is characterized by a drastic, discontinuous reduction in credit (for $p < p^*$), once II loans are not sustainable and only a discontinuously smaller IS can be obtained. With a single-sided information acquisition in Chapter 3 a crisis is characterized by a smooth, continuous reduction in credit (for $p < p^{Ch}$), once IS loans generate more profits than II loans. In short, with two-sided information acquisition, a preferred II loan is not feasible because the size of the loan is either too low for borrowers or too high for lenders to avoid information. To see this differently, previously we assumed that $\gamma_b = \infty$, which means that the constraint represented by the horizontal dotted line is never binding, and then output does not change discontinuously at p^*.

Another important element to notice is that as the mass of active firms, η, increases, there is a reduction of the probability of success, $\widehat{q}(\eta)$. This has three effects that induce less credit in the economy. First, the information-insensitive region where firms can obtain the optimal loan size (the first range) shrinks, as p^H decreases with $\widehat{q}(\eta)$. Second, the loan size in the information-insensitive region that is binding by information acquisition (the second range) declines. Finally, the information-sensitive region (the third range) widens, as p^* decreases with $\widehat{q}(\eta)$.

While we previously studied the effects of moving the average quality of collateral $\widehat{p}$ over the horizontal line, here we focus on changes in the average quality of projects $\widehat{q}$ that move the solid curve, then affecting the threshold p^* at which regimes change. In other words, while in the previous chapter we focused on exogenous changes in $\widehat{p}$ around p^*, here we focus on endogenous changes in p^* around $\widehat{p}$.

4.3   Credit and Growth Accounting

The previous section was based on credit for a single match of a household (young agent) and a firm (old agent) in a given period t. Now we can aggregate the results to articulate growth accounting in our model and construct the model's counterparts of the main macro variables we analyzed in the data.

Expressing the model in terms of growth accounting shows how we link to the standard macroeconomic measures in the literature. Since we decompose productivity in two parts—the probability of a firm's success, q, and the productivity conditional on success, A—we exploit the useful approach of growth accounting to shed light on the role of each component and of credit in explaining output growth and the determinants of the Solow residual.

To generate a model counterpart of productivity, assume that households are not born with numeraire $\overline{K}$ but instead produce it linearly with an endowment of labor $\overline{L}$. This implies that the total output of households in every period t is $Y_h = \overline{K}$. The total net output (after deducting the use of intermediate inputs) of a single firm that has land of quality p, conditional on η_t active firms operating in the economy, is $Y_{f,t} = K(p|\widehat{q}(\eta_t))(\widehat{q}(\eta_t) A - 1)$, where $K(p|\widehat{q}(\eta_t))$ is the credit obtained by the firm according to equation (4.8). Thus, aggregating, total credit in the economy is

$$Cr_t(\widehat{q}(\eta_t)) = \int_0^1 K(p|\widehat{q}(\eta_t))f_t(p)dp,$$

where $f_t(p)$ is the distribution of beliefs about collateral types in period t. Given the Leontief production function, the total labor used in firms' production is given by $L_f = Cr_t(\widehat{q}(\eta_t))$.

Summing over the net output of all households and firms, GDP in our model is

$$Y_t = Y_h + Y_{f,t} = \overline{K} + Cr_t(\widehat{q}(\eta_t))(\widehat{q}(\eta_t)A - 1). \tag{4.9}$$

Agents are risk neutral, so welfare is just given by aggregate consumption. The numeraire consumption good is perishable, so there is no intertemporal reallocation and then total welfare is just total output, $W_t = Y_t$. As a benchmark, note that in the unconstrained first best (the case in which output was verifiable, for example) all firms are active (i.e., $\eta = 1$) and operate with $K^* = L^*$, regardless of beliefs p about the collateral. This implies that the unconstrained first-best aggregate consumption (and output) can be defined as

$$W^* = \overline{K} + K^*(\widehat{q}(1)A - 1). \tag{4.10}$$

Since collateral with relatively low p is not able to sustain loans of K^*, the deviation of consumption from the unconstrained first best critically depends on the distribution of beliefs p in the economy. When this distribution is biased toward low perceptions of collateral values, financial constraints hinder the productive capacity of the economy. This distribution also introduces heterogeneity in production, purely given by heterogeneity in collateral and financial constraints, not by heterogeneity in technological possibilities.

In Chapter 2 we focused on studying the relationship between the growth rates of credit over GDP, TFP, and labor productivity. To construct the model's counterparts of these growth rates (that we generically denote by g in what follows) we first compute the growth rate of total output,

$$g_Y = \frac{Y_h}{Y}g_{\overline{K}} + \frac{Y_f}{Y}g_{Cr} + \frac{Y_f}{Y}\left[\frac{\widehat{q}ACr}{Y_f}(g_{\widehat{q}} + g_A) + \frac{(\widehat{q}A - 1)\widehat{q}\frac{\partial Cr}{\partial \widehat{q}}}{Y_f}g_{\widehat{q}}\right].$$

Defining $w_f = \frac{Y_f}{Y}$ as the share of firms' output of total output and recalling that $L_h = \overline{K}$ and $L_f = Cr(\widehat{q})$ are the measured labor inputs in the household and firm sectors, respectively, we can obtain the Solow residuals as

$$g_{TFP} = g_Y - (1 - w_f)g_{\overline{K}} - w_f g_{Cr},$$

which can be further rewritten as

$$g_{TFP} = w_f \left[\frac{\widehat{q}A}{(\widehat{q}A - 1)} g_A + \left(\frac{\widehat{q}A}{(\widehat{q}A - 1)} + \varepsilon_{Cr,\widehat{q}} \right) \left(\varepsilon_{\widehat{q},\psi} g_\psi + \varepsilon_{\widehat{q},\eta} g_\eta \right) \right], \qquad (4.11)$$

where $\varepsilon_{Cr,\widehat{q}} > 0$ is the elasticity of total credit to the average probability of success in the economy, $\varepsilon_{\widehat{q},\psi} > 0$ is the elasticity of the average probability of success to the exogenous shock ψ, and $\varepsilon_{\widehat{q},\eta} < 0$ is the elasticity of the average probability of success to the endogenous mass of active firms η. Notice that there are two sources of exogenous shocks to TFP growth: ψ increases the probability of success of firms' projects and A increases output conditional on success. There is also an endogenous source of TFP decline, η, which evolves with total credit in the economy.

In our setting labor productivity (LP) growth is identical to TFP growth. The reason is that $g_{LP} = g_Y - g_L$, where $g_L = (1 - w_f)g_{L_h} + w_f g_{L_f}$. Since $L_h = \overline{K}$ and $L_f = Cr$, the result follows.

Finally, the growth rate of credit over GDP is simply defined by $g_{Cr/GDP} = g_{Cr} - g_Y$. Since $g_{\overline{K}} = 0$, then $g_{Cr/GDP} = (1 - w_f)g_{Cr} - g_{TFP}$.

In the model, the state variable that evolves over time is the distribution of beliefs, $f(p)$, which affects the fraction of operating firms η and then the total credit in the economy, $Cr_t(\widehat{q}(\eta_t))$. In the next section we study how an economy that does not replenish information each period experiences a clustering of p values at the mean $\widehat{p}$, which increases η. The increase in η reduces total factor and labor productivity (if not compensated for by exogenous changes in ψ or A), which reduces output for a level of credit, increasing the ratio of credit to GDP. At the same time, the increase in η has a first-order effect of increasing credit. Even though more credit also generates more output, the ratio of credit over GDP increases because the output of households does not change with credit. In the next section we study the intricate dynamics (and potential for completely endogenous cycles) of credit, productivity, and production.

Relation with Literature on Growth Accounting.   There is a rich literature that explores the role of micro-level distortions (restrictions on labor contracts, information asymmetries, etc.) on aggregate productivity (e.g., Hopenhayn and Rogerson 1993; Guner, Ventura, and Yi 2008; Cole, Greenwood, and Sanchez 2016; and David, Hopenhayn, and Venkateswaran 2016). The effect of financial frictions on aggregate productivity and output through misallocation is a subset of this literature and has been focused on long-term growth. (For a recent and complete survey, see Matsuyama 2007 and for recent quantitative applications Jeong and Townsend 2007 and Buera, Kaboski, and Shin 2011.)

This literature focuses on long-term effects of financial development and usually considers such development exogenous. In this book we have focused on the short-term fluctuations of growth accounting when the aggregate productivity (q) is endogenous to credit, and credit moves cyclically from its endogeneity to productivity. In contrast to such literature, beliefs about collateral affect the strength of financial constraints in the economy, the allocation of resources that can be used productively by firms, and the measured productivity over the cycle.

4.4   Model Dynamics

We, as before, assume that each unit of land changes quality over time, mean reverting toward the average quality of land in the economy. We study how endogenous information acquisition shapes the distribution of beliefs over time, characterize the three possible stationary distributions, and discuss the evolution of credit, productivity, and production during transitions between these stationary distributions.

With the simple stochastic process for idiosyncratic shocks described in Chapter 3, the belief distribution has a three-point support: 0, $\widehat{p}$, and 1. Since firms holding land that is known to be bad $(p = 0)$ are inactive, the mass η of active firms is the fraction of firms with beliefs $\widehat{p}$ and 1. Then $\eta = f(\widehat{p}) + f(1)$.

4.4.1   Stationary Equilibria

Here we study the possible steady states as a function of technology—the fraction of high-quality projects, ψ. We first define three critical levels of ψ to characterize three possible steady states.

First, we introduce definitions that allow us to characterize stationary equilibria. Define first $\chi \equiv \lambda \widehat{p} + (1 - \lambda)$, a benchmark parameter that represents the lowest possible fraction of active firms after a single round of idiosyncratic shocks starting from a situation in which all land types are known: a fraction λ of the $\widehat{p}$ of firms that were known to have a good collateral remains so (then having beliefs $p = 1 > 0$), while a fraction $(1 - \lambda)$ of all collateral suffers the shock and their perceived quality, absent information acquisition, is $\widehat{p} > 0$. These are then active firms.

Fix the average quality of land, $\widehat{p}$. Assuming $\eta = \chi$ average productivity is $\widehat{q}(\chi|\psi) = \frac{\psi}{\chi} q_H + \left(1 - \frac{\psi}{\chi}\right) q_L$ and from equation (4.5) there is a technology level $\underline{\psi}$ such that $\widehat{p} = p^*(\widehat{q}(\chi|\underline{\psi}))$. Assuming now $\eta = 1$ (all firms are active), average productivity is $\widehat{q}(1|\psi) = \psi q_H + (1 - \psi) q_L$ and from equation (4.5) there is technology level $\overline{\psi}$ such that $\widehat{p} = p^*(\widehat{q}(1|\overline{\psi}))$. Finally, when $\eta = 1$, from equation (4.6) there is also a technology level $\overline{\psi}^H$ such that $\widehat{p} = p^H(\widehat{q}(1|\overline{\psi}^H))$.

The next lemma shows the relation between $\underline{\psi}$, $\overline{\psi}$, and $\overline{\psi}^H$.

Lemma 2. $\underline{\psi} < \overline{\psi} < \overline{\psi}^H$.

Proof. By construction $\widehat{p} = p^*(\widehat{q}(\chi|\underline{\psi})) = p^*(\widehat{q}(1|\overline{\psi}))$. Using equation (4.5), fixing all other parameters, $\widehat{q}(\chi|\underline{\psi}) = \widehat{q}(1|\overline{\psi})$. Then $\underline{\psi} = \chi\overline{\psi}$ and the first inequality follows as $\chi < 1$. The second inequality arises because $p^* < p^H$ for all $\widehat{q}$, p^H is decreasing in $\widehat{q}$, and $\widehat{q}$ is increasing in ψ. $\qquad\square$

The next three propositions characterize the stationary equilibrium of the economy in three regions of ψ, *low technology* ($\psi < \underline{\psi}$), *intermediate technology* ($\psi \in [\underline{\psi}, \overline{\psi}]$), and *high technology* ($\psi > \overline{\psi}$).

Proposition 9 (Low Technology: Symmetric Information—Low, Steady Consumption). If $\psi < \underline{\psi}$, the steady state is characterized by repeated information acquisition about collateral and constant consumption in every period at

$$\overline{W}(\widehat{p}) = \overline{K} + \widehat{p}(K^* - \gamma_b(1 - \lambda))(\widehat{q}(\widehat{p})A - 1) < W^*. \qquad (4.12)$$

Proof. In this case, as $\psi < \underline{\psi}$ then $\widehat{p} < p^*(\widehat{q}(\chi|\psi))$. Assuming an $\eta \geq \chi$, then $p^*(\widehat{q}(\eta|\psi)) \geq p^*(\widehat{q}(\chi|\psi))$ and $\widehat{p}$ is always in the region where information-insensitive debt is not feasible. This implies that in the steady state there is always information acquisition and in every period $f(1) = \lambda\widehat{p}, f(\widehat{p}) = (1 - \lambda)$ and $f(0) = \lambda(1 - \widehat{p})$. Since

$$W_t^{IS} = \overline{W}(\widehat{p}) = \overline{K} + [\lambda\widehat{p}K(1) + (1 - \lambda)K(\widehat{p})](\widehat{q}(\widehat{p})A - 1),$$

as $K(0) = 0$, $K(1) = K^*$ and $K(\widehat{p}) = \widehat{p}(K^* - \gamma_b)$. Then consumption is constant at the level at which information is reacquired every period, from equation (4.12), which is less than the optimal consumption from equation (4.10). The economy remains in the symmetric information regime. $\qquad\square$

In words, when the technology is poor and the probability of default is large there are high incentives for information acquisition about the collateral, even when there are few active firms. The steady state is characterized by a continuous renewal of information in the economy. In this case, as long as exogenous shocks are absent, the economy does not face any fluctuations and consumption remains below its potential.

We say that there are "*information cycles*" if the economy fluctuates between booms with no information acquisition and crashes with information acquisition. The next proposition shows this is the case when there is an intermediate technological level, that is, $\psi \in [\underline{\psi}, \overline{\psi}]$.

Proposition 10 (Intermediate Technology: Information Cycles—Sequence of Bad Booms). If $\psi \in [\underline{\psi}, \overline{\psi}]$ there is a deterministic length of the boom $t^*(\psi)$ at the end of which credit and consumption crash to the symmetric information consumption, restarting the cycle. Furthermore, $t^*(\psi)$ is increasing in ψ (the better the technology in this range, the longer the boom before it crashes).

Proof. In this case, as $\psi \in [\underline{\psi}, \overline{\psi}]$ then $\widehat{p} \geq p^*(\widehat{q}(\chi|\psi))$ and $\widehat{p} \leq p^*(\widehat{q}(1|\psi))$. Assume $\eta_1 = \chi$, and there are no incentives to acquire information about the collateral with beliefs $\widehat{p}$. Then there is no information acquisition in the first period. In the second period, $f(1) = \lambda^2 \widehat{p}$ and $f(\widehat{p}) = (1 - \lambda^2)$, implying that $\eta_2 > \eta_1$, which implies that $\widehat{q}(\eta_2) \leq \widehat{q}(\eta_1)$ and $p^*(\widehat{q}(\eta_2)) \geq p^*(\widehat{q}(\eta_1))$.

Repeating this reasoning over time, information-insensitive loans become infeasible when η_{t*} is such that $\widehat{p} = p^*(\widehat{q}(\eta_{t*}))$. We know there is such a point because in this region $\widehat{p} \leq p^*(\widehat{q}(1|\psi))$. As $W_{t*}^{II} > W_0^{II}$, the change in regime implies a crash. This crash is larger, the longer and larger the preceding boom.

Furthermore, as $\widehat{p}$ is given, then $\widehat{q}(\eta_{t*}) = \frac{\psi}{\eta_{t*}} q_H + \left(1 - \frac{\psi}{\eta_{t*}}\right) q_L$ is also given. The larger ψ is the higher η_{t*} is and the larger $t^*(\psi)$, which is the length of the boom. $\square$

The intuition for information cycles is the following. In a situation of symmetric information, in which only a fraction $\widehat{p}$ of firms gets financing, the quality of projects in the economy, in terms of their probability of success, is relatively high and there are no incentives to acquire information about collateral, and a credit boom starts. As the boom evolves over time, information decays, more firms are financed, and the average quality of projects declines.

The reduction in projects' quality increases both the probability of default in the economy and the incentives for information acquisition. At some point, when the credit boom is large enough, default rates are also large and may induce information acquisition—a change in regime from symmetric ignorance to symmetric information. A crash is characterized by only a fraction $\widehat{p}$ of firms (those with good land) obtaining credit. Then a new boom starts.

The better the technology ψ the longer the period that a bad boom lasts until it crashes. Note that there are no "shocks" needed to generate information cycles, as the steady state of the economy displays deterministic cycles. Cycles arise from the endogenous evolution of the distribution of collateral beliefs in credit markets.[5]

Finally, the next proposition characterizes the steady state when the technology is high, $\psi > \overline{\psi}$.

Proposition 11 (High Technology: Symmetric Ignorance—High, Steady Consumption). If $\psi > \overline{\psi}$, the steady state is characterized by no information acquisition about collateral and constant consumption in every period. Furthermore, if $\psi > \overline{\psi}^H$ consumption is at the unconstrained optimal level in equation (4.10).

Proof. In this case, as $\psi > \overline{\psi}$ then $\widehat{p} > p^*(\widehat{q}(1|\psi))$. Assume any $\eta \leq 1$, then $p^*(\widehat{q}(\eta|\psi)) \leq p^*(\widehat{q}(1|\psi))$ and there are never incentives to acquire information. Furthermore, if $\psi > \overline{\psi}^H$ all firms obtain a loan K^* in steady state and consumption is at the unconstrained optimum level given by equation (4.10). $\square$

In this last region, when technology is high, there are no incentives to acquire information about collateral. Over time all collateral looks alike, and the economy converges to a situation in which all firms obtain a loan and produce without spending resources on information acquisition. If the technology is high enough, output is at the unconstrained first best. This is because financial frictions are not operational given the low expected default probabilities. This is naturally the optimal situation as the economy is stable and with the maximum level of consumption. This suggests that there are also reasons from a credit market perspective for which high productivity and success probabilities are beneficial for the economy, in terms of both level and stability of activity.

Remark on Balanced Growth Paths.   Notice first that absent any exogenous shock in the economy the symmetric information and ignorance regions are *deterministic steady states*, as η is fixed, and then $g_{Cr} = 0$ and $g_{TFP} = 0$, while the asymmetric information region is a *stochastic steady state* as η is fluctuating deterministically over time; the probabilities of the various states will be repeated and remain constant. Second, notice that in case A grows at a constant rate the three regions will be on a balanced growth path, with TFP and consumption growing at the same rate, but without changing the characterization of information acquisition in credit markets or the availability of credit in each one of them.

4.4.2   Stationary Equilibria with Phase Diagrams

The next corollary summarizes the previous three propositions. The economy can be in a stationary *good boom* equilibrium (in which all firms receive credit), a stationary *no boom* equilibrium (in which only a fraction of firms receives credit), or a stationary *cyclical bad boom* equilibrium, with a deterministic sequence of booms and busts.

Corollary 4.   Define η^* the mass of active firms such that $p^*(\widehat{q}(\eta^*)) = \widehat{p}$ and $\underline{\eta} \equiv 1 - \lambda + \lambda\widehat{p}$ the lowest possible mass of active firms (all firms that suffer an idiosyncratic shock and all firms with good-quality collateral that do not face an idiosyncratic shock). Then the evolution of active firms is

$$\eta_{t+1} = 1 - \lambda + \lambda[\mathbb{I}_C\widehat{p} + (1 - \mathbb{I}_C)\eta_t],$$

where $\mathbb{I}_C = 1$ for all $\eta_t > \eta^*$ and 0 otherwise. The stationary equilibria are:

1. <u>No Boom:</u> If $\eta^* \leq \underline{\eta}$, information is replenished every period and $\eta_{SS} = \underline{\eta}$.
2. <u>Good Booms:</u> If $\eta^* \geq 1$, information is never generated and $\eta_{SS} = 1$.
3. <u>Cycles of Bad Booms:</u> If $\eta^* \in (\underline{\eta}, 1)$, information is generated only when $\eta_t > \eta^*$.

When there is no crisis (this is $\mathbb{I}_C = 0$), $\frac{\partial \eta_{t+1}}{\partial \eta_t} = \lambda$ and when there is a crisis (this is $\mathbb{I}_C = 1$), $\frac{\partial \eta_{t+1}}{\partial \eta_t} = 0$. We illustrate this next using a phase diagram. The first panel of Figure 4.4 shows the first case of the proposition, in which the mass of active firms is constant and at the minimum, as information is replenished every period. The second panel shows the

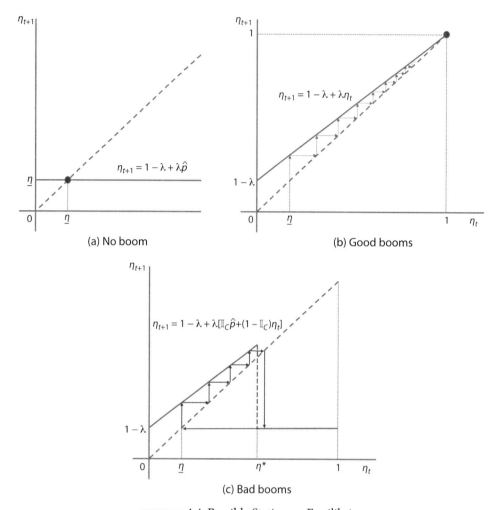

FIGURE 4.4. Possible Stationary Equilibria

second case of the proposition, in which an economy with information transits to a steady state without information about any collateral and all firms are active (a *good boom*). The third panel shows the last case of the proposition, in which the economy cycles between booms that end in crises once the mass of active firms (η^*) is high enough, just to restart the process again from $\underline{\eta}$.

4.4.3   *Transitions*

In the previous section we described the three possible stationary equilibria of the economy when technology ψ is fixed. In this section we discuss how the economy reacts to shocks to ψ such that the economy has to transit from one steady state to another. As steady states are ranked in terms of the productivity level, ψ, these shocks can be positive or negative. On the one hand, positive shocks boost credit to a new steady state, but how the credit boom ends depends on the size of the positive shock. On the other hand, negative shocks have the potential to generate crises in which credit suddenly collapses, more in line with standard views of crises driven by exogenous contemporaneous negative shocks.

If the economy experiences a technological improvement, the dynamics of the economy depend both on the size of the improvement and on the initial technological condition. If the technology is low and increases dramatically (say to high), then the economy transitions from a calm and inefficient symmetric information regime to a calm and more efficient symmetric ignorance regime—a good boom. If the technological improvement is not as dramatic (say from low to intermediate), the economy moves from a stable environment with low consumption to a cyclical environment with higher output but more volatility, characterized by a sequence of booms and busts. If the initial condition of technology is intermediate and improves (say to high), the economy moves from an unstable cyclical situation to a stable economy with higher output.[6]

Our model then captures a view that is akin to Schumpeter's (1930) argument that new products and technologies give rise to "gales of creative destruction," which would have an impact for a long time. Mokyr (1990) argues that technological progress is discontinuous and that occasional seminal inventions are the key sources of economic growth (examples include the steam engine, telegraph, and electricity).[7] Our model shows that these technological breakthroughs also play a critical role in shaping the cyclical properties of aggregate economic activity and the recurrence of financial crises.

On the other hand, if the technology is already high (say, for example, that the economy had experienced a good boom in the past), it does not imply that the economy cannot suffer a negative technological shock that induces a crisis and moves it to a worse (either less efficient or more volatile) steady state. In this situation the model also generates interesting insights. A reduction in ψ can always induce a crisis, which is more likely if the shock is larger or if the economy has been in a long boom. In other words, a negative shock can induce a crisis even in the absence of a preceding boom. This story is more in line with the standard view of crises as generated by negative contemporaneous shocks. Also in our setting a negative contemporaneous shock in productivity induces an otherwise stable credit situation to collapse and then transforms what would have been just a recession into a sudden crisis.

In the next section we illustrate numerically the difference between good and bad booms by showing the reaction of the economy to positive shocks to ψ. Negative shocks to ψ just push the economy to a trivial, but potentially permanent, destruction of credit. Even though our informational mechanism is different than most other stories in the literature, we will dispense with illustrating those cases of negative shocks to ψ as the transitions are sudden and relatively trivial.

Relation with Literature on Endogenous Cycles. The view that economic activity may cycle endogenously, and not necessarily when battered by exogenous shocks, has a long tradition in economics but has recently been abandoned. Early incarnations of this view can be traced back to Kaldor (1940) and Hicks (1950) with revisits in the 1980s with the contributions of Benhabib and Nishimura (1985) and Grandmont (1985) among others, which was surveyed in Boldrin and Woodford (1990). A recent study that revives the discussion of purely endogenous cycles, as in our setting, is Beaudry, Galizia, and Portier (2020). In their case, cycles are determined by complementarities between aggregate employment and consumption, which induce smooth deterministic cycles. In our case there are complementarities between the volume of credit and the incentives for information acquisition. Since this complementarity is not relevant unless information constraints bind, our model displays deterministic cycles that are not smooth—long booms that suddenly and dramatically end in crises. The sharp reversals after lending booms have been documented by Gopinath (2004) and Ordoñez (2013b) among others, but in our case they are generated by the evolution of information-acquisition incentives and not from search frictions or learning inertia.

Remark on Policy Implications.   There is a clear externality in our setting. When firms decide to take an information-insensitive loan, they do not internalize its effect on reducing the average productivity in the economy and increasing the incentives to acquire information. In other words, firms do not internalize the effect of their loan on the feasibility of a "symmetric ignorance" regime. A planner would take this effect into consideration, keeping average productivity from declining too much. More specifically, a planner would never allow credit booms in which the fraction of firms operating exceeds η_{t^*} to occur, for example by restricting credit or leverage, or by producing extra information, but interestingly with the main objective of avoiding too much information from being produced privately. In contrast to the dynamic intervention explored in the previous chapter, in which the planner would like to subsidize information production to prevent a boom from growing too much and then reducing the expected costs of a crisis generated by a negative exogenous shock, in this chapter the planner could prevent a crisis altogether by restricting credit once the average productivity of projects has reached a critical level.

4.4.4   Numerical Illustration

In this section we illustrate how small differences in the exogenous process of productivity can lead to large differences in the cyclical behavior of measured credit, productivity, and output. For the illustration we assume idiosyncratic shocks happen with probability $(1 - \lambda) = 0.1$ per period, in which case the collateral becomes good with probability $\widehat{p} = 0.88$. Firms' labor is $L^* = K^* = 7$, households' labor is $\bar{L} = \bar{K} = 20$ (the endowment is large enough to allow for optimal investment), and $C = 15$ (good collateral is good enough to sustain an optimal loan size). The costs of information are $\gamma_l = 0.35$ for households in terms of numeraire and $\gamma_b = 0.05$ for firms in terms of labor. Finally, a fraction ψ of projects (which we will vary) has a probability of success $q_H = 0.7$ and the rest a lower one, $q_L = 0.4$. Conditional on success the firm produces $A = 15$ units of numeraire.

First, we show how three different levels of technology (captured by ψ) generate three very different steady states as described in Propositions 9, 10, and 11 in Section 4.4.1.

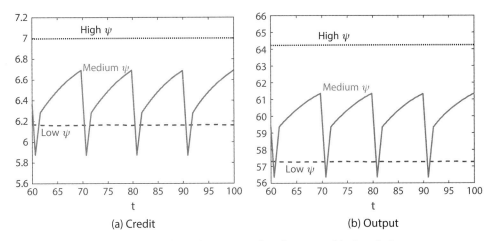

FIGURE 4.5. Credit and Output: The Three Possible Steady States

Given the previous parameters, when the technology level is low ($\psi = 0.52$), the economy displays a low credit and low output steady state with continuous information replenishment, as characterized in Proposition 9. This situation is depicted by the dashed line in Figure 4.5.

When there are more good projects ($\psi = 0.62$) the technology is high and the steady state is characterized by Proposition 11. Credit and output are also stable but higher than in the previous case. This result arises from high levels of credit (as all firms obtain credit and operate) and high levels of GDP (both because there is more activity and because TFP is higher). This situation is depicted by the dotted black line in Figure 4.5.

Finally, for an intermediate level of technology ($\psi = 0.57$), the steady state is in a cyclical situation, with a sequence of bad booms as characterized in Proposition 10. In this situation both credit and GDP fluctuate periodically, with periods above the level of an economy with worse technology (when credit is growing) but also with periods below it (when there are crises). This situation is depicted by the solid line in Figure 4.5.

Now, based on Section 4.4.3, we illustrate transitions. We focus on how an economy that is originally in an information-sensitive regime, with a low and stable output, responds to an exogenous positive and permanent productivity shock that increases the average probability of projects succeeding. We show that if this change is not large enough, the economy will transition to a regime with deterministic credit booms followed by crises— a sequence of bad booms. When the shock is followed by a series of other small positive shocks that make further technological improvements, the economy may experience a credit boom that drives the economy toward the first best, where the credit boom gets exhausted without experiencing a crisis—a good boom.

More precisely, as above we assume that ψ changes from 0.52 to 0.59. In itself this change will make the economy transition to a cyclical steady state. We plot the evolution of the two main variables we measured in the data, credit over GDP (solid light grey) and TFP (dashed light grey), in Figure 4.6. To compare to a good boom, we assume another

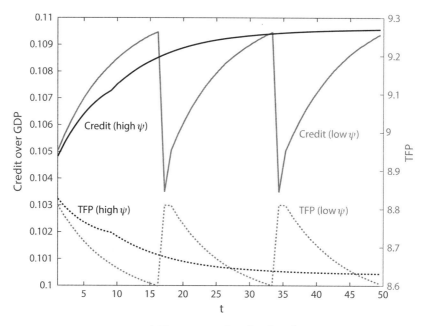

FIGURE 4.6. Transitions: Good and Bad Booms

situation in which, after the shock, ψ keeps increasing at a rate of 1% for 10 periods, reaching a level of 0.60. This higher level of technology that is achieved during the boom makes the economy transition into a different, information-insensitive steady state—a good boom. This second possibility is depicted by the dark line in the figure.

The credit boom generates an endogenous decline in TFP; however, we have assumed an exogenous force that compensates this decline in the second case. When the decline in productivity is less severe, crises are less likely (not likely in this illustration) to end in crisis, which is consistent with our main empirical findings. Credit growth is the same in both types of booms, but productivity (and output) is higher during a good boom. This implies that credit over GDP is higher during bad booms. This is, however, in contrast to the common interpretation of excessive leverage in the literature, as in our model credit grows at the same rate in both cases, but during a bad boom such credit goes to projects that are less productive, which puts on pressure for information acquisition and crises. This relation justifies why large credit booms predict crises—they are based on a situation in which credit increases faster than the output it sustains. Note that our setting does not predict the numerator being different across good booms and bad booms but instead that GDP is lower in bad booms, as productivity is lower. We examine this empirically below.

These numerical examples illustrate the rich interactions between productivity and credit in an economy and their implications for its cyclical behavior. An economy may experience credit booms that take the economy from a low, stable output level to a higher level of stable output without financial crises, which we have denoted as "good booms." It can also experience a movement from a low, stable output level to a sequence of booms and busts that exist even without fundamental changes, which we have denoted as "bad booms."

4.5   The Financial Crisis of 2007–2008: A Case of a Bad Boom

The Financial Crisis of 2007–2008 was unexpected and, unlike earlier bank runs, was not seen except by those on trading floors. And those on trading floors did not understand what they were seeing because the run was not on demand deposits at banks but on another form of short-term debt, sale and repurchase agreements (repo). Repo is used in the wholesale market, while demand deposits are an instrument for the retail market.

This crisis involved all the forces and factors that we have included in our model. First, there was a positive productivity shock a decade before the crisis. Second, there was a credit boom starting about nine years before the crisis onset. Third, this credit boom was sustained by the creation and structuring of collateral. And finally, there was the crisis, and informational crisis, that coincided with a decline in the value of underlying collateral and with a slowdown in productivity.

We start by briefly describing the transformation of banking in the United States in the decade that preceded the crisis and the buildup to the crisis. Then we discuss the role of repo and the crisis itself.

4.5.1   The Transformation of Banking

The transformation of the U.S. banking system is dramatically seen in Figure 4.7 (from Gorton, Lewellen, and Metrick 2010). It shows the components of privately produced safe debt as a ratio to total privately produced safe assets. The transformation of the U.S. banking system started in the late 1970s and accelerated in the 1990s. The figure shows the rise of the "shadow banking system." By the start of the financial crisis in 2007, the shadow banking system was larger than the traditional banking system.

The darkest part of the figure at the bottom is demand deposits (as a percentage of total privately produced safe debt). Demand deposits have fallen from almost 80 percent of privately produced safe assets to about 30 percent. The next component from the bottom is money market instruments, including repo, various kinds of commercial paper, and money market funds. Finally, AAA/Aaa tranches of securitizations (the most senior tranche of a portfolio backed by loans, notably home mortgages, but also credit card receivables, auto loans, student loans, and others) are indicated by horizontal lines.

The two banking systems are symbiotic. Loans originating in the traditional banking system are securitized into bonds and the AAA/Aaa part is used as collateral to back repo and asset-backed commercial paper.[8] Xie (2012) shows that 85 percent of a securitized loan portfolio is AAA/Aaa. Indeed, the purpose of securitization is to produce "safe" debt that can be used as collateral for credit purposes. Since securitization is the process of pooling and tranching assets of heterogeneous qualities, this is consistent with the

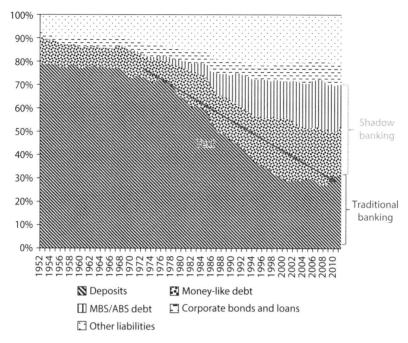

FIGURE 4.7. Components of Privately Produced Safe Debt
(as % of Total Private Safe Assets)
Source: Gorton, Lewellen, and Metrick (2012).

elements we introduced to the model and that led to the discussion of collateral design in Section 2.2.5.

The transformation of the financial system had been going on for decades prior to the crisis. Behind the figure there are many forces at work that turned the banking system into a wholesale system rather than a retail system. One was the enormous increase in global wealth, which resulted in various types of agents, such as institutional investors, financial firms, pension funds, and sovereign wealth funds, controlling billions and billions in cash for investment. Before the cash is invested, these agents need a "demand deposit," an instrument where the money can be invested for a short period of time and earn interest. The repo contract accomplishes such a goal. These investors receive collateral with a market value equal to the loan amount.

The collateral for repo was often asset-backed or mortgage-backed securities. Privately produced safe debt was used in part because of the global savings glut, during which the United States saw large and sustained capital inflows from foreigners seeking U.S. assets to store value, largely restricting their purchases to U.S. Treasuries and Agency debt.[9]

Putting this all together, traditional banking worked like this: the bank would borrow in the demand deposit market, paying, say, 3 percent, and lend the money to a borrower buying a home, a mortgage contract, where the bank earns 6 percent. Thus, the bank earns 6–3, which is why banking is called a spread business. With securitization, the home mortgages are securitized and can be used for collateral for repo. The depositor/lender earns 3

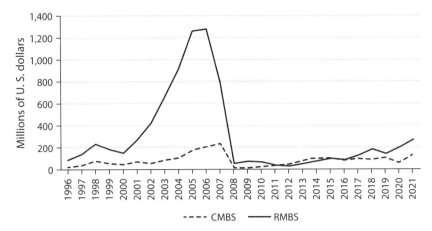

FIGURE 4.8. Issuance of RMBS and CMBS
Source: Securities Industry and Financial Markets Association

percent and the dealer bank provides mortgage-backed securities (MBS) as collateral. Say the MBS collateral earns 6 percent. This money accrues to the borrowing dealer bank. So, the dealer bank earns 6–3, where the "depositor" is an institution depositing in the repo market.

4.5.2   Buildup to the Crisis

The buildup to the financial crisis involved three important forces: (1) a positive shock to productivity, which then tails off significantly prior to the crisis; (2) a credit boom most notably in residential mortgages; and (3) a shortage of safe debt to be used for collateral. We discussed the link between good booms, bad booms, and productivity growth in Chapter 1. The Financial Crisis of 2007–2008 was a bad boom. The pattern of productivity growth during the period leading up to the crisis was as described in that chapter. The shortage of collateral was solved by securitization, which is the process of producing "safe" debt from bank loans, as we described in Section 2.2.5.

The positive shock to productivity occurred in the mid-1990s. Kahn and Rich (2007) detect a regime switch from a low-productivity period to a high-productivity period in 1997. As Cette and colleagues wrote: "There was a burst of innovation and reallocation related to the production and use of information technology in the second half of the 1990s and the early 2000s. That burst ran its course prior to the Great Recession" (2016, 3). There was also a credit boom, as shown in Figure 4.8. The credit boom induced bank loans, particularly residential mortgages, to be securitized into AAA/Aaa safe collateral, which became important because of a shortage of highly rated collateral in the economy.[10] From the lens of our model this captures a decline in the average quality of collateral in the economy as the credit boom evolves (i.e., a gradual reduction in $\widehat{p}$ as credit grows). The system partially reacted to this decline in quality by making securitization and financial products increasingly complex (this is an increase in the cost of information γ), but the pressures for information acquisition also were building up.

4.5.3   Repo

To understand the financial crisis, let's first look at some of the mechanics of repo. In a repo transaction, one side, the lender or depositor, gives, say, $100 to a dealer bank.[11] The dealer bank gives $100 worth of collateral (at market prices) to the lender and promises to pay interest overnight. The collateral is provided to make the deposit or loan safe, as in our model, facilitating credit. According to the contract, if one side of the transaction goes bankrupt the solvent side can unilaterally terminate the contract and keep the collateral or cash. A repo contract is the closest contract to an insured demand deposit. The limit on deposit insurance, $250,000 in the United States ($80,000 before the crisis), makes deposits unsecure for institutions that are seeking to store large amounts overnight safely, and earn interest.

For our purposes it is important to understand what a repo "haircut" is. Take a simplified version of the above repo transaction. Suppose the dealer bank rushes out to the market and buys $100 worth of AAA/Aaa mortgage-backed securities (MBS) to give to the lender as collateral. In this case, the lender of the $100 financed the entire MBS, and the dealer bank earns the return on the MBS even though it is held by the lender as collateral. The next day suppose the lender is nervous about the macroeconomy and asks to keep the $100 of collateral but wants the dealer to return $10 of the original deposit (or loan). This will mean that the lender is overcollateralized. In effect, the lender has withdrawn $10 that the dealer bank must make up to finance the bond. This is called a 10 percent haircut. In the crisis, to raise the $10 the dealer will have to sell assets (issuing new securities is not practicable).

Standard finance theory would say that the lender should demand a higher overnight interest rate to compensate for the perceived increase in risk. This did happen at the start of the crisis in early 2007, but then the haircut became positive. Why is there a haircut? The collateral is information-insensitive debt. It is complicated to examine securitized bonds, which no one can really value. The bonds are accepted at par for collateral. It must be this way. When the lender appears to lend $100 and the dealer bank offers the $100 of MBS as collateral, the lender cannot say, "Well, I need my credit team to analyze this MBS to see if it is really AAA/Aaa." Overnight repo or, in general, short-term repo could not work this way. The privately produced collateral must be information insensitive. A haircut compensates for the essentially unknown risk of the MBS. This is captured in our model by the reduction in the loan that the firm (akin to the dealer bank in our story) can sustain without collateral turning information sensitive to households (akin to the lender in this story), and captured by equation (2.6).

There are no official statistics on the overall size of the bilateral repo market. The Federal Reserve collects data only from the primary dealers (banks authorized to transact with the Fed's open market desk). The Fed's numbers are inadequate (see Gorton, Metrick, and Ross 2020). Hordahl and King report that the amount traded in repo markets doubled since 2002, "with gross amounts outstanding at year end 2007 of roughly $10 trillion in each of the U.S. and euro markets, and another $1 trillion in the UK repo market"

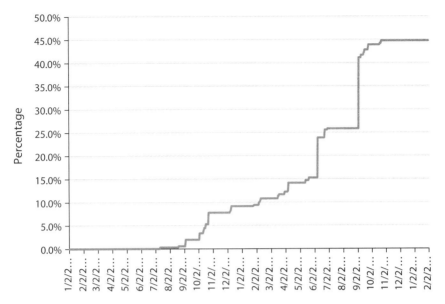

FIGURE 4.9. Average Repo Haircut on Structured Debt

(2008, 37). They also report that the U.S. repo market exceeded $10 trillion in mid-2008, including double counting. Gorton and Metrick (2012) and Singh and Aitken (2010) also estimate the pre-crisis U.S. repo market size to be around $10 trillion.

4.5.4   The Panic

The crisis began in the first quarter of 2007, as discussed in Gorton, Metrick, and Xie 2014. During this period, the maturities of short-term debt began to shorten, repo spreads widened, and there was a run on asset-backed commercial paper conduits, as documented in Covitz, Liang, and Suarez (2013). Repo haircuts first rose in October 2007. On December 12, 2007, the Federal Reserve announced the opening of the Term Auction Facility (TAF) to provide liquidity to the market. The TAF was a mechanism under which the Federal Reserve auctioned collateral-backed short-term loans to depository institutions.

The shortening of maturities on short-term debt continued, as did the rise in repo haircuts, culminating in the collapse of Lehman Brothers, the fourth largest investment bank, with $600 billion in assets and 25,000 employees. The bankruptcy of Lehman Brothers was the largest in U.S. history. A firm the size of Lehman could only go bankrupt over a weekend if it was significantly financed with overnight repo, which were loans that were not going to be rolled over the following Monday.

The panic is illustrated in Figure 4.9. The figure shows the increase in the equally weighted average haircut on twelve structured products, that is, various kinds of securitization collateral. Figure 4.10, which presents an incomplete picture (because the flow of funds data are incomplete), nevertheless shows the dramatic fall in repo during the panic.

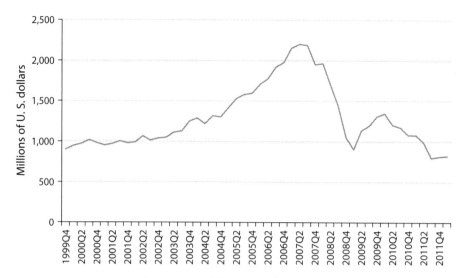

FIGURE 4.10. Net Funding Received from Repo (Dealer and Commercial Banks)

A back-of-the-envelope calculation is as follows. The average haircut went from essentially zero to, say, 30 percent and the size of the repo market was $10 trillion. That means that $3 trillion was withdrawn from the banking system. Raising that amount of money meant selling assets and eventually going to various emergency lending facilities set up by the Federal Reserve.

What led to the panic? The forces highlighted by our model were all present. First, there was a positive shock to productivity in the 1990s, which then tailed off prior to the crisis. As documented by Fernald (2012), there was a productivity slowdown starting in 2005, which according to our model increases the likelihood of default and the incentives to acquire information about underlying collateral (in our model, this manifests as an increase in p^*). Second, there was a prolonged and large credit boom, which resulted in collateral quality declining (in our model, a reduction in $\widehat{p}$). Third, there was a reduction in the price of housing that started in 2005 in the United States, which also manifested as a reduction in the expected value of collateral (again, akin to a reduction in $\widehat{p}$). Fourth, there was a large amount of short-term debt outstanding with short maturities and high reliance on collateral, making the economy very fragile.

4.6   The Roaring Twenties: Another Case of a Bad Boom

To understand the role of credit granted to households and to corporations during a credit boom ending in a crisis, we briefly look at the Roaring Twenties in the United States, the famous credit boom leading up to the Great Depression. The Roaring Twenties illustrates the variety of credit granted during a boom as well as the decline or maturing of the technological innovations that started at the beginning of that decade, leading up to the crisis, which we have modeled as a decline in average productivity over a bad boom.

The Roaring Twenties was also an investment boom, as more generally shown in Table 1.2. It was a period of intense technological innovation, deemed by Field to be "the most technologically progressive decade of the century" (2006, 203). There seems to have been a sharp upward movement in TFP at the start of this era, a technology shock. In Solomon Fabricant's introduction to John Kendrick's study of productivity trends in the United States, he noted: "A distinct change in trend appeared sometime after World War I. By each of our measures, productivity rose, on the average, more rapidly after World War I than before. . . . The change in trend . . . is one of the most interesting facts before us" (1961, xliii). David and Wright also note "a marked acceleration of productivity growth in U.S. manufacturing occurred after World War I" (1999, 1).

According to Field, "Manufacturing contributed almost all 83 percent of the growth of total factor productivity in the U.S. private non-farm economy between 1919 and 1929" (2006, 203). "The extraordinary TFP growth in manufacturing in the 1920s was largely driven by floor space savings and improved materials flow associated with newly laid out factories. The rearrangements were made possible by the removal of the straightjacket previously imposed by a mechanical distribution of internal power" (227). There was also a large increase in the use of electric power (see Devine 1983). Other examples of this burst of innovation include the radio and other electrical appliances, assembly-line production for cars, petrochemicals, and new materials like Teflon and nylon (see Field 2003, 2006; Raff 1991). Further, the National Research Council data show that between 1919 and 1928 inclusive, companies founded an average of 66 R&D labs per year (see Field 2003). According to Gordon: "The rise in output of cars, trucks, and accessories accounted for roughly a third of the total increase in the flow of finished commodities between 1909–13 and 1923–1929. Comparing the flow of finished commodities from the automobile industry with the total flow of all finished commodities, both in producers' 1913 prices, for selected years between 1909 and 1929, we find that by 1920, the output of the motor industry had already expanded some 2 billion, in 1913 prices, since 1990" (1951, 189). Smiley (2008), Oshima (1984), and Soule (1947) provide further overviews of technological change prior to and during the Roaring Twenties.

What types of credit were granted during the Roaring Twenties? Table 4.1 shows the changes in the quantity of different types of credit granted during the period. The percentage changes, in the last column, show that real estate loans, including urban home mortgages, had the highest growth. Commercial mortgages also grew a great deal. Non–real estate loans and corporate bond issuance also grew, but not by as much. The credit boom, it seems, consisted of a variety of different types of credit, but mortgages were the largest component. Although, as Gordon points out: "It is difficult to say to what extent the housing boom should be considered an independent influence in the '20's. In part it arose out of the changes created by the automobile. This was true also of commercial building. In part the housing boom was due to the war, which tended to push forward into the '20's a good deal of private investment that otherwise would have occurred earlier" (1951, 212).

Table 4.1. Credit during the Roaring Twenties

Changes in Credit by Type (in Millions of U. S. Dollars) during the Roaring Twenties			
Type of Credit	1920–1924	1925–1929	1920–1929
Total Loans and Investments	841	7,566	17%
Real Estate Loans	2,723	2,600	114%
Non–Real Estate Loans	841	7,566	34%
Domestic Corporate Bond Issuance	10,138	13,739	35%
Urban Home Mortgages	20	41.5	108%
Urban Commercial Mortgages	16.3	31.6	94%

The Roaring Twenties is also an illustration of the technological change slowing or "maturing." Gordon put it this way:

> The investment boom of the '20's resulted from a concentrated flowering of investment opportunities, created by the rapid maturing of a series of new industries and new services. . . . The "gestation period" for the new industries of the '20's was short compared with that of the railroads or steel in an earlier period. By 1929 automobiles, electric power, road-building, the new service industries, and so on were at or near maturity; they no longer needed, for replacement or for further growth, the same volume of investment as formerly. (1951, 211)

In other words, the new technologies ran out of steam, resulting in a crisis, the Great Depression. The Roaring Twenties is an example of a bad boom.[12]

4.7   Some Empirical Tests

In this section we test an assumption we use in the model and two predictions that the model delivers.

The assumption we test is that default is a component of measured TFP. While measured TFP is a residual that may contain several factors, in our model TFP growth is a combination of the growth of the probability of success $(\widehat{q})$ and the growth of output conditional on success (A), as shown in equation (4.11). We have deliberately constructed the model such that only $\widehat{q}$, not A, affects incentives to examine collateral in credit markets. Then our model is based on the insight that there is a component in our measure of TFP that drives the probability of default and then affects debt markets, while there is another component that determines the gains in case of success (and then repayment), which affects equity markets, not debt markets. Based on this we show that changes in TFP are correlated with changes in a measure of firm fragility (likelihood of failure).

The two predictions we test relate to the different behavior of default frequency and GDP growth during good and bad booms. The first prediction of the model is that firms are increasingly more fragile over bad booms, relative to good booms. The second prediction, as we discussed in the numerical example, is that while the growth in total credit is the same during both types of booms, productivity and output grow less during bad booms, and then credit over GDP grows more during bad booms.

4.7.1   Firm Default Is a Component of TFP

Testing the assumption that default is a component of TFP is hard because we do not have bankruptcy data, nor do we have business failures for our panel of countries. We can, however, use equity data to produce a measure of firm fragility introduced and studied by Atkeson and colleagues (2013). As a measure of firm fragility, they introduce distance-to-insolvency (DI), based on Merton (1975) and Leland (1994). DI measures the adequacy of a firm's equity cushion relative to its business risk. They show that this is a good proxy for the probability of default and that it can be measured with the inverse of the volatility of a firm's equity returns.[13] We construct $\frac{1}{vol_{j,t}}$ for a country j at year t, based on daily stock price data for all listed companies for each country in our sample. The period for which these data are available differs somewhat across countries. Also, the number of listed firms changes over time. See Table B.6 in Appendix B for details. More specifically, for a given country we calculate the monthly stock return volatility for each listed company based on daily data. We then take the median of the monthly volatilities for each firm in a year. This is the annual measure of firm fragility we use for each country in each year, $vol_{j,t}$.

Note that a decrease in $\frac{1}{vol_{j,t}}$ corresponds to an economy becoming more fragile (as volatility is larger). To test our assumption we examine versions of the following regressions, with and without fixed effects:

$$\Delta(TFP)_{j,t} = \alpha + \beta \Delta \frac{1}{vol_{j,t-i}} + \epsilon_{j,t}.$$

In Table 4.2 the results are shown for changes in the variables over different horizons, that is, $i = 1$ year, 2 years, out to 5 years, confirming that a significant component of measured TFP is firm fragility.

These results suggest that firms' fragility, which is the productivity component that we highlight in this book as affecting credit markets the most, is an important part of TFP. In Figure B.3 in Appendix B we show a scatter plot of this regression for all countries as well as specific examples for some countries that illustrate the robustness of this relationship.

4.7.2   Firms Default More during Bad Booms

Atkeson, Eisfeldt, and Weill (2013) show that in the United States the measure of fragility for the entire economy was uniquely low for the Great Depression, the recession of

Table 4.2. Default as a Component of TFP

	$(i=1)$		$(i=2)$		$(i=3)$		$(i=4)$		$(i=5)$	
α	0.00		0.01		0.02		0.02		0.03	
t-Statistic	3.97		5.32		7.18		8.57		9.49	
β	0.02	0.02	0.02	0.02	0.02	0.03	0.02	0.02	0.02	0.02
t-Statistic	4.10	4.32	3.97	4.33	4.32	4.83	3.43	3.99	2.84	3.50
R^2	0.02	0.07	0.02	0.11	0.02	0.16	0.01	0.19	0.01	0.22
N	871	871	839	839	807	807	775	775	743	743
FE	No	Yes	No	Yes	No	Yes	No	Yes	No	Yes

Table 4.3. Firm Fragility over Good Booms and Bad Booms

	Whole Sample	Booms	Booms with a Crisis	Booms without a Crisis	t-Stat for Means
Number of Booms		87	34	53	
1/Volatility	2.75	2.82	2.61	3.03	−4.24

1938–1939, and the crisis of 2007. Table 4.3 shows that our first prediction is borne out just comparing means. Firms are significantly more fragile, on average, over bad booms compared to good booms.

We formalize these results with the following regression, which is a version of regression (1.2) but using fragility instead of productivity changes.

$$Pr(BadBoom_{j,t})|Boom_{j,t}) = F_L\left(\alpha + \beta\,\frac{1}{vol_{j,t-1}}\right).$$

Table 4.4 shows that the coefficient on this variable is significantly negative, meaning that the likelihood of being in a bad boom, conditional on being in a boom, is increasing as the fragility of the firms in the economy increases.

4.7.3   GDP Grows Less during Bad Booms

In our model, total credit grows at the same rate during both good and bad booms, but productivity and output grow more during a good boom. This implies that credit over GDP grows faster during bad booms, which is confirmed in the first row of Table 1.2. We can probe into this further by looking at the numerator and the denominator separately. The second row of Table 1.2 shows that total credit (the numerator) grows on average 13.95% in bad booms and 13.03% in good booms, with this difference not statistically significant ($t=-0.7$). The third and fourth rows of Table 1.2 decompose the sources of total credit

Table 4.4. $\frac{1}{vol}$, Good Booms and Bad Booms

	Volatility		
	LOGIT		LPM
α	0.97	0.72	
t-Statistic	3.79	12.56	
β	−34.79	−8.03	−10.40
t-Statistic	−4.04	−4.24	−6.03
Marginal	−0.10	−0.09	−0.12
R^2		0.03	0.66
N	522	522	522
FE	No	No	Yes

growth. While corporate credit grows at roughly the same rate in both booms (around 3.6%), credit to households indeed grows less during bad booms (8.5% versus 6.7%), which contradicts the common view that credit booms that end in crises are fueled by particularly strong boosts of credit toward households. In fact, the seventh row of Table 1.2 shows that real GDP grows on average 2.4% in bad booms and 3.1% in good booms, with this difference statically significant ($t = 3.28$). So, this model prediction not only is confirmed but also differentiates our model from others that are driven by total credit instead of being driven by what the credit finances. This finding, consistent with our model, suggests that a crisis is more likely to be predicted not by monitoring the growth of total credit but instead the growth of productivity that such increase in credit generates.

Remark on Testing the Informational Mechanism. Even though these empirical results confirm two predictions of the model, we have not directly tested the mechanism of information, under which the crisis is caused by a switch to producing information about collateral from a previous state of not producing information about collateral. Our data limits what we can analyze, but others have produced consistent direct evidence. Benmelech and Bergman (2018) show that when the price of bonds falls, they become very illiquid, corresponding in our model to collateral becoming unusable for borrowing. They also show that the causality runs from prices going down (information being produced) and not the other way around (prices go down in anticipation of future illiquidity). In addition, they demonstrate that the effects show a distinct nonlinearity as the value of a bond nears the default point. Their study is not, however, about crises.

In our model, a financial crisis is a sudden switch from information-insensitive debt to information-sensitive debt. Brancati and Macchiavelli (2019) provide evidence for this switch. They find that at the onset of a crisis more analysts are assigned to cover banks and that these analysts produce significantly more precise information, measured by the standard deviation of their bank ROA forecasts. The precision of the ROA forecasts has a larger impact on bank credit default swap spreads in a crisis compared to non-crisis periods. Also, they show that more precise information has a larger impact on banks that are expected to do poorly, those banks with prior "bad" ROA forecasts. In short, in a crisis more precise information amplifies market expectations of default risk and increases default risk for banks that are expected to perform poorly. These effects are not present in non-crisis times. Dang and colleagues (2020) summarize other empirical studies on the mechanism.

Further, as mentioned above, in our model TFP growth is a combination of the growth of the probability of success (q) and the growth of output conditional on success (A). In other words, one component of TFP that drives the probability of default affects debts, while the other component, which affects the gains in case of success, affects equity markets, not debt markets. We will examine this in the next chapter.

4.8   Alternative Model with Mortgages

Consider a single-period economy, with a mass 1 of risk-neutral households and deep-pocket lenders. Households have an exogenous endowment c of numeraire good at the beginning of the period and can work during the period to obtain a wage w at the end of the period. The lender verifies that the household is employed at the beginning of the period, but employment is uncertain. With probability q the household maintains his work and with probability $(1 - q)$ he is laid off. Households obtain utility from homeownership. A house of size K (in terms of the price in units of numeraire) generates marginal utility $A > 1$ for $K \leq K^*$, and 0 for $K > K^*$. This assumption just guarantees an optimal housing size of K^*.

If labor income were verifiable, state contingent contracts would implement the optimal consumption of housing. In this case, households would borrow $K^* - c$ from lenders, promising 0 in case of being unemployed and $\frac{K^* - c}{q}$ in case of being employed. As long as $w > \frac{K^* - c}{q}$, lenders break even and all households would consume housing of size K^*, obtaining an expected utility of

$$E(U)_{opt} = K^* A + q \left(w - \frac{K^* - c}{q} \right) = c + qw + K^*(A - 1).$$

If labor income is non-verifiable, households can use the house they buy as collateral. We assume that a lender who seizes a house of size K in case of default can resell it at K with probability p, but cannot resell it at all with probability $1 - p$ (then generating 0 to the lender, as the lender does not obtain any utility from holding the house). We assume the lender can analyze the housing market to determine the value of the house at a cost γ_l in terms of the numeraire good. Households can also endeavor in such analysis at a cost γ_b in terms of housing. As in the main text, the question is whether there is information about the (marketability of the) house or not at the time of issuing the mortgage.

Information-Sensitive Mortgage.   Lenders are competitive and they break even when

$$p[qR_{IS} + (1 - q)x_{IS}K] = p(K - c) + \gamma,$$

with $\gamma = \min\{\gamma_l, \gamma_b\}$. As in the main text, truth telling implies that households should pay the same in case of success or failure, $R_{IS} = x_{IS}K$. Then $x_{IS} = \frac{p(K-c)+\gamma}{pK} \leq 1$. Expected total utility of households (both from consumption and housing) is $c + qw + p(KA - x_{IS}K)$. Then, plugging x_{IS} in equilibrium, and as households buy a house of size K^* when obtaining a mortgage, *expected net utility* (net of the endowment and expected labor income $c + qw$) from an information-sensitive mortgage is

$$E(U|p, q, IS) = \max\{pK^*(A - 1) - \gamma, 0\}.$$

Intuitively, with probability p the households can obtain a mortgage for K^*, which generates a net utility of $K^*(A - 1)$ of housing services, and with probability $(1 - p)$ the house does not have any resale value and then the household cannot obtain a mortgage. Notice this is almost identical to the expected profits from information-sensitive loans we derived in the main text.

Information-Insensitive Mortgage.   Another possibility for households is to borrow such that there is no information acquisition about the house that will serve as collateral. As in the text, information acquisition is private. Lenders break even when

$$qR_{II} + (1 - q)x_{II}pK = K - c,$$

subject to truth telling, $R_{II} = x_{II}pK$. Then $x_{II} = \frac{K-c}{pK} \leq 1$.

For this contract to be information insensitive, we have to guarantee that neither lenders nor borrowers have incentives to deviate and check the value of collateral privately before the loan is negotiated and to take advantage of such private information before it becomes common knowledge. Lenders want to deviate because they can lend at beneficial contract provisions if the house has a market for sure and not lend at all if the house cannot be resold. Borrowers want to deviate because they can borrow at beneficial contract provisions if the house cannot be resold and they can renegotiate even better conditions if the house can be resold.

Formally, lenders do not want to deviate if the expected gains from acquiring information, evaluated at x_{II} and R_{II}, are smaller than the private losses, γ_l, from acquiring information,

$$p[qR_{II} + (1 - q)x_{II}K - (K - c)] < \gamma_l \qquad \Rightarrow \qquad K < c + \frac{\gamma_l}{(1-p)(1-q)}.$$

As mortgages are never larger than K^*,

$$K < K^l(p|q, II) \equiv \min\left\{K^*, c + \frac{\gamma_l}{(1-p)(1-q)}\right\}. \tag{4.13}$$

Similarly, borrowers do not want to deviate if the expected gains from acquiring information, evaluated at x_{II} and R_{II}, are smaller than the losses from acquiring information.

Specifically, if borrowers acquire information, their expected benefits are $p(K^*(A-1) - \gamma_b) + (1-p)K(A-1)$. With probability p the house has a resale value and the household borrows K^*. Recall that for simplicity we have assumed that the information cost is in terms of housing and then it only applies if the house can be resold, with probability p. With probability $1-p$ the house does not have any resale value and the household borrows the original contract K. If borrowers do not acquire information, their benefits are $K(A-1)$. Hence borrowers do not acquire information if

$$K > K^b(p|q, II) \equiv K^* - \frac{\gamma_b}{(A-1)}. \tag{4.14}$$

An information-insensitive mortgage is only feasible when conditions (4.13) and (4.14) are both satisfied. In this case the expected net utility of households becomes

$$E(U|p, q, II) = \max\{K^l(p|q, II), K^b(p|q, II)\}(A-1).$$

Notice again that the problem is almost identical in structure to the one in the main text. In particular constraint (4.14) does not depend on q, while constraint (4.13) does. This implies that, as q declines, the range of p for which an information-insensitive mortgage is feasible shrinks, making crises more likely for a given average resalability of houses $\widehat{p}$.

Dynamics.   The same dynamics hold in this case. Denote by η the volume of mortgages in the economy; this is the leverage and indebtedness of households for homeownership. One possibility is that the increase in household indebtedness in the economy increases labor supply by a dominating wealth effect, reducing the likelihood of finding a job for each individual, reducing q. Our setting has the same dynamic implications as in the main text as long as $q(\eta)$ declines with household leverage. Another possibility is that the increase in household leverage reduces the probability a house can be resold on average. If $\widehat{p}(\eta)$ is a decreasing function of η, information-insensitive mortgages are more difficult to sustain and then the system is also more prone to suffer a crisis.

4.9   Summary

In this chapter, we provided a model that relates productivity, credit booms, and financial crises in a way that is consistent with the facts of Chapter 1. Investments based on a positive technological shock may be financed by information-insensitive debt that has the potential to generate deterministic business cycles. When technology is good enough there are no incentives to examine the collateral that backs the debt. As information about collateral decays there is a credit boom that endogenously reduces the quality of projects that are financed and increases the incentives to acquire such information. Once this pressure is large enough, there is a wave of collateral examination, which destroys credit and generates a crash (recession or depression).

In our setting the change of technological opportunities is exogenous for simplicity. In reality innovation is an endogenous process, usually subject to sudden discoveries. The diffusion of technology takes time because firms need financing. As the credit boom develops, more firms get financing and the technology diffuses. But if over time there is decreasing productivity of marginal projects, then a crisis will eventually occur. The innovation runs out of steam, so to say. This endogenous process is outside the scope of this work, but a fruitful path for future research is to understand how endogenous growth and financial crises relate.

Even though in this chapter we have highlighted the critical role of information in credit markets, in relation with the endogenous evolution of macroeconomic variables, most notably productivity, we have abstracted from the operation of another important market in the economy for which information is also critical: stock markets in which firms are traded. In the next chapter we add stock markets and study the dynamic interaction between the information revealed in those markets about firms and the information concealed in credit markets about collateral. We show that stock markets have an additional benefit, on top of the well-known allocative role in the economy, in preventing financial crises. If that happens, however, it is at the cost of restricting credit to efficient firms. In few words, we will show that stock markets constitute an endogenous, and costly, macroprudential mechanism.

5

The Crisis Prevention Role
of Stock Markets

5.1   Chapter Overview

Here we add stock markets to the model of the previous chapter. Stock markets reveal information so it is natural to ask how the presence of a stock market changes anything important in relation to the results in previous chapters. We show that stock markets act as a macroprudential tool in the sense that they may sometimes relax the pressures for information acquisition about collateral in credit markets that, as we discussed, lead to crises.

In stock markets agents produce information about the dividend stream expected from firms. This information is then impounded in prices, improving the allocation of resources in the economy. Stock prices are information sensitive. Credit markets, particularly collateralized credit markets, perform better when information about collateral is not produced—when debt is information insensitive. In a financial crisis, information production about collateral in credit markets cannot be prevented, and the size of the loan adjusts to zero (a run).

These two systems, one a price system and one a quantity system, interact dynamically through the cross-incentives to acquire information. In this chapter we propose a model in which information production in stock markets is about firms' productivities and determines the allocation of credit, while information production—or the lack thereof—in credit markets is about the firms' collateral and determines the volume of credit granted.

Lack of information production about collateral increases the amount of credit available in credit markets. The volume of credit determines total output in the economy and the average productivity of projects (as before, the more projects are undertaken, the lower the productivity of the marginal project). This reduction in the average quality of projects in the economy induces information acquisition in stock markets. When information is produced in stock markets, weak firms (those with relatively lower project quality) are identified and cannot participate in credit markets. This *cleansing effect* of stock markets' information on credit markets' composition discourages information acquisition about the collateral of the firms remaining in credit markets, slowing down credit growth and potentially preventing a crisis. A stock market acts as an *automatic macroprudential tool*; it slows down credit and stabilizes the economy.

This dynamic interaction between stock and credit markets through information acquisition highlights the delicate balance of their functions in macroeconomics. When credit is booming because there is scarce information about collateral, output also booms but the average productivity declines. Both forces make the economy more fragile. On the one hand, lenders are more worried about the quality of collateral backing their loans, which is concerning as information production about a high volume of collateral of uncertain quality (the type fueling the credit boom) is a crisis. On the other hand, increasingly worse average project quality induces investors in stock markets to investigate firms. Information from stock markets, however, feeds back into the composition in credit markets and reduces the incentives for information acquisition in credit markets and, if strong enough, can prevent a crisis altogether.

As the linkage between these two markets operates through the evolution of the average quality of projects, the model incorporates technology shocks in a different way than standard macroeconomic models. Credit booms are triggered by a positive technology shock (defined, as in the previous chapter, as the fraction of high-quality projects in the economy), generating a credit boom and giving rise to the aforementioned dynamics. Similarly, negative technological shocks can induce a crisis as we saw in Chapter 3, regardless of the amount of information produced in stock markets. This chapter highlights the informational interactions between these two markets, with opposite informational properties but complementary informational implications.

The macroprudential role of stock markets is enhanced if the cost of producing information in stock markets is *low*, and crises are less likely if the cost of acquiring information in credit markets is *high*. This rationalizes the endogenous push in markets toward facilitating information about firms in stock markets (large investment in fast computers and detailed analysis of projects), while hampering information about collateral in credit markets by the design of complex, opaque securities that back credit.

The model generates empirical counterparts of information acquisition in stock markets, which can be proxied by the evolution of the cross-sectional dispersion of stock returns. We also obtain the empirical counterparts for the average quality of projects from a credit perspective, which can be proxied by the average time-series volatility of stocks—as we have discussed, a proxy of average fragility. As we want to capture the relation between stock markets and financial crises, we implement an empirical analysis exploiting data for many countries over a relatively long period of time so that we can include enough crisis events.

5.2   Model

This model highlights the interaction between the incentives to acquire information in stock markets (about projects) and in credit markets (about collateral). The challenge is to capture the joint functioning of three markets—of firms (stock markets), of loans (credit markets), and of collateral (asset markets)—in a dynamic setting that is tractable enough to characterize business cycles and financial crises and to map to data counterparts.

5.2.1   Environment

To include stock markets in the economy, and gain mileage on testable implications, we have to extend our environment more fundamentally than in the previous chapter. As we move on with the exposition we will detail the specific role of each additional assumption.

Agents and Goods.   To model who buys, who operates, and who sells firms, we extend the overlapping generation structure, such that in each calendar period t, three (not just two as in previous chapters) overlapping generations coexist: young, middle-aged, and old; each generation has *mass 1* of a continuum of agents. There are two goods in the economy—*numeraire* and *land*. Numeraire, again denoted by K, is productive, re-producible, and non-storable, while land is again storable, not productive, and not reproducible. Each generation is again risk neutral and derives utility from consuming numeraire at the end of the period, without discounting.

Technology.   We assume that middle-aged agents are heterogeneous. A third are *entre-preneurs*, who each come up with an idea for a productive *project*. They can form *a firm* by combining the idea with a unit of land. Entrepreneurs cannot operate the firm, but the rest of the middle-aged agents are *managers* and can operate firms. An entrepreneur can sell his firm to a manager in *a stock market*. The assumption that there are two buyers per seller just simplifies the modeling of information acquisition in stock markets later. This additional generation then will be critical in modeling stock markets.

Upon becoming old, the manager who bought a firm when middle-aged needs K^* units of numeraire to operate the same technology described in the previous chapters, charac-terized by the stochastic production function in equation (2.1), with probability of success depending on the mass of active firms η and technology ψ as in equation (4.1). Again we assume *all projects are efficient* and it would be optimal for all firms to operate at optimal scale K^*.

An Agent's Lifetime.   The lifetime of an individual agent is as follows: At the start of a period, say t, the individual is born young with endowment $\overline{K}$. The agent can use this numeraire to lend to a firm against collateral in credit markets. In period $t + 1$ the agent becomes middle-aged. At the end of the period, all agents obtain a new endowment $\overline{K}$ but only a third get an idea.[1] These entrepreneurs buy land to combine with their ideas and to create firms, which are then sold to managers in a stock market. In period $t + 2$ the agent becomes old, and does not obtain any endowment. Those who own a firm (managers who bought a firm the previous period) can borrow numeraire K^* in credit markets to productively operate the project. Firms produce, loan contracts are settled, and land is sold to middle-aged agents at the end of the period. Consumption takes place at the end of each calendar period.

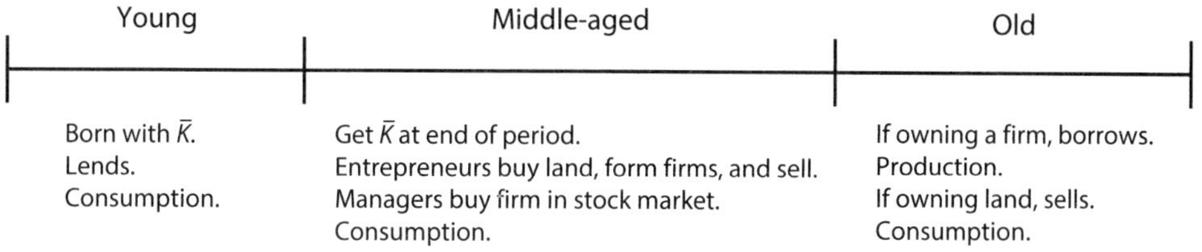

Young	Middle-aged	Old
Born with $\bar{K}$. Lends. Consumption.	Get $\bar{K}$ at end of period. Entrepreneurs buy land, form firms, and sell. Managers buy firm in stock market. Consumption.	If owning a firm, borrows. Production. If owning land, sells. Consumption.

FIGURE 5.1. An Agent's Lifetime

This timeline guarantees that resources are in the wrong hands and so there are gains from trade. Entrepreneurs cannot operate firms, so there are gains to sell them to managers in stock markets. Managers who own firms do not have numeraire to operate the firms when old, so there are gains from borrowing in credit markets. Finally, at the end of the period old agents already used the land in a firm, so there are gains from selling land in asset markets to entrepreneurs to create new firms. The assumptions about who has these different roles are just expositional, as they clearly identify who buys and who sells in each of these three markets. We summarize the agent's lifetime in Figure 5.1.

Land as Collateral.   At the time of production (the start of each calendar period), young agents have numeraire available while firms have a project that needs numeraire to produce. Again firms can hide the numeraire output but cannot hide land, which makes land useful as *collateral*. The land's properties are the same as modeled in previous chapters, with the same process of idiosyncratic shocks.

Markets.   We model trading between a random pair of an old manager and a young agent in *credit markets* as in the previous chapter (with two-sided information-acquisition incentives). We also model trading between a random pair of a middle-aged entrepreneur and an old manager who already produced in *asset markets* as in Chapter 4, in which the price is given by the fundamental expected value, pC.

In the new market, the *stock market*, a middle-aged manager can buy a firm from a middle-aged entrepreneur. As there are twice as many buyers as sellers, we model the stock market as a random matching of two potential managers to one entrepreneur. Each buyer submits an individual bid in a sealed envelope to the seller, who then sells the firm to the highest bidder. Before submitting the bid, *a bidder can privately acquire information about the firm's productivity* at a cost γ_q in terms of numeraire. In the case of acquiring information we assume the bidder not only observes the project's quality q but also learns whether his competitor has also acquired information. This last part is not relevant to the mechanism but greatly simplifies the exposition.

5.2.2   Timing and Equilibrium

We have discussed the environment, preferences, technologies, markets, and information structures. Here we are explicit (at the risk of some repetition with respect to previous chapters) about the timing in a single period and the definition of equilibrium.

1. <u>Credit Market:</u> There is random matching between a young agent and an old agent. If the old agent does not own a firm, this market is irrelevant. If the old agent owns a firm, both the lender (l) and borrower (b) know the probability p that the land owned by the borrower is good and observe the price at which the firm was traded in the previous period (then making an inference about the project's quality q). The borrower makes a take-it-or-leave-it offer for a loan K, the face value R to be repaid, and the fraction of collateral that should be transferred to the lender in case of default, x. The loan contract also specifies whether the lender or borrower is to acquire information (an information-sensitive loan contract, denoted IS) or not (an information-insensitive loan contract, denoted II). The lender either accepts or rejects the offer.

2. <u>Firms' Production and Land Shocks:</u> Production takes place and all information generated about land at the time of the loan (information privately acquired) gets revealed. Loan contracts are settled. Then, land realizes the mean-reverting idiosyncratic shocks, as before.

3. <u>Asset Market:</u> Middle-aged agents obtain endowment $\bar{K}$. A third become entrepreneurs and the rest become managers. Entrepreneurs want land to combine with ideas to form firms, so they randomly match with old agents (who have already used land in their own firms) or with young agents (who have received land as collateral for a defaulted loan).

4. <u>Stock Market:</u> There is a random match between a middle-aged (m-a) entrepreneur and two middle-aged managers. Among these firms, some will hold land with low enough p such that they will not be able to obtain credit. The rest, *active firms*, will draw the quality of the project q, according to the process (4.1). Two managers are randomly assigned to an entrepreneur and bid for the firm. All agents know p, but the bidders do not know the project of quality q, and they can choose to become informed about it at a cost γ_q before submitting the bid.

5. <u>Consumption:</u> Numeraire goods will perish at the end of the period and so are consumed.

We summarize this timeline of a single period t in Figure 5.2. As we will discuss, periods are only linked by the evolution of beliefs about land quality, p.

Now we can define the equilibrium. As the asset market is mechanical, with the price pinned down by the expected value of land and the traded land given by random matching, we focus on the remaining two markets.

Definition 5.1. *Equilibrium.*

- *In the credit market borrowers choose the loan contract type ($i \in \{IS, II\}$, K_i, R_i and x_i) to maximize expected profits conditional on the lender's participation constraint; the borrower repays when the project succeeds and defaults when the project fails (truth-telling constraint); and there are no private incentives to acquire information in the information-insensitive contract (incentive-compatibility constraint).*
- *In the stock market bidders choose to acquire information or not before submitting a bid for a firm, conditional on knowing collateral type p of a randomly assigned seller,*

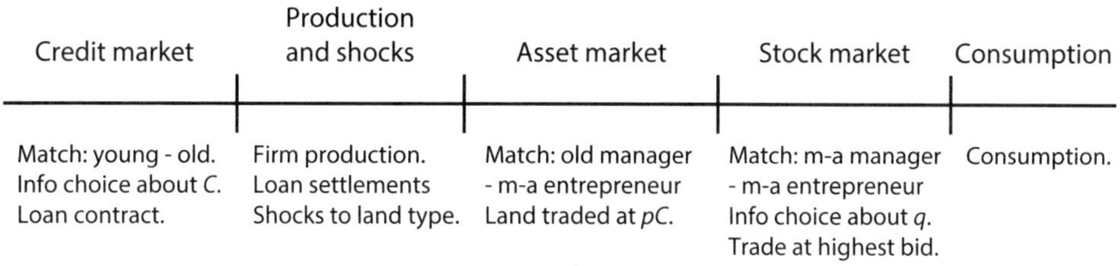

Credit market	Production and shocks	Asset market	Stock market	Consumption
Match: young - old. Info choice about C. Loan contract.	Firm production. Loan settlements Shocks to land type.	Match: old manager - m-a entrepreneur Land traded at pC.	Match: m-a manager - m-a entrepreneur Info choice about q. Trade at highest bid.	Consumption.

FIGURE 5.2. Timeline in Period t

and the mass of active firms (η). The stock price for each firm is determined by the highest bid.

We have crafted the extension of the setting such that the characterization of the solution in credit markets is the same as described in the previous chapter. This characterization is depicted for a firm with project of expected probability of success $\widehat{q}$ and with land with expected quality p as in Figure 4.3. We then characterize the novel addition in this chapter: stock markets and their information content.

5.2.3 The Stock Market

Take a firm with expected project quality $\widehat{q}$ and expected land quality p; the bidders' choice to acquire information about the realized q depends on the expected functioning of credit markets (how p maps into credit once the manager tries to borrow). At the time, information about the project determines the informativeness of firms' stock prices about q, which is then used in credit markets to determine whether information about land will be produced in credit markets. Here we explore this intricate relation. Then we study its dynamic implications.

Both the seller and potential buyers agree on the belief about the firm's land quality (p). Buyers also know the fraction of active firms in credit markets (η) and then the probability of bidding for a firm with a q_H-project, which we define as $z(\eta) \equiv Pr(q_H) = \frac{\psi}{\eta}$. A firm's value is composed of two parts, one is the expected value of its collateral pC and the other is the expected profit generated by the project according to Figure 4.3. We define $V_H(p)$ as the value of a firm with a q_H-project and $V_L(p)$ as the value of a firm with a q_L-project.

Define $y(p)$ to be the fraction of uninformed bidders among firms with land of expected quality p and let $P_U(p)$ be the *pooling price* (i.e., the bid submitted by an uninformed bidder for a firm known to have collateral with belief p). These two variables are jointly determined in equilibrium by the bidding and information production of potential buyers.

In what follows, and unless there is risk of confusion, we dispense with the explicit reference to the dependence on p. The expected gains of an *uninformed bidder* are:

$$\Pi^U = z\left[\frac{y}{2}(V_H - P_U)\right] + (1-z)\left[\left(1 - y + \frac{y}{2}\right)(V_L - P_U)\right].$$

In words, an uniformed bidder always bids the pooling price in equilibrium P_U. When facing another uninformed bidder, he buys with a probability $1/2$, regardless of the firm's project quality. When the uninformed bidder faces an informed bidder, he never buys a good firm in equilibrium (as the informed bidder would bid $P^U + \epsilon$ for a good firm) and the uninformed bidder always buys a low-quality firm (as the informed bidder would bid less than P_U). Similarly, the expected gains of an *informed bidder* are:

$$\Pi^I = zy(V_H - P_U).$$

In words, an informed bidder always bids the value of the firm when facing another informed bidder, a bit above the pooling price when facing an uninformed bidder and the firm is of high quality, and less than the pooling price when facing an uninformed bidder and the firm is of low quality.

Hence, there is no information acquisition in stock markets for firms p as long as

$$\mathcal{V}_{stock} = \Pi^I(p) - \Pi^U(p) < \gamma_q.$$

Notice that bidding competition across uninformed bidders implies that $\Pi^U = 0$, otherwise there are incentives to marginally increase the bid P_U and discreetly raise the probability of buying the firm. This implies that P_U should be such that, for a given y, the pooling price P_U balances the gains of buying a good firm and the losses of buying a bad one. Hence

$$P_U = \omega V_H + (1 - \omega) V_L \qquad \text{with} \qquad \omega(z, y) = \frac{zy}{zy + (1 - z)(2 - y)}. \qquad (5.1)$$

The fraction of uninformed bidders y affects the price that uninformed bidders bid for a firm. When no bidder is informed (i.e., when $y = 1$), $P_U = zV_H + (1 - z)V_L$, the ex ante value of the firm. When all bidders are informed (i.e., when $y = 0$), then $P_U = V_L$, as the only firms that are available for the uninformed to buy are those of low quality.

All bidders for a firm p acquire information (i.e., $y = 0$) when $\mathcal{V}_{stock} > \gamma_q$. When $y = 0$, $\omega = 0$ and $P_U = V_L$. This implies that $\Pi^U(y = 0) = 0$ and $\Pi^I(y = 0) = 0$, then there is no positive cost of information for which all buyers are informed. At the other extreme, no bidder acquires information (i.e., $y = 1$) when $\mathcal{V}_{stock} < \gamma_q$. When $y = 1$, $\omega = z$ and $P_U = zV_H + (1 - z)V_L$. This implies that $\Pi^U(y = 1) = 0$ and $\Pi^I(y = 1) = z(1 - z)(V_H - V_L) > 0$, and then we can express the condition for no bidder being informed as $\overline{\gamma}_q \equiv z(1 - z)(V_H - V_L) < \gamma_q$. In words, when the cost of information is very large no bidder has incentives to deviate and become informed. This is the case in which the stock market is the least informative as all firms with land of expected quality p are traded at the same price, P_U.

Hence, there is a relatively low cost ($\gamma_q < \overline{\gamma}_q$) in which the equilibrium is given by $\mathcal{V}_{stock} = \gamma_q$, with an interior y that has to be consistent with equilibrium prices P_U. In this

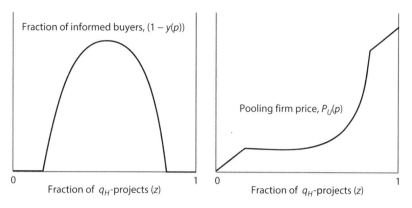

FIGURE 5.3. Fraction of Informed Bidders and Pooling Price

case y^* is the solution to the following equation:

$$\frac{zy^*(1-z)(2-y^*)}{zy^* + (1-z)(2-y^*)}(V_H - V_L) = \gamma_q, \tag{5.2}$$

and P_U^* is determined by equation (5.1) evaluated at y^*.

The first panel of Figure 5.3 shows how the fraction of informed investors $(1 - y(p))$ depends on the fraction of active firms with q_H-projects (this is $z = \psi/\eta$, on the x-axis). This has an inverted-U shape. When all firms have q_H-projects, bidders do not acquire information. As there are more and more active firms (during a credit boom, for instance), eventually more of the projects will be q_L firms and will attract information in stock markets. The incentives to acquire information are maximized when there is relatively large uncertainty about the composition of projects in the market.

The second panel shows the pooling price, $P_U(p)$, also as a function of the fraction of active firms with q_H-projects. Not surprisingly, as the composition of projects in the market worsens, $P_U(p)$ declines. As more informed bidders participate in the market they force a faster decline in the pooling price because those bidders "cream skim" the market. Note that the two kinks in the second panel correspond to the points at which no bidder becomes informed, because almost all the projects are q_H (RHS) or q_L (LHS) so it does not pay to produce information.

Notice that the solution y^* determines *the information content of the stock market.* The distribution of observed prices in the economy determines beliefs about q. A fraction $z(1 - y^*)^2$ of firms with land p trades at price V_H, which reveals that the firm has a q_H-project, a fraction $(1 - z)(1 - y^*)^2$ trades at price V_L, which reveals that the firm has a q_L-project, and a fraction $1 - (1 - y^*)^2$ trades at the pooling price P_U, which is uninformative about q. As can be seen, the higher the fraction of informed bidders (the lower y^*), the more information about q is revealed in stock markets, which affects the fraction of firms that are able to raise funds with information-insensitive loans in credit markets.

5.3   Credit and Stock Markets: Dynamic Interactions

In this section we show how information about collateral in credit markets and information about projects in stock markets interact dynamically.

5.3.1   Credit Booms, Busts, and the Evolution of Beliefs

The idiosyncratic shock process for collateral generates depreciation of credit market collateral information. Given our assumed mean-reverting process, a unit of land falls into one of three possible categories: it is known to be good ($p = 1$), known to be bad ($p = 0$), or of uncertain quality ($p = \widehat{p}$). We denote the mass of land in each category $p \in \{0, \widehat{p}, 1\}$ after period t production (i.e., after idiosyncratic shocks to land but *before* the stock market opens) as $m(p)_t$. As the mass of *active firms* is given by all firms that may have good collateral,

$$\eta_t = m(\widehat{p})_t + m(1)_t. \tag{5.3}$$

In what follows we assume that $\widehat{p} < p^*(q_L)$ (there is information production about collateral of unknown quality for firms known to operate with q_L-projects) and that $\widehat{p} > p^*(q_H)$ (there is no information production about collateral of unknown quality for firms known to operate with q_H-projects). These parametric assumptions allow us to focus attention on an environment in which information about firms' projects affects their performance in credit markets. Otherwise, information about collateral in the credit market does not depend on the availability of information about projects in the stock market, muting any interaction between stock and credit markets.

In credit markets at $t + 1$, a fraction v_{t+1} of land of unknown quality (i.e., of $\widehat{p}$) will be investigated. The mass of land in each belief category after credit markets (which we denote by $(t + 1)'$) changes to:

$$m(\widehat{p})_{(t+1)'} = (1 - v_{t+1})m(\widehat{p})_t$$

$$m(1)_{(t+1)'} = m(1)_t + v_{t+1}\widehat{p}m(\widehat{p})_t$$

$$m(0)_{(t+1)'} = m(0)_t + v_{t+1}(1 - \widehat{p})m(\widehat{p})_t.$$

After production at $t + 1$, the mass of land in each belief category (after idiosyncratic shocks), which determines the collateral belief distribution in the next period, is:

$$m(\widehat{p})_{t+1} = \lambda m(\widehat{p})_{(t+1)'} + (1 - \lambda)$$

$$m(1)_{t+1} = \lambda m(1)_{(t+1)'}$$

$$m(0)_{t+1} = \lambda m(0)_{(t+1)'}.$$

Putting these elements together, the mass of active firms in period $t + 1$ is

$$\eta_{t+1} = m(\widehat{p})_{t+1} + m(1)_{t+1}$$

$$= \lambda[1 - v_{t+1}(1 - \widehat{p})]m(\widehat{p})_t + \lambda m(1)_t + (1 - \lambda). \tag{5.4}$$

The first term corresponds to land $\widehat{p}$ that has not suffered an idiosyncratic shock and either was not examined during the credit market or was examined and found to be good. The second term corresponds to land known to be good (i.e., $p = 1$) that has not suffered an idiosyncratic shock. The last term corresponds to all land that has suffered an idiosyncratic shock.

Combining equations (5.3) and (5.4), *a credit boom* is defined as the change in the mass of firms that are actively participating in credit markets,

$$\eta_{t+1} - \eta_t = (1 - \lambda)(1 - m(1)_t) - [1 - \lambda(1 - v_{t+1}(1 - \widehat{p}))]m(\widehat{p})_t$$
$$= (1 - \lambda)m(0)_t - \lambda v_{t+1}(1 - \widehat{p})m(\widehat{p})_t. \tag{5.5}$$

The credit boom is given by the old collateral known to be of bad quality that suffered an idiosyncratic shock and started in the pool of unknown collateral, minus the unknown collateral that was investigated and found to be bad collateral.

Now, we can put structure on the fraction of collateral v_{t+1} that is investigated in period $t + 1$. First, the mass of active firms η_t reduces the fraction $z_t = \frac{\psi}{\eta_t}$ of q_H-projects in the economy. This fraction reduces the average quality of projects, $\widehat{q}_t = z_t q_H + (1 - z_t)q_L$, and, as depicted in Figure 5.3, determines information acquisition in the stock market, $(1 - y_t)$. Among firms with collateral $\widehat{p}$, a fraction $(1 - z_t)(1 - y_t)^2$ is identified in the stock market as q_L-firms, a fraction $z_t(1 - y_t)^2$ as q_H-firms, and the rest are not explored in the stock market. If $p^*(\widehat{q}_t) \leq \widehat{p}$ there is no information production about the third group, just about the first group. If, in contrast, $p^*(\widehat{q}_t) > \widehat{p}$ there is also information production about the third group, which we denote *a crisis*. Denoting by $\mathbb{I}_{C,t+1}$ a crisis indicator function in period $t + 1$, with $\mathbb{I}_{C,t+1} = 1$ in case of a crisis and 0 otherwise,

$$v_{t+1} = (1 - z_t)(1 - y_t)^2 + \mathbb{I}_{C,t+1}\left[1 - (1 - y_t)^2\right]. \tag{5.6}$$

In short, when $\mathbb{I}_{C,t+1} = 0$ and there is no information production about collateral of unknown quality of a firm with unknown project quality, $v_{t+1} = (1 - z_t)(1 - y_t)^2$ (only the collateral of q_L-projects are investigated). In contrast, during a crisis (this is $\mathbb{I}_{C,t+1} = 1$) only the collateral of known q_H-projects is not investigated, and then $v_{t+1} = 1 - z_t(1 - y_t)^2$.

The fraction of collateral that is examined in credit markets in $t + 1$, v_{t+1}, is a function of the mass of active firms in the economy, η_t, and changes in the following way.

$$\frac{\partial v_{t+1}}{\partial \eta_t} = \begin{cases} \frac{\psi(1-y_t)}{\eta_t^2}\left[(1 - y_t) + 2(1 - z_t)\frac{\partial y_t}{\partial z_t}\right] & \text{if } \mathbb{I}_C = 0 \text{ (i.e., } \eta_t < \eta^*) \\ \frac{\psi(1-y_t)}{\eta_t^2}\left[(1 - y_t) - 2z_t\frac{\partial y_t}{\partial z_t}\right] & \text{if } \mathbb{I}_C = 1 \text{ (i.e., } \eta_t > \eta^*), \end{cases} \tag{5.7}$$

where η^* is the mass of active firms for which $p^*(\widehat{q}_t(\eta^*)) = \widehat{p}$.

This derivative shows that information in credit markets changes with the volume of credit in the economy (the mass of active firms) through two channels. The first is by triggering a *financial crisis*, in which v_{t+1} increases discontinuously after a certain volume of credit requests. From equation (4.5), $p^*(\widehat{q}_t)$ decreases with $\widehat{q}_t$ (which increases with η_t), and then the indicator $\mathbb{I}_{C,t+1}$ switches from 0 to 1 when η_t gets large enough.

The second channel is more continuous and comes from changes in *information in stock markets*. When there is no crisis, there is more collateral examination when there is *more* information in the stock market and there are more q_L-projects identified. If a crisis is triggered, there is more collateral examination when there is *less* information in the stock market, but more q_L-projects. Given these relations, the next lemma characterizes the evolution of credit in the economy.

Lemma 3.   *The mass of active firms follows the following first-order difference equation.*

$$\eta_{t+1} = 1 - \lambda + \lambda[v_{t+1}(\eta_t)\widehat{p} + (1 - v_{t+1}(\eta_t))\eta_t] \tag{5.8}$$

and then

$$\frac{\partial \eta_{t+1}}{\partial \eta_t} = \lambda(1 - v_{t+1}(\eta_t)) - \lambda(\eta_t - \widehat{p})\frac{\partial v_{t+1}}{\partial \eta_t} \tag{5.9}$$

with $\frac{\partial v_{t+1}}{\partial \eta_t}$ given by equation (5.7).

Proof. Among collateral with known quality (i.e., $1 - m(\widehat{p})_t$), a fraction $\widehat{p}$ is of good quality. Then, $m(1)_t = \widehat{p}(1 - m(\widehat{p})_t)$. Substituting into equation (5.3), we can express $m(\widehat{p})_t$ as a function of η_t. This is,

$$\eta_t = \widehat{p} + (1 - \widehat{p})m(\widehat{p})_t \qquad \Longrightarrow \qquad m(\widehat{p})_t = \frac{\eta_t - \widehat{p}}{1 - \widehat{p}},$$

and we can rewrite equation (5.4) as

$$\eta_{t+1} = (1 - \lambda) + \lambda(m(\widehat{p})_t + m(1)_t) - \lambda v_{t+1}(1 - \widehat{p})m(\widehat{p})_t$$

$$= (1 - \lambda) + \lambda \eta_t - \lambda v_{t+1}(1 - \widehat{p})m(\widehat{p})_t.$$

Replacing $m(\widehat{p})_t$ in this equation we obtain the equation (5.8) in the lemma. $\square$

This lemma constitutes a generalization of the equation that characterizes dynamics in the absence of stock markets, in Corollary 4. The framework with a stock market nests the previous chapter without a stock market by assuming $\gamma_q = \infty$, and then there are no incentives to acquire information about the project (i.e., $y_t = 1$ in all t). The situation without a stock market was characterized graphically with the phase diagrams in Figure 4.4, which show the three possible steady states in that situation (no boom, good booms, and bad booms) as a function of the available technology ψ and collateral average value $\widehat{p}$. Next, we show the role of information in stock markets in affecting the dynamics in the economy.

5.3.2   *The Stock Market as a Macroprudential Mechanism*

In this section we obtain three results. First, we study an extreme situation in which stock markets reveal full information about the quality of all firms' projects. Here we show that the economy just has one stationary equilibrium with an intermediate level of active firms, and there is never a crisis. Second, we assume that information in stock markets is constant and we point out that a lot of information prevents crises but even if the information produced is not enough to avoid a crisis, it still reduces the crisis magnitude. Finally, we consider the more general setting in which information in stock markets is endogenous to the credit boom. This case, with a two-way interaction between stock and credit markets, shows that information in stock markets endogenously builds up when a crisis becomes more likely, then serving as a market-generated, automatic, macroprudential tool. Furthermore, even though avoiding a financial crisis, endogenous information may induce *deterministic non-crisis cycles.*

First, assume full information in stock markets. This is just a benchmark that would be supported by $\gamma_q = 0$, such that all agents weekly prefer to have free information, and $y_t = 0$ in all t. The economy just has one stationary equilibrium with an intermediate level of active firms, and there is never a crisis.

Proposition 12 (Steady Steady with Full Information in Stock Markets).   Assuming $\gamma_q = 0$, $y_t = 0$ in all t. From equation (5.6), $v_{t+1} = 1 - z_t$ in all t. Then

$$\eta_{t+1} = 1 - \lambda + \lambda[(1 - z_t)\widehat{p} + z_t \eta_t] \qquad \text{with } z_t = \min\left\{\frac{\psi}{\eta_t}, 1\right\}.$$

There is a unique steady state in which $\eta_{SS} \in (\underline{\eta}, 1)$.

The proof follows directly from the dynamics in equations (5.8) and (5.9). When there is perfect information in the stock market, only collateral of unknown quality is investigated if it is backing q_L-projects. This is why there are no crises, as there are only two possible thresholds for information acquisition, $p^*(q_L) > \widehat{p}$ and $p^*(q_H) < \widehat{p}$. The credit boom is continuous, strictly increasing at a decreasing rate, as there are more q_L-firms operating in the economy. Formally, from equation (5.9), $\frac{\partial \eta_{t+1}}{\partial \eta_t} = \frac{\lambda \widehat{p} \psi}{\eta_t^2}$ (positive and decreasing in η). Figure 5.4 shows this result graphically.

This result is a first indication of the role of stock markets in preventing crises. When the stock market reveals which firms are very likely to repay and which are more likely to default, this informs the credit market about which collateral to investigate. When, during a credit boom, there are more and more firms that are less likely to repay, there is more information acquisition in credit markets but no sudden change in that process—no crisis. Information in the stock market generates a stationary equilibrium that is mediocre (i.e., low consumption because fewer firms get credit) but stable.

Now we assume information in the stock market is constant over time (i.e., $y_t = y \in (0, 1)$) for all t. The next proposition shows that even when information in the stock

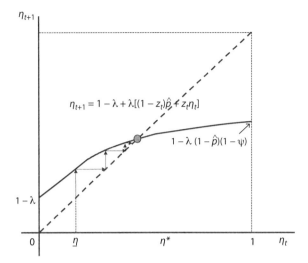

FIGURE 5.4. Full Information in the Stock Market

market is not enough to prevent a crisis (y is relatively high), the crisis is smaller than in an alternative scenario without information in stock markets.

Proposition 13 (The Macroprudential Role of Stock Markets). Assume bad booms in the absence of information in stock markets. Information in the stock market prevents crises, and if not, it reduces their magnitude.

Proof. When there is some information in stock markets, this result follows from a credit boom growing at a slower rate than without information when there is no crisis, and from the mass of active firms being larger than without information when there is a crisis. Formally, the first condition implies $\frac{\partial \eta_{t+1}}{\partial \eta_t}|_{\mathbb{I}_C=0,y_t=y} < \frac{\partial \eta_{t+1}}{\partial \eta_t}|_{\mathbb{I}_C=0,y_t=1}$ from equation (5.9). This is the case because $\frac{\partial \eta_{t+1}}{\partial \eta_t}|_{\mathbb{I}_C=0,y_t=y} = \lambda[1-(1-z_t)(1-y)^2] - \lambda(\eta_t - \widehat{p})\frac{\psi}{\eta_t^2} < \lambda$, and because $1-(1-z_t)(1-y)^2 < 1$ and $\eta_t > \underline{\eta} > \widehat{p}$. The second condition implies $\eta_{t+1}|_{\mathbb{I}_C=1,y_t=y} > \eta_{t+1}|_{\mathbb{I}_C=1,y_t=1}$ from equation (5.8). This is the case because $\eta_{t+1}|_{\mathbb{I}_C=1,y_t=y} = 1-\lambda+\lambda\widehat{p}+\lambda z_t(1-y)^2(\eta_t - \widehat{p}) > \underline{\eta}$, and because $\underline{\eta} = 1 - \lambda + \lambda\widehat{p}$. $\qquad\square$

Figure 5.5 is based on the parametric combination that generates bad booms in the absence of information in the stock market (third panel of Figure 4.4). The first panel displays the case with relatively high information production in the stock market (that is, relatively low y). This information slows down the credit boom so much that the economy comes to a steady state without triggering a crisis. The second panel displays the case with relatively low information in the stock market (that is, relatively high y). This information slows down the credit boom, but not so much to prevent a crisis. However, the information acquired in the stock market allows some q_H-projects to avoid collateral examination and decreases the magnitude of the crisis relative to the situation without information in the

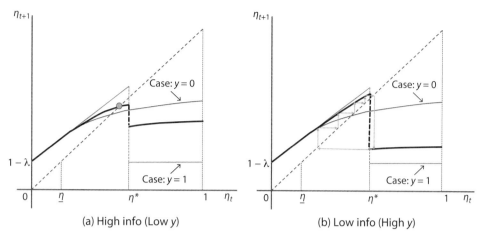

FIGURE 5.5. Some Information in the Stock Market

stock market. In other words, information acquisition in stock markets may prevent crises, and if not, it reduces the volatility of deterministic boom-bust cycles.

Finally, we take the general setting with endogenous information in stock markets (i.e., y is endogenous to the credit boom, as in Figure 5.3). The next proposition shows that information in stock markets reacts endogenously at the peak of the credit boom, when more in need given the proximity of a crisis. Even though this reaction most likely prevents a crisis, it also has the possibility to induce *non-crisis cycles*.

Proposition 14 (Endogenous Information in Stock Markets).   When information in the stock market is endogenous, it may prevent crises but create non-crisis cycles.

Proof. From the proof of Proposition 13, $\frac{\partial \eta_{t+1}}{\partial \eta_t}|_{\mathbb{I}_C=0, y_t=y} > 0$. Combining equation (5.9) from Lemma 3 with equation (5.7), $\frac{\partial \eta_{t+1}}{\partial \eta_t}|_{\mathbb{I}_C=0, y^*}$ can be negative. The reason is that, as credit booms increase $\frac{\partial z_t}{\partial \eta_t} < 0$, and from equation (5.7), $\frac{\partial y_t}{\partial z_t} > 0$. If this derivative is large enough the derivative is negative and can generate a cyclical steady state with a cycle that does not involve a crisis.   □

The first panel of Figure 5.3 shows how y_t changes with z_t and then with η_t. That information in the stock market reacts to availability of credit changes the nature of the stationary equilibrium. If stock markets attract information acquisition before crises develop, then not only does information production in the stock market prevent a crisis but it may also generate *non-crisis cycles*. Figure 5.6 shows this possibility: the evolution of η_t bends as information acquisition in the stock market changes. If at some point information starts being acquired in the stock market, the difference equation transitions gradually from the case without information ($y = 1$) to the case of full information ($y = 0$). Once the credit moves back to a situation with low information acquisition in the stock market, the difference equation transitions back to the case $y = 1$.

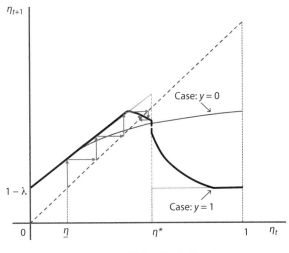

FIGURE 5.6. No-Crisis Cycles

The shape of the difference equation critically depends on the shape of the first panel of Figure 5.3. In the case depicted, the economy cycles before suffering a crisis. The cycle still displays less volatility than the one involving crises. More in general, however, the phase diagram is contained between the benchmarks of $y = 0$ and $y = 1$ depending on how information in stock markets reacts to the credit boom. The shape of the phase diagram determines whether the crisis is avoided with a non-crisis cycle, avoided with a non-cyclical steady state, or not avoided at all.

Relation with Literature on the Real Effect of Stock Markets.   Our view of stock markets is consistent with a large literature on stock prices being informative and feeding back onto real variables, such as Dow and Gorton (1997). In this literature, the information content in asset markets directs managers' investment decisions and allows for a better allocation of resources in the economy. In the work here, however, information in stock markets has another, previously unexplored, positive role in the economy beyond its pure allocative use: it endogenously acts as a macroprudential tool to reduce the likelihood of a financial crisis. While information about firms' collateral can be counterproductive by reducing aggregate credit in the economy, information in stock markets can be beneficial in allocating such credit. A scarcer literature explores the interaction between stock and credit markets. One branch is mostly empirical and focuses on pricing interactions, such as Beck and Levine (2004) and Gilchrist, Yankov, and Zakrajsek (2009). Another branch is theoretical, such as Dow, Goldstein, and Guembel (2017), and studies how managers and creditors take actions based on information in stock markets, creating feedback effects on the determination of stock prices that magnify shocks. Our work differs by explicitly defining the concept of a crisis and highlighting an informational interaction between these two markets. In our setting stock prices perfectly reveal information. The complementarity does not come from a feedback between choices and information about firms but instead from a feedback between information acquisition about firms and about collateral. Furthermore, we explore this interaction through its impact on macroeconomics, providing a contribution to most standard macroeconomic models. While those models focus on the stock pricing implications of macro, we focus on the macro implications of the informational content of stock prices.

5.3.3 Policy Implications

Our setting offers a clear characterization of the unconstrained first best: since we have assumed that all firms have a positive net present value project and their financing is feasible, the first best specifies that all firms operate in all periods, which would be achieved in the absence of financial frictions. Then, what makes our economy depart from the first best is the reliance on collateral with heterogeneous quality and the possibility of private information acquisition in both markets. While information in stock markets does not affect allocations directly, it does so by affecting information production in credit markets.

The first best is implemented in equilibrium in the situation we denoted as "good booms" in Proposition 4 (depicted in the second panel of Figure 4.4). In all other steady states the equilibrium implements lower welfare than in the first best, either because it displays recurrent crises (as in the case of bad booms) or because it displays less production than optimal (as in the case with full information in stock markets).

What can a government do in those situations to bring the economy near the first best? The answer depends on the available policy tools. Here we assume the government can implement a set of policies (regulations, restrictions, controls, etc.) that induce *shadow taxes and subsidies* to the cost of information production and processing, both about projects in stock markets (which we denote by τ_q in proportion to the private cost) and about collateral in credit markets (which we denote by τ_C).

Policies that induce a shadow tax on information acquisition in credit markets include all interventions that make it more difficult for a lender to obtain information about collateral, for instance, deregulating opaque over-the-counter markets, facilitating the use of complex structured products and rehypothecation, or relaxing regulatory constraints that punish the use of non-standard contracts such as those specified in Dodd-Frank. Policies that induce a shadow tax to information acquisition in stock markets include all interventions that make it more difficult for an investor to obtain information about firms, for instance, relaxing accounting guidelines and restrictions of reporting practices such as those specified in the Sarbanes-Oxley Act.

If the government could intervene in both markets, it would like to discourage information in credit markets to a point at which there is no crisis even if all firms operate ($\eta^* = 1$) and also in stock markets, which would lose their macroprudential role and only induce an inefficient reduction of credit in the economy.

Proposition 15 (Optimal Information Policies in Both Markets).   If the government can intervene in both markets, it would like to discourage information in both. To implement the first-best allocation with stable high production, the set of policies should induce a "shadow tax" to the cost of information in credit markets (about collateral) such that $\tau_C \geq \frac{(1-\widehat{p})(1-\widehat{q}_t(1))K^*}{\gamma_C} - 1$ and in stock markets (about projects) such that $\tau_q \geq \psi(1-\psi)(q_H - q_L)AK^* - 1$.

Proof. The government would like to implement all firms operating ($\eta^* = 1$) but without crises. This implies $p^*(\widehat{q}_t(\eta^* = 1)) < \widehat{p}$, or using equation (4.5), $1 - \frac{\gamma_C(1+\tau_C)}{(1-\widehat{q}_t(1))K^*} < \widehat{p}$, where τ_C captures the shadow cost of restrictive policies and regulations. The condition in the proposition follows, with $\widehat{q}(1) = \psi q_H + (1-\psi)q_L$. To avoid information in stock markets, from equation (5.2) evaluated at $y^* = 1$ and at $\eta^* = 1$ (which implies $z(\eta^* = 1) = \psi$), the condition to prevent information is $\psi(1-\psi)(V_H - V_L) < \gamma_q(1+\tau_q)$. Since, evaluated at the situation in which all firms get credit, $V_H - V_L = (q_H - q_L)AK^*$, the equation in the proposition follows. □

The desirability of discouraging information production in stock markets arises from the possibility of discouraging information production in credit markets so as to avoid crises, and then eliminating the macroprudential benefit of information in stock markets. If direct interventions in credit markets were not feasible, intervening in stock markets would still help. The next proposition shows the optimal level of difficulty to obtain information that can be implemented in stock markets when facing the possibility of a crisis.

Proposition 16 (Optimal Informational Policies in Stock Markets). If the government cannot intervene in credit markets and there is a crisis at a credit boom η^*, the optimal amount of information in stock markets is given by

$$(1 - y^*) = \left[\frac{(1-\lambda)(1-\eta^*)\eta^*}{(1-\psi)(\eta^* - \widehat{p})} \right]^{0.5},$$

which can be induced by policies that implement a "shadow tax/subsidy" such that equation (5.2) holds.

Proof. If there is a mass of active firms η^* that triggers a crisis, it implies that the fraction of informed bidders in stock markets for firms with collateral $\widehat{p}$ is low enough to prevent it (as in the second panel of Figure 5.5). The maximum amount of production that is stable is η^*. This credit volume is maintained in steady state when equation (5.8) in Lemma 3 holds when evaluated at η^*, which implies evaluating v_{t+1} as $\left(1 - \frac{\psi}{\eta^*}\right)(1-y^*)$, from equation (5.6). The equation in the proposition follows. The fraction $(1 - y^*)$ represents the minimum fraction of informed bidders that prevent a crisis. It can be implemented by reducing the cost of information to γ_q in equation (5.2) evaluated at the target y^* for $z = \frac{\psi}{\eta^*}$ and $V_H - V_L = (q_H - q_L)AK^*$. □

Intuitively, there is a crisis once the credit boom reaches a mass η^* of active firms and there is not enough information in stock markets to prevent it (as in the second panel of

Figure 5.5). The proposition shows the minimum amount of information in stock markets that prevents a crisis exactly at that point. The government would not like to have more information than the volume characterized in the proposition because it would just reduce production without further gains in terms of stability (as in the first panel of Figure 5.5). In other words, if the government cannot directly discourage information in credit markets it may want to encourage information in stock markets to indirectly discourage information in credit markets and avoid a crisis. Still, discouraging information directly in credit markets is superior as it can avoid a crisis while at the same time increasing the feasible magnitude of the credit boom.

5.4   Testing Aggregate Information Dynamics

In this section, we test a number of implications of the model. First, we explain the empirical measures that we use in our analysis. Motivated by our setting, we use stock market price data to construct an empirical proxy of information produced in the economy and a measure of economy-wide fragility that captures the probability of default in credit markets. We then discuss our data set. Finally, we turn to the hypotheses tests.

5.4.1   Measures of Information and Fragility

Corresponding to the model we examine two measures that capture information encoded in stock markets and a stock-based measure of fragility or default probability in credit markets.

The first is a stock price-based measure of information in the economy. If information is produced in stock markets, firms are distinguished by the quality of their project, which gets embedded in firms' stock prices. Our empirical counterpart is a cross-section characterization, more specifically the cross section of firms' average stock returns. In particular we look at the standard deviation of firms' average returns: *CsAvg*.[2] We label this variable *Information*.

The second measure also comes from the model and corresponds to default probability in credit markets, which has implications for the likelihood of information acquisition about collateral, and then credit. It is a stock price-based measure of economy-wide fragility. When ψ is low, eventually there are more q_L firms in the economy and these firms are more likely to default because $q_L < q_H$. We measure fragility (the extent of low-quality projects operating in the economy) with the inverse of the time-series volatility of a stock, which we denote by $1/Vol$ and label as *Fragility*.[3]

As we discussed previously in Section 4.7.1, this definition of fragility is from Atkeson, Eisfeldt, and Weill (2013). Based on Leland's (1994) and Merton's (1975) structural models, these authors develop two concepts of default: distance-to-insolvency and distance-to-default. They then show that the variable one over the firm's equity volatility ($1/Vol$) is bounded between these two measures. Intuitively, when a firm's equity volatility is high, the firm is more likely to default (for given leverage). The fragility of an economy moves over time and spikes significantly during a crisis. Based on $1/Vol$, Atkeson, Eisfeldt, and Weill (2013) study the United States over 1926–2012 and show that 1932–1933, 1937, and 2008 stand out as especially fragile periods.[4]

5.4.2 Data

The measures of *Information* and *Fragility* are constructed using daily stock price data from Thomson/Reuters DataStream. We use daily stock price data from 52 countries over 1973–2012, which amounts to approximately 105 million observations.[5] Tables B.5 and B.6 in Appendix B show the countries and the time period covered for each country. The panel is unbalanced. We follow Laeven and Valencia (2012) for the dating of financial crises.

We proceed as follows. To measure *CsAvg* in each country we compute the cross-sectional standard deviation of the average of firms' monthly stock returns in the stock market of that country. For $1/Vol$, we compute the average of firms' monthly stock return volatilities in each country. For stability of these figures, we take these two monthly series and average them across months to create quarterly series. The annual series that we study next is formed using the last quarter observation of the quarterly series.

5.4.3 Three Tests

In this section we test three hypotheses that follow from the model.

(1) *Information* and *Fragility* predict financial crises.   As the credit boom goes on, the economy is becoming increasingly fragile. This is because the marginal project is of lower quality and higher fragility than the average (in the model, more q_L projects are undertaken and they are more likely to default than q_H projects). As this occurs, information is increasingly produced in the stock market, leading up to the crisis. Table 5.1 addresses this hypothesis. The left-hand side variable is a dummy variable indicating that there was a crisis in a specific country that year when equal to 1, as per Laeven and Valencia (2012). We provide results from Linear Probability Model (LPM) and LOGIT specifications (controlled by GDP, credit, and productivity, as well as clustering). We confirm the hypothesis, as an increase in *Information* (i.e., an increase in *CsAvg*) and an increase in *Fragility* (i.e., a decline in $1/Vol$) both tend to precede and predict financial crises.

(2) *Information* and *Fragility* do not predict financial crises when the preceding credit boom happens jointly with high-productivity growth.   The theoretical analysis showed that the relative abundance of q_H-projects, ψ, is important to drive credit booms and to determine the dynamic interaction between stock and credit markets. More specifically, when ψ is high, the probability of default in the $\widehat{q}(\eta)$ is lower for all η and the condition $p^*(\widehat{q}(\eta^*)) = \widehat{p}$ at which a crisis happens implies η^* is larger and that crises are less likely, regardless of information in stock markets. Indeed, in Chapter 2 we showed that good booms (those that do not end in a crisis) are characterized by high total factor productivity (TFP) growth while bad booms (those that do end in a crisis) display a TFP growth path that starts to decline leading up to the crisis.

Table 5.1. Information Measures, Macroeconomic
Variables, and Financial Crises

	(1) LPM	(2) LOGIT
$1/Vol_{t-2}$	−0.052 (−1.48)	−0.796[+] (−1.65)
$CsAvg_{t-2}$	0.743[+] (1.80)	7.555* (2.18)
$\Delta(1/Vol)_{t-1}$	−0.087** (−2.82)	−1.337*** (−6.21)
$\Delta CsAvg_{t-1}$	0.551[+] (1.84)	4.983[+] (1.87)
$\Delta rGDP_{t-1}$	−4.052***	−45.629***

Note: The table summarizes the predictive power of information measures ($1/Vol$, $CsAvg$, $\Delta(1/Vol)$, $\Delta CsAvg$) and macroeconomic variables ($\Delta rGDP$, $\Delta Credit$, ΔTFP, $\Delta Labor\,Productivity$) on the occurrence of financial crises. The linear probability model regression specification is: $\mathbb{I}_{n,t}(Crisis) = \alpha_n + \beta' X_{n,t-1} + \epsilon_{n,t}$ and the logit regression specification is: $\mathbb{I}_{n,t}(Crisis) = \alpha_n + \beta' X_{n,t-1} + \epsilon_{n,t}$, where $X_{n,t-1} = (1/Vol_{n,t-1}, CsAvg_{n,t-1}, \Delta Vol_{n,t-1}, \Delta CsAvg_{n,t-1}, \Delta rGDP_{n,t-1}, \Delta Credit_{n,t-1}, \Delta TFP_{n,t-1}, \Delta LP_{n,t-1})'$. The data are annual and span a period from 1973 until 2012. All regression specifications take into account country fixed effects and standard errors are clustered at both a country and time level.

Similar to the previous chapter, we define a credit boom as follows. The beginning of a credit boom is marked by three consecutive years of credit growth greater or equal to 3% and the end by two consecutive years of negative credit growth. Empirically, we distinguish between high TFP and low-TFP credit booms by dividing the booms around the mean growth in TFP across all the identified booms. Since low and high-TFP are indeed interpreted as low and high *Fragility*, we dispense from *Fragility* in the regression. Table 5.2 shows that indeed *Information* predicts financial crises during low-TFP booms but not in high-TFP booms.

(3) Information production in stock markets negatively predicts future credit during credit booms. As highlighted when comparing the two panels in Figure 5.5, information in stock markets delays credit growth during a credit boom (the first panel shows a faster decline in the growth rate of credit than the second). In words, more information production in stock markets reduces the amount of future credit because a larger fraction of weak firms is revealed as such, their collateral is examined, and they are cut out of the credit market when found out with bad collateral.

To test this hypothesis and to track the role of information in different phases of the credit boom, we interact the change in the measure of *Information*, $\Delta CsAvg$, with the year of the credit boom, for example, first year, second year, and so on. Table 5.3 shows the results. For boom years one, two, and three the coefficients on the interaction terms are

Table 5.2. Information Production during Low- and
High-Productivity Credit Booms

	(1) All Booms	(2) Low TFP	(3) High TFP
$\Delta CsAvg_{t-1}$	0.691* (2.13)	0.741* (2.22)	0.367 (0.56)
$CsAvg_{t-2}$	0.829* (2.54)	0.811* (2.36)	0.583 (0.61)
ΔLP_t	−1.404 (−0.89)	−2.578 (−1.16)	0.074 (0.04)
ΔGDP_{t-1}	−0.648+ (−1.74)	−1.245 (−1.33)	−0.265 (−1.19)
ΔTFP_{t-1}	0.647 (0.91)	0.684 (1.31)	0.490 (0.39)
ΔINV_{t-1}	−0.771* (−2.51)	−0.649 (−1.22)	−0.799+ (−1.96)
N	382	235	147
R^2	0.34	0.33	0.31
F	4.19	5.87	0.87
Cluster (Boom)	YES	YES	YES
Cluster (time)	YES	YES	YES
FE (Boom)	YES	YES	YES

t-statistics in parentheses
$+p < 0.10$, $*p < 0.05$, $**p < 0.01$, $***p < 0.001$
Note: The table summarizes the predictive power of $\Delta CsAvg$ interacted with dummy variables indicating years into the credit boom on future $\Delta Credit$. The regression specification is: $\mathbb{I}_{n,t}(Crisis) = \alpha_n + \beta \Delta CsAvg_{n,t-1} + \gamma CsAvg_{t-2} + \delta' X_{n,t-1} + \epsilon_{n,t}$, where $X_{n,t-1} = (\Delta rGDP_{n,t-1}, \Delta TFP_{n,t-1}, \Delta LP_{n,t-1}, \Delta INV_{n,t-1})'$. The data are annual and span a period from 1973 until 2012. All regression specifications take into account country fixed effects and standard errors are clustered at both a country and time level.

negative and significant, implying that, indeed, when there is more information generated in stock markets during a credit boom there is a decline in subsequent credit growth.

5.5   Measures of Information and Business Cycles

We have identified from the model measures of information that are related to financial crises. How does such information evolve over the business cycle? The main challenge in identifying this relation is to define business cycles. We do that next.

5.5.1   What Is the "Business Cycle"?

The rise and fall of aggregate economic activity is called the "business cycle." Here we review conceptualizations of the business cycle and then conjecture an alternative. We will show that the alternative is consistent with our measures of fragility and information.

Table 5.3. Future Credit in Relation to Information Production during Credit Booms

	(1)	(2)	(3)
$\Delta CsAvg_t$	−0.128[+]	−0.177	
	(−1.72)	(−0.97)	
$\mathbb{I}_t(Boom)$	0.034	0.037	0.033[+]
	(1.63)	(1.29)	(1.77)
$\Delta CsAvg_t \times \mathbb{I}_t(Boom=1)$	−0.021	−0.150	
	(−0.07)	(−0.36)	
$\mathbb{I}_t(Boom=1)$	0.057*	0.054[+]	0.059**
	(2.49)	(1.79)	(2.82)
$\Delta CsAvg_t \times \mathbb{I}_t(Boom=2)$	−0.006	−0.012	
	(−0.03)	(−0.04)	
$\mathbb{I}_t(Boom=2)$	0.046***	0.032	0.048***
	(3.39)	(1.28)	(3.35)
$\Delta CsAvg_t \times \mathbb{I}_t(Boom=3)$	−0.281*	−0.280[+]	
	(−2.42)	(−1.93)	
$\mathbb{I}_t(Boom=3)$	0.003	−0.022	0.003
	(0.20)	(−1.10)	(0.21)
$\Delta CsAvg_t \times \mathbb{I}_t(Boom=4)$	0.214	0.136	
	(1.30)	(0.28)	

Note: The table summarizes the predictive power of $\Delta CsAvg$ interacted with dummy variables indicating years into the credit boom on future $\Delta Credit$. The regression specification is: $\Delta Credit_{t+1} = \alpha_n + \beta' \sum_{k=1}^{5} \Delta CsAvg_{k,t-1} \times \mathbb{I}_{n,t}(Boom\text{-}year = k) + \gamma' X_{n,t-1} + \epsilon_{n,t}$, where $X_{n,t} = (\Delta Credit_{-1}, \Delta(1/Vol)_t, \Delta CsAvg_t, \Delta rGDP_{n,t}, \Delta Credit_{n,t}, \Delta TFP_{n,t}, \Delta LP_{n,t})$. The data are annual and span a period from 1973 until 2012. All regression specifications take into account country and year fixed effects, and standard errors are clustered at both the country and year level.

There are two conceptualizations of business cycles. One comes from a long line of investigators, including importantly Mitchell (1913, 1927), and Burns and Mitchell (1946). Burns and Mitchell examined levels of a large number of series and viewed cycles in terms of four phases (prosperity, crisis, depression, revival), identifying peaks and troughs by examining the coherence and "turning points" of many series. This is essentially the procedure the U.S. National Bureau of Economic Research follows and has been formalized by Harding and Pagan (2002) and Bry and Boschan (1971). This conceptualization imposes structure on the data in that it requires that peaks follow troughs and troughs follow peaks. There is no theoretical basis for this structure, a criticism made by Koopmans (1947) and Kydland and Prescott (1990).

The other approach was proposed by Lucas (1977), who defined business cycles as the deviations from a trend. Hodrick and Prescott (1997) specified an econometric procedure for determining the trend and hence the deviations. The idea that there is a phenomenon called a "deviation" that is conceptually distinct from the "trend" is based on the Solow (1970) growth model. Conceptually, the Solow model determines the "trend" and the residual is the "business cycle." In this view, the "business cycle" corresponds to "shocks" that take the economy away from the trend temporarily. In other words, business cycles are deviations from trend. After a shock the economy converges back to the steady state. So, in the traditional view, the economy is fundamentally stable. This traditional view, however, has no room for financial crises unless pushed by exogenous large and financially specific shocks.

In Chapter 3 we invoked shocks to show that a financial crisis can occur even when the "shock" is small, if the credit boom has gone on long enough. But the idea of a "shock" is shorthand for something we do not understand. If we understood it, then we could incorporate it endogenously into a model. Consequently, in this chapter, and the previous one, we have not relied on shocks. In these chapters the relevant aggregate state is the financial crisis, but the crisis is the outcome of the implications of idiosyncratic shocks to collateral that result in the credit boom. These models are deterministic and the steady states displayed a range of rich dynamics. Still, to move from one steady state to another requires invoking a "shock," and we do not know what such a shock might be. Relying on exogenous "shocks" that are mysterious in their origins is not much of a theory.

Now we will conjecture a definition of aggregate states of the economy and then we will look at our information and fragility measures to determine if they predict the starts of recessions, for example. This will be a joint hypothesis that our definition is correct and that our information and fragility measures are predictive of this alternative conceptualization of business cycles.

To define the business cycle, we do not want to impose a great deal of preconceived structure on the data such as detrending or defining peaks and troughs because there is no theoretical justification for this. Instead, we will define recessions and growth periods differently, as follows. At date t^* we look backward four years and determine if the level of real GDP (rGDP) today is below that level by a threshold of $\alpha \leq -0.005$. If it is, then we say that a *recession* has started from the previous peak and it continues until this previous peak is again attained. In Figure 5.7, looking back from today, date t^*, to date t_0 real GDP at date t^* is below the peak at t_0 by α, and so we say that a recession has started at t_0. The recession continues until the level of real GDP is at least the level it was at date t_0. This definition is based on the level of GDP. As Burns and Mitchell put it: "Aggregate [economic] activity can be given a definite meaning and made conceptually measurable by identifying it with gross national product" (1946, 72).

In the figure, a financial crisis starts at date t^C during the recession and continues until date t^{**}, which is the end of both the crisis and the recession. A crisis may come anywhere during a recession and in a few cases the crisis is not associated with a recession. In what follows we will look at predictive regressions to try to explain the starting date of recessions (date t^*) and the starting dates of crises (date t^C). We also look at *growth* periods. A period of *growth* is said to occur when, by the same backward-looking procedure, we find that rGDP has increased by 0.01. So, there are four states that macroeconomy may be in: growth, recession, recession with crisis, or normal, where "normal" is the complement of the first three states.

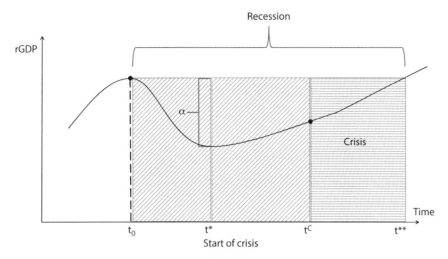

FIGURE 5.7. Definition of Recessions.
Note: A recession period is identified when the minimum quarterly real GDP change over a period of n quarters $(t^*\text{-}t_0)$ is less than a specified threshold (α). The recession begins at the highest GDP level (t^0) prior to the drop and continues until the previous peak is again attained (t^{**}). A financial crisis can occur at any point over the course of a recession (t^C).

Table 5.4. Duration of Economic Events

	Count	Mean	StDev	Min	Max
Normal Times	133	2.49	1.83	1	9
Growth	106	1.61	1.17	1	8
Recessions	109	2.78	1.26	1	7
Recessions with Crises	25	2.96	0.84	1	5
Recessions with No Crises	96	2.39	1.15	1	5

Note: The table summarizes the total number and duration of the following economic events: normal times, growth, recessions, recessions with crises, and recessions without crises. The economic episodes are computed using quarterly real GDP data from the OECD iLibrary over a period of thirty years from 1973 until 2010.

Note that the structure imposed on real GDP is only the choice of the thresholds. We do not detrend, which imposes much more structure. And we do not require that a peak follow a trough and a trough follow a peak. Lastly, we impose the same threshold on all countries. Under our definitions, there can be a pattern of aggregate activity such as the following: recession, normal, recession, growth, normal, recession with a crisis, normal. This pattern would not be possible using a peaks and troughs structure.

Recessions fall into two types: recessions with a crisis and recessions with no crisis. We make this classification by first defining recessions and then checking Laeven and Valencia (2012), which provides crisis dates worldwide since 1970. Based on the data discussed below we identify these different types of aggregate economic activity shown in Table 5.4.

The column labeled "Count" in Table 5.4 shows the number of each type of episode across the countries of our sample. As expected, episodes of "normal times" predominate. There are 106 growth episodes and 109 recessions, among which 25 are associated with crises and 96 include instances of no crises.[6] After the column labeled "Count" are statistics on the average duration in years of each event type. The average duration of a recession with a crisis episode is longer than that of a recession with no crisis. Growth episodes are the briefest.

5.5.2   Information Measures over Business Cycles

We first present univariate comparisons of our measures of information, fragility (this is the inverse of the $1/Vol$), and the cross-sectional dispersion of average returns and of firm-level volatility (this is $CsAvg$ and $CsVol$), before the beginning of different types of aggregate events. Table 5.5a shows a univariate comparison of key variables *four quarters prior* to the beginning of a recession with a crisis episode versus the beginning of a recession with no crisis episode. Leading to a recession with a crisis, growth in real GDP ($\Delta rGDP$) is lower and α is negative. Prior to recessions with crises, we observe a higher level of fragility ($1/Vol$ is smaller). The significant difference in fragility is natural. As an economy heads toward a crisis, the distance to default of the average firm decreases. Leading to a recession with a crisis, both $CsAvg$ and $CsVol$ are significantly higher. This is an indication of a higher dispersion of volatility and returns among companies, which we interpret as an increase in the information produced by agents in the economy. None of the other measures are significantly different.

Table 5.5b reports the results of a univariate comparison of the same variables *four quarters prior* to the beginning of a recession versus the beginning of a growth period. The only variables that are statistically different between the two events are fragility and $CsAvg$ with the first being lower and the second higher prior to a growth episode. This suggests that the short-lived (average duration of 1.55 years) growth stage is associated with higher levels of fragility and more production of information.

Table 5.5 suggests that information measures have predictive content. Figure 5.8 corroborates that finding. It shows plots of the two information measures averaged over recessions with a crisis and recessions without a crisis, starting fifteen quarters *before* the start of the average recession with a crisis and the average recession without a crisis. It is apparent that these measures of information and fragility vary depending on whether the coming recession will involve a financial crisis or not. We observe that fragility is higher and more information is produced prior to the beginning of a recession with crisis episode.[7] In what follows we explore the results in the figures econometrically.

We also conduct univariate comparisons of variables *during* the course of different types of aggregate events. Table 5.6b shows a univariate comparison of key variables *during* recessions versus periods of no recession (the complement of recession). By definition of a recession, growth in real GDP ($\Delta rGDP$) is lower and so α is negative. Recessions display a higher level of fragility, that is, $1/Vol$ is smaller in recessions than in non-recession periods. None of the other measures are significantly different.

Table 5.5. Difference in Mean Values: Four Quarters Prior (all countries)

(a) Recessions with Crises vs. Recessions with No Crises				(b) Recessions vs. Growth		
	No-Crisis	Crisis	Mean Diff.		Recession	Growth	Mean Diff.
$\Delta rGDP$	0.031	−0.011	0.042***	$\Delta rGDP$	0.023	0.044	−0.021***
			(12.83)				(−10.00)
α	0.003	−0.030	0.033***	α	−0.005	0.007	−0.012***
			(23.04)				(−10.33)
$1/Vol$	3.311	2.547	0.763***	$1/Vol$	3.250	3.185	0.065
			(12.11)				(1.56)
$CsVol$	0.423	0.606	−0.183***	$CsAvg$	0.128	0.130	−0.002
			(−7.95)				(−0.45)
$CsAvg$	0.120	0.163	−0.043***	$\Delta(1/Vol)$	−0.009	0.017	−0.025
			(−8.58)				(−1.10)
$\Delta(1/Vol)$	0.007	−0.077	0.084*	$\Delta CsAvg$	0.001	0.001	0.000
			(2.41)				(0.04)
$\Delta CsVol$	−0.000	0.030	−0.030	N	163	235	
			(−1.51)				
$\Delta CsAvg$	−0.000	0.007	−0.007				
			(−1.58)				
N	124	26					

t-statistics in parentheses
$^{+}p < 0.10$, $^{*}p < 0.05$, $^{**}p < 0.01$, $^{***}p < 0.001$
Note: The table summarizes mean values for $\Delta rGDP$, α, $1/Vol$, $CsAvg$, $\Delta(1/Vol)$, and $\Delta CsAvg$ four quarters prior to instances of: (i) recessions with crises vs. recessions with no crises, and (ii) recessions vs. growth. The third column reports the difference in means and the t-statistic of the difference. The data are quarterly and span a period from 1973 until 2010.

Table 5.6a shows the comparison of recessions with a crisis to recessions with no crisis. Recessions with a crisis are significantly deeper in terms of the level of the real GDP decline. Fragility is significantly higher ($1/Vol$ is smaller) as are both $CsAvg$ and $CsVol$, that is, the standard deviation of returns and the standard deviation of volatility. These two measures are higher, that is, there is more dispersion of volatility and returns among companies. None of the other measures are significantly different. In Table 5.6a we get a glimpse of recessions with crises being different.

Definitions of the "business cycle" have an arbitrariness to them. That's why we wanted to look at the joint hypothesis that our definition of a recession is related to our information measures. We take this as some confirmation that this definition of recessions is on the right track. But clearly there's a lot more to do.

5.6   Summary

In this chapter we explored the interaction of credit markets subject to crises and the other main financial market, stock markets, showing a novel macroprudential role for

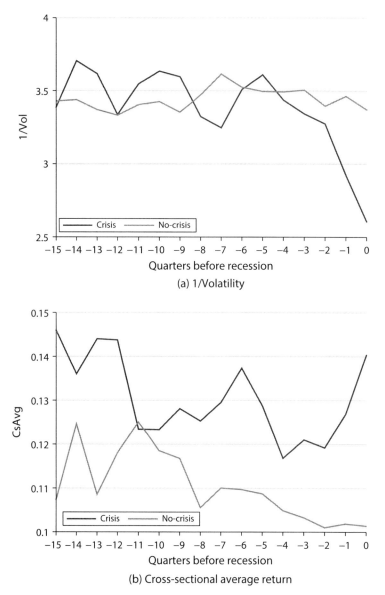

FIGURE 5.8. Information Variables prior to a Recession with and without a Crisis.
Note: The figure summarizes the evolution of average distance-to-insolvency ($1/Vol$) and
cross-sectional average returns ($CsAvg$) over 15 quarters prior to the beginning of: (*a*) a
recession with a crisis, and (*b*) a recession without a crisis. The variables are averaged
across all countries in the sample. The data are quarterly from 1973 until 2010.

stock markets. We allow participants in both markets to acquire information about their
respective objects of interest, firms' projects in stock markets and firms' collateral in credit
markets. As credit booms evolve and average projects' quality declines, there are greater
incentives to acquire information not only about collateral but also about firms in stock
markets. Once weaker firms are discovered and stop participating in credit markets, there

Table 5.6. Difference in Mean Values (all countries)

(a) Recessions with Crises vs. Recessions with No Crises				(b) Recessions vs. Growth		
	No-Crisis	Crisis	Mean Diff.		Recession	Growth	Mean Diff.
$\Delta rGDP$	−0.005	−0.017	0.013** (3.17)	$\Delta rGDP$	−0.008	0.073	−0.081*** (−34.76)
α	−0.024	−0.056	0.033*** (13.59)	α	−0.033	0.018	−0.051*** (−35.95)
$1/Vol$	3.159	2.440	0.720*** (12.32)	$1/Vol$	2.950	3.242	−0.291*** (−6.55)
$CsAvg$	0.123	0.191	−0.068*** (−8.94)	$CsAvg$	0.143	0.124	0.019*** (3.85)
$\Delta(1/Vol)$	0.020	0.023	−0.002 (−0.06)	$\Delta(1/Vol)$	0.021	−0.025	0.046+ (1.70)
$\Delta CsAvg$	0	0.006	−0.005 (−0.93)	$\Delta CsAvg$	0.002	0.002	−0 (−0.11)
N	798	332		N	1130	794	

t-statistics in parentheses
$^{+}p < 0.10, {}^{*}p < 0.05, {}^{**}p < 0.01, {}^{***}p < 0.001$
Note: The table summarizes mean values for $\Delta rGDP$, α, $1/Vol$, $CsAvg$, $\Delta(1/Vol)$, and $\Delta CsAvg$ for instances of: (i) recessions with crises vs. recessions with no crises, and (ii) recessions vs. growth. The third column reports the difference in means and the t-statistic of the difference. The data are quarterly and span a period from 1973 until 2010.

is a relaxation of the incentives to acquire information about the collateral of participating firms, potentially preventing a crisis.

By playing an unexplored positive macroprudential role in the economy, stock markets become an automatic stabilizer of credit markets. This cleansing effect of stock markets' information on credit markets' composition of firms can prevent crises. On the one hand, when stock markets do not convey too much information we may observe more crises. On the other hand, when stock markets convey too much information, credit markets may not function at full potential. Weighing this credit-crisis trade-off of stock markets, we discussed normative implications that guide policy restrictions that may have effects on information incentives in both markets.

We tested three hypotheses from the model. These tests relied on two stock price-based measures called *Information* and *Fragility*. We confirmed the three hypotheses. We also extended the empirical work to business cycles generally. In standard macroeconomics a "business cycle" is a deviation from trend. But here that makes no sense, so we defined a business cycle and showed how our measure of information interacts with other macroeconomic variables, in particular, measures of productivity.

So far we have studied a comprehensive dynamic model with information about collateral in credit markets, information about firms in stock markets, and endogenous evolution of productivity. This model generates the facts we documented in Chapter 1 and predicted others that we have tested as well. We have not, however, introduced financial intermediaries (in particular banks) explicitly, which are natural players in credit markets. Further, we have studied the role of stock markets in preventing a crisis, but if a crisis is not prevented, what can central banks do? Given our unique stand on the role of information in linking booms and busts, it is natural to ask what can a central bank do to manage information in the midst of a crisis that affects banks. We tackle this extension in the next chapter.

6

The Crisis-Fighting Role
of Central Banks

6.1   Chapter Overview

In this chapter we add banks and central banks in our setting and study their role *when a crisis occurs*. The previous chapter showed how stock markets, by generating information in the economy, can prevent crises. In this chapter we imagine that the crisis was unavoidable and we study the role of central banks in taming the generation of information that pervades credit in the economy. Central banks do this by opening emergency lending facilities. We study the optimal design of those facilities in affecting information in credit markets and restoring confidence.

As lending facilities operate through banks, we explicitly introduce financial intermediaries in this chapter. Households are born with endowments already deposited in a bank. A bank is an institution that also has its own funds and has the proprietary access to two productive investment opportunities. One, which we denote *collateral,* generates an asset that is pledgeable and the other, which we denote *project,* is stochastic, ex ante efficient, and not pledgeable. The first will be financed with its own resources and is then used to collateralize the deposits to finance the second. Put simply, banks use assets in their portfolio as collateral for deposits to finance new assets.

The underlying problem in the economy, as in previous chapters, is a scarcity of good collateral in banks' portfolios. When good collateral is scarce, an efficient substitute, as before, is ignorance about which private assets used as collateral are good and which are bad, as in the absence of information even banks with bad collateral can maintain their deposits and invest in the project.

A crisis happens when an (exogenous) event occurs (a fall in home prices, for instance) causing depositors to run, defined here as the demand to examine the bank's portfolio and withdraw if the bank has bad collateral. If this happens, banks can react by reducing their investment scale, thus reducing the incentives for depositors to examine the portfolio and run. As in Chapter 3, depositors have less to worry about when the borrower (the bank in this case) takes less risk. This can avoid information acquisition, or they can give in to the run, be examined by depositors, and hope the depositors find out that the collateral is good so it can invest at the optimal scale. In either case, absent government intervention, aggregate consumption falls during a crisis.

We then introduce a government, whose goal is to prevent a *systemic run*, which means avoiding information acquisition about *all banks' portfolios*. How does a government, operating through a central bank, end a crisis in our model? First, the central bank opens an emergency lending facility (which we call the *discount window*) that exchanges government bonds for private collateral at a haircut (*discount*).

Because one of the most discussed complications for banks using lending facilities is the existence of stigma that may prevent banks' participation, we extend the model in a second dimension, making the heterogeneous quality of collateral persistent. Then, which banks go to the discount window depends on their private information about their portfolio quality and on the central bank's discount. The central bank can adopt a policy of *opacity* in which the identities of banks going to the discount window are not revealed, or a policy of *transparency* in which identities are revealed. We provide conditions under which opacity is the socially preferred policy, characterize the optimal discounting, and we show that an opaque policy is implementable because stigma prevents individual banks from deviating by revealing their participation status.

Why is opacity optimal? It is socially beneficial because restoring confidence during crises means raising the perceived average quality of all bank assets in the economy. With opacity, lending government bonds to some banks increases the *expected* bank portfolio value for all banks. In a way, secrecy creates an information externality by raising the average quality of assets in the banking system without replacing all assets under suspicion, mitigating the desire of depositors to examine all banks' assets. As above, a crisis here is an information event and as such its solution has a strong information content. Lending facilities re-create confidence and avoid inefficient examination of banks' portfolios. Secrecy minimizes the social cost of resorting to lending facilities.

What is the optimal discount on the assets the central bank accepts at the discount window? The central bank's choice of the discount rate controls how many banks participate in the discount window and by doing so the perceived average quality of private collateral remaining in the economy, calibrating not to intervene more than necessary to restore confidence.

But even when the central bank may prefer secrecy to reduce intervention costs, individual banks could have different plans, individually disclosing their participation (or lack thereof) and making the intended secrecy unsustainable. How can opaque lending facilities be sustainable in equilibrium? As participating banks are those with lower-quality collateral on average, they do not want to individually reveal their participation and face a higher likelihood of an idiosyncratic run in the future (they fear stigma). Similarly, nonparticipating banks cannot credibly signal a high quality of collateral in the future by revealing no participation, because they would then face a run during the ensuing crisis. *Endogenous participation and stigma are what make the opacity policy sustainable in equilibrium.*

Our view of stigma is in contrast to the more standard view in the literature, usually thought of in the context of normal, non-crisis times in which a single bank does not want to be identified as weak by borrowing from the discount window for fear of a run. Neither the bank nor the central bank wants this bank-specific information revealed. But a financial crisis is a state of the world in which *the whole banking system* is stigmatized. The run is already happening: holders of short-term debt doubt all banks' backing for their debt. Addressing this with a policy of opacity is intended to create the rational belief that the *system* is solvent. Here, opacity is not the means to avoid stigma and a run on a single bank but instead stigma is the means to avoid transparency and a run on the whole system.

The use of opaque lending facilities is indeed ubiquitous in dealing with financial crises. During the Financial Crisis of 2007–2008, for instance, the Federal Reserve introduced a number of new emergency lending programs, including the Term Auction Facility, the Term Securities Lending Facility, and the Primary Dealers Credit Facility, which provide public funds to financial intermediaries in exchange for private assets. Also as part of their Emergency Economic Stabilization Act, the U.S. Treasury implemented similar programs, such as the Troubled Asset Relief Program (TARP). What these facilities had in common was their initial specific design to hide borrowers' identities.[1] Secrecy was also integral to the special crisis lending programs of the Bank of England and the European Central Bank.[2] Plenderleith, asked by the Bank of England to review their Emergency Lending Facilities (ELA) during the financial crisis, wrote: "Was secrecy appropriate in 2008? In light of the fragility of the markets at the time . . . ELA is likely to be more effective if provided covertly" (2012, 70). Even before the Federal Reserve came into existence, private bank clearinghouses opened emergency lending facilities during banking panics, keeping the identities of borrowing banks secret. (See Gorton and Tallman 2018.)

The secrecy of these lending facilities is not without controversy. Hiding the identities of weak or insolvent banks has been widely criticized, resulting in fierce calls for transparency. During the recent crisis, for instance, Bloomberg and Fox News sued the Fed (under the Freedom of Information Act) to obtain the identities of borrowers.[3] Similarly, TARP was initially designed to maintain secrecy of borrowers, but this was quickly overturned by the Senate Congressional Oversight Panel.[4]

6.2   Model

6.2.1   Environment

As the goal of this chapter is to understand the government's intervention when there is a crisis, it is not necessary to discuss all the dynamics, so we can go back to the single period of Chapter 3. Since we want to model stigma, however, which mostly relies on a future cost of participating in the discount windows, we want at least two periods. This is what we will do next: assume a two-period economy.

Because we want to understand the intervention of central banks in the financial system through discount windows opened to banks, instead of modeling households and firms we model depositors and banks. More specifically, the economy is populated by a mass 1 of depositors and a mass 1 of banks. Also, as we want to focus on the use of banks' portfolios as collateral, instead of interpreting collateral as land, we will use the assets in the banks' portfolios as collateral, still subject to heterogeneity and information issues.

Depositors live for a single period, are risk neutral, and are indifferent between consuming at the beginning or at the end of the period in which they live. Each depositor is born with an endowment D of consumption good (numeraire), which is already deposited in a bank, but it is available for withdrawal at no cost at the beginning of the period.

Banks live for two periods and are also risk neutral. Each bank is matched with a single depositor, has its own funds (bank equity), and has two single-period investment opportunities in each period. One investment opportunity generates output that is observable and verifiable in court. The other does not. This structure guarantees that the bank finances the former with its own funds and uses it to collateralize the depositors' funds to finance the latter project. Accordingly, we call the first, verifiable, project *the collateral* and the second simply *the project*.

Collateral.   With probability p_{it} the collateral of bank i in period t is of *good type*, in which case it delivers C units of numeraire at the end of the period. With the complementary probability, the collateral is of *bad type* and does not deliver any numeraire at the end of the period. The collateral types are independent and identically distributed across periods and across banks. We refer to p_{it} as the *quality of the collateral* held by bank i in period t. The quality of collateral depends on an aggregate component and on an idiosyncratic component, $p_{it} = \bar{p}_t + \eta_i$. The aggregate component, $\bar{p}_t$, is time-varying and captures the average quality of collateral in the economy. The idiosyncratic component, η_i, is persistent and captures heterogeneity of banks' ability to manage good collateral, where $\eta_i \sim F[-\bar{\eta}, \bar{\eta}]$, with $E(\eta_i) = 0$ and $\bar{\eta}$ such that $p_i \in [0, 1]$.[5]

While the aggregate component is the same force as we introduced in Chapter 3 and affects all collateral in the economy, the idiosyncratic component is a new element in this chapter. Extending the characteristics of collateral in this way captures persistence in the quality of the borrower and then the possibility of endogenous stigma. It also adds asymmetric information about collateral between lenders (depositors) and borrowers (banks).

Collateral Information.   In terms of information, no agent (neither the bank nor the depositor) knows the collateral type at the beginning of the period but there is asymmetric information about its quality: while both banks and depositors know the average quality of collateral in the economy, $\bar{p}_t$, each bank privately observes its own idiosyncratic component η_i, so the bank has a better assessment of its own collateral quality, p_{it}. At the end of the period, *after all contracts are settled*, the collateral type becomes public knowledge. Even though no agent knows the collateral type at the beginning of the period, depositors have a technology to *privately investigate the collateral type at the beginning of the period* at a cost γ in terms of numeraire. Using this technology they can determine whether the collateral will deliver C units of numeraire at the end of the period.[6] As in the rest of the book, we assume that acquiring information is a private activity, but the depositor can credibly disclose (*certify*) such private information immediately upon acquisition if it is in his best interest to do so. This information technology induces depositors to learn about the bank's collateral type before deciding whether or not to keep their funds in the bank.

Project. The project of the bank has the same form as that of the project of firms in previous chapters. The project pays $A \min\{K, K^*\}$ with probability q and 0 otherwise, where K^* is the maximum feasible scale of production. As mentioned, the result of the project (whether it succeeds or fails) is known by the bank but it is neither observable nor verifiable by the depositors. We maintain the following parametric assumptions about the project's payoffs:

Assumption 1.   Project Payoffs.

- $qA > 1$. It is ex ante optimal to finance the project up to a scale K^*.
- $D > K^* + \gamma$. It is feasible to implement the optimal investment just using deposits.
- $C > K^*$. Good collateral is sufficient to cover the optimal loan size.[7]

6.2.2   Timing

The timing during a single period is as follows. At the beginning of the period, a bank offers a contract to its depositor that consists of an investment plan (the commitment to invest a certain amount K in the project), an interest rate for the deposits (a promised repayment $R \geq D$ at the end of the period), and the collateral that secures the deposits (a fraction x of the collateral to be delivered to the depositor in case the bank defaults). Conditional on this contract, depositors choose whether or not to examine the bank's collateral and then decide whether or not to withdraw the deposits at the beginning of the period. At the end of the period, two sequential events take place. First, projects pay and loan contracts are fulfilled. Then, collateral types are revealed and banks sell their collateral (the fraction not handed out to lenders because of default) to households (making a take-it-or-leave-it offer to a randomly matched household).

Formally, we have a sequential game between a bank and its depositors in which a bank chooses a contract to maximize profits conditional on the constraints imposed by information acquisition and withdrawal choices of depositors. Modifying the announced investment, the bank can (in effect) change these choices. The main timing difference compared with the model inhabited by households and firms in Chapter 3, in which the lenders (households) hold the funds and decide whether to transfer the funds or not to borrowers (firms), is that here the borrowers (banks) hold the funds and the lenders (depositors) choose whether to withdraw the funds from borrowers.

As in Chapter 3, borrowers (firms there and banks here) can restrict the project size to reduce the risk exposure of lenders (households there and depositors here) and relax the incentives to acquire information about collateral. The main difference is that in this chapter borrowers have superior information about their own collateral (because of the idiosyncratic component), which will affect the offered contract (good banks are less worried about collateral examination). Depositors, however, understand this and take the offered contract as a signal of the idiosyncratic component and then of the quality of collateral. We study these more complicated contracts (vis-à-vis Chapter 3) in the following section.

6.3   Runs and Investments

We first study the withdrawal decisions of depositors and then, considering these choices, the investment choices of banks.

6.3.1   Withdrawal Choices

We say there is a *run* on a bank when its depositor examines the bank's collateral at the beginning of the period and withdraws the funds upon finding out that the collateral is bad. Here we characterize the optimal contract in case of a run and in case of no run. While the bank knows its own collateral quality p_{it}, households just have an expectation about the probability that a particular bank's collateral is good, which we denote as $E(p_{it}|\mathcal{I})$, where $\mathcal{I}$ is the information set of depositors at the time of deciding whether to withdraw at the beginning of the period. In this section we focus on a single bank and a single period, so we dispense with the subindex *it*.

6.3.1.1 BANK RUN (DEPOSITOR EXAMINES THE BANK).   Assume the depositor examines the bank's collateral at the beginning of the period, spending γ of numeraire. When examination occurs both the depositor and the bank learn the type of collateral at the beginning of the period. If the collateral is good, it is enough to guarantee the recovery of deposits at the end of the period, even if the bank finances the project at the optimal scale K^* and the project fails. This is because $C + D - K^* > D$ by assumption. If the collateral is bad, the depositor withdraws the deposits at the beginning of the period because if the bank were to finance the project it can always claim the project has failed and turn over the worthless collateral to the depositor.

What is the bank contract triplet (R_r, x_r, K_r) (the promised repayment at the end of the period, the fraction of collateral that backs the loan, and the investment scale) that induces the depositor to examine the collateral and allows for investment if the collateral is good? To begin to answer this first define the expected quality of collateral of a bank offering a contract that induces a run as $E^r(p) \equiv E(p|run)$, which is an equilibrium object. With probability $E^r(p)$ the depositor's expected payoffs are $qR_r + (1-q)(D - K_r + x_r C) - \gamma$. With probability $(1 - E^r(p))$, the depositor always withdraws and loses the cost of examination, then obtaining $D - \gamma$.

The *truth-telling condition* discussed in Chapter 3 imposes $R_r = D - K_r + x_r C$. Expected payoffs for a depositor are then $E^r(p)(R_r - \gamma) + (1 - E^r(p))(D - \gamma)$, independent of K_r. Assuming as in previous chapters that lenders (depositors in this case) do not have negotiation power and break even, $D = E^r(p)R_r + (1 - E^r(p))D - \gamma$. This participation constraint pins down the interest rate:

$$R_r = D + \frac{\gamma}{E^r(p)}, \tag{6.1}$$

which is independent of q (the probability the project pays off).

The contract that maximizes the bank's payoffs under runs is then a triplet, (R_r, x_r, K_r), where R_r is given by equation (6.1), $x_r = \frac{R_r - D + K_r}{C}$ (from the truth-telling condition) and $K_r = K^*$ (from feasibility of optimal investment upon finding the collateral is good). Now we can compute the bank's ex ante expected profits given this contract. As the bank knows its collateral is good with probability p, and that it will suffer a withdrawal in case its collateral is bad, its ex ante expected profits are $p(D + qAK^* - K^* - R_r) + pC$. Substituting R_r in equilibrium, the period *expected profits* (net of the expected price of the collateral at the end of the period, pC) from inducing a run are:

$$E_r(\pi \,|\, p, E^r(p)) = \max\left\{ pK^*(qA - 1) - \frac{p}{E^r(p)}\gamma, 0 \right\}. \tag{6.2}$$

These expected profits depend not only on the probability that the bank's collateral is good, p, but also on the average quality of the collateral of all other banks inducing a run. This implies that, with the asymmetric information extension in this chapter, there is cross-subsidization among banks that face a run: banks with $p > E^r(p)$ end up paying more to compensate depositors for the information costs in expectation, as $\frac{p}{E^r(p)} > 1$. The opposite happens for banks with $p < E^r(p)$.

6.3.1.2 NO BANK RUN (DEPOSITOR DOES NOT EXAMINE THE BANK).

Another possibility is that the depositor does not examine the bank's portfolio and does not withdraw. In this case, the depositor expects to obtain R_{nr} in case of repayment. And in the case of default, a fraction x_{nr} of the collateral of expected value $E^{nr}(p)C$ (where $E^{nr}(p) \equiv E(p \,|\, no\ run)$ is the expected quality of collateral among banks that offer a contract that does not trigger examination); this is $D - K_{nr} + x_{nr}E^{nr}(p)C$. In this case the truth-telling constraint is given by $R_{nr} = D - K_{nr} + x_{nr}E^{nr}(p)$. If $R_{nr} < D - K_{nr} + x_{nr}E^{nr}(p)C$, the bank can sell the collateral at a price $E^{nr}(p)C$ (recall information about the type is revealed after contracts are settled) and repay always. In contrast, if $R_{nr} > D - K_{nr} + x_{nr}E^{nr}(p)C$, the bank would always default. Then, $x_{nr} = \frac{R_{nr} - D + K_{nr}}{E^{nr}(p)C}$.

The depositor is indifferent between withdrawing or not if $D = R_{nr}$, which implies that no run is feasible if and only if $x_{nr} = \frac{K_{nr}}{E^{nr}(p)C} \leq 1$. This gives the first technological constraint on investment from this contract,

$$K_{nr} \leq E^{nr}(p)C. \tag{6.3}$$

The second, informational, constraint on investment comes from guaranteeing that the depositor does not have an incentive to deviate and examine the bank's collateral privately at the beginning of the period. Depositors want to deviate if the expected gains from acquiring information, evaluated at R_{nr} (and then at x_{nr}), are greater than the gains from not acquiring information. This is

$$(1 - E^{nr}(p))D + E^{nr}(p)\left[qR_{nr}^R + (1-q)[D - K_{nr} + x_{nr}C]\right] - \gamma > D.$$

Substituting in the definitions of R_{nr} (and then x_{nr}), there is no incentive to privately deviate and examine the bank's collateral if:

$$K_{nr} < \frac{\gamma}{(1-q)\left(1 - E^{nr}(p)\right)}. \tag{6.4}$$

Intuitively, the gains from examining the bank's portfolio and withdrawing if it is bad are increasing in the investment size and in the risk of default. If the bank scales down the project (hence the loan), the depositor has less of an incentive to acquire information about the bank's collateral.

Imposing constraints (6.3) and (6.4), the project size that is consistent with a no-run contract is

$$K_{nr}(E^{nr}(p)) = \min\left\{K^*, \frac{\gamma}{(1-q)\left(1 - E^{nr}(p)\right)}, E^{nr}(p)C\right\}, \tag{6.5}$$

and the bank's expected profits (net of the expected price of the collateral at the end of the period, pC) are

$$E_{nr}(\pi \mid E^{nr}(p)) = K_{nr}(E^{nr}(p))(qA - 1). \tag{6.6}$$

6.3.2   Investment Choices

The bank would like to invest at optimal scale, but that may trigger collateral examination. By choosing the investment level, a bank can then choose between facing a run or not. The optimal decision of how much to invest in the project is then isomorphic to the bank announcing an investment strategy that finances the project either at the optimal scale (triggering a run) or at a restricted scale (avoiding a run). All banks' decisions, however, must be consistent in the aggregate. Even though banks are not fundamentally linked to each other, their choices of whether to trigger examination or not affect the inference of depositors about the quality of their collateral.

As we have shown, the expected profits of a bank suffering a run (equation 6.2) depend on both p and $E^r(p)$ while the expected profits of a bank without a run (equation 6.6) only depend on $E^{nr}(p)$. Since $E_r(\pi)$ increases in p while $E_{nr}(\pi)$ is independent of p, if a bank with collateral of quality p announces an investment plan that induces a run, then all $p' > p$ will also. Similarly, if a bank with a collateral of quality p announces an investment plan that avoids a run, then all $p' < p$ will also. Intuitively, a bank with high collateral quality is more willing to open the portfolio for examination and to face the lottery that a run represents.

Hence, banks with better collateral in expectation are more inclined to announce large investments that induce examination.

This implies that the optimal investment strategy is given by a cutoff rule under which all banks with $p < p^*$ restrict their investments to avoid runs and all banks with $p > p^*$ invest at the optimal scale and open themselves to examination of the collateral (a run), where p^* is the collateral quality that makes a bank indifferent between a run or not.

$$E_r(\pi | p^*, E^r(p)) = E_{nr}(\pi | E^{nr}(p)),$$

and where $E^r(p) = E(p | p > p^*)$ and $E^{nr}(p) = E(p | p < p^*)$.

More formally, allowing for corner solutions in which all banks either face a run or not, the equilibrium cutoff is such that

$$p^* = \begin{cases} \overline{p} + \overline{\eta} & \text{if} & E_r(\pi | \overline{p} + \overline{\eta}, \overline{p} + \overline{\eta}) < E_{nr}(\pi | \overline{p}) \\ p^* & \text{s.t.} & E_r(\pi | p^*, E(p | p > p^*)) = E_{nr}(\pi | E(p | p < p^*)). \\ \overline{p} - \overline{\eta} & \text{if} & E_r(\pi | \overline{p} - \overline{\eta}, \overline{p}) > E_{nr}(\pi | \overline{p} - \overline{\eta}) \end{cases}$$

(6.7)

As both $E^r(\pi | p^*, E(p | p > p^*))$ and $E^{nr}(\pi | E(p | p < p^*))$ increase with p^* there may be multiple p^* in equilibrium. In what follows we focus on the largest p^*; this is the *best equilibrium* that guarantees the highest sustainable output. The next proposition shows that in such an equilibrium the threshold p^* increases with the average quality of collateral in the economy, $\overline{p}$. That is, the higher the average quality of collateral in the economy the fewer the banks that face runs and collateral examination.

Proposition 17 (Beliefs and Runs). In the best equilibrium, the threshold p^* is increasing in $\overline{p}$. There exist beliefs $p^H > p^L$ such that if $\overline{p} > p^H$ no bank faces a run and if $\overline{p} < p^L$ all banks face runs.

Notice that in this extended setting, in which the borrower has some superior ex ante information about the quality of collateral, nests the setting in Chapter 3, in which all borrowers were symmetrically uninformed about the collateral quality and then all choose the same contract, given p. Here, in equilibrium, some borrowers will induce examination of collateral, and some others not, even though sharing the lenders' perception of collateral p. Corner situations are still possible depending on the conditions specified in the proposition.

Remark on Off-Equilibrium Beliefs. When the threshold p^* is a corner (either $p^* = \overline{p} - \overline{\eta}$ or $p^* = \overline{p} + \overline{\eta}$), the expected quality of the collateral of a bank following a strategy that is off-equilibrium is not well-defined. If $p^* = \overline{p} + \overline{\eta}$ no bank faces a run and then $E^r(p)$ is not well-defined as it is an off-equilibrium strategy. The same is the case for $E^{nr}(p)$; if $p^* = \overline{p} - \overline{\eta}$, then all banks are expected to face a run. Following the Cho and Kreps (1987) criterion, we assume that if a bank follows a strategy not supposed to be followed in equilibrium, depositors believe the bank holds a collateral that maximizes its incentives to deviate from the expected strategy. That is, if $p^* = \bar{p} + \bar{\eta}$ and a depositor observes a bank investing in a large project so as to induce a run, then the depositor believes that the bank has the highest-quality collateral available, $E^r(p) = \bar{p} + \bar{\eta}$. Similarly, if $p^* = \bar{p} - \bar{\eta}$ and a depositor observes a bank investing in a project that discourages examination of the collateral, then the household believes that the bank has the lowest-quality collateral available, $E^{nr}(p) = \bar{p} - \bar{\eta}$.

6.4   Crises and Interventions

In this section we restrict attention to a situation in which the economy suffers a *crisis* in the first period and gets back to normal in the second period. How the economy fares during the crisis in the first period will also determine output in the second period.

The crisis in the first period comes from a shock to the economy as follows. First, we capture the informational nature of crises by assuming that $\bar{p}_{t=1} = p_L < p^L$, as defined in Proposition 17, such that all banks face examination (runs) in the absence of intervention. Second, we capture the turbulent nature of crises by assuming that absent interventions, there are potential *information leakages*; with probability ε the bank's collateral type is revealed.[8] In the second period the economy goes back to *normal*, which we capture by assuming that $\bar{p}_{t=2} = p_H > p^H$, as defined in Proposition 17, such that, absent a crisis in the first period, there would not be a run on any bank.

When the economy is in normal times, absent a previous crisis, it achieves the maximum potential consumption: depositors consume D and all banks invest at the optimal scale, producing an additional amount $K^*(qA - 1)$ of numeraire to consume. Aggregate consumption is then

$$W_N = D + p_H C + K^*(qA - 1).$$

During crises, however, absent government intervention, all banks face runs, depositors examine all banks' collateral, and only a fraction p_L of banks retains their deposits, at an information production cost γ, while the remaining fraction $(1 - p_L)$ faces withdrawals at the beginning of the period and is not able to finance their projects. In this case, aggregate consumption is

$$W_C = D + p_L C + p_L K^*(qA - 1) - \gamma < W_N.$$

6.4.1   Tools to Fight the Crisis: Lending Facilities

We now introduce a central bank, a benevolent planner that manages a particular set of lending facilities that can be used to relax the incentives to acquire information in the economy and boost investment and consumption during the crisis in the first period. This is the timing of these facilities.

1. The central bank opens a *discount window* that exchanges B government bonds (hereafter "bonds" for short) per unit of collateral, to be paid in numeraire at the end of the period. It also announces whether it will reveal the identities of banks

participating at the discount window (a policy of *transparency*) or not (a policy of *opacity*). The central bank chooses both B and the disclosure strategy, committing to the announced policy.[9]

2. Conditional on the announced policies, banks choose whether to go to the discount window (*participate*) or not and, critically, whether to disclose such participation to its depositors, potentially in opposition to the government's intended disclosure policy. If a bank does not participate, its collateral type is revealed with leakage probability ε. If a bank participates, and its participation becomes public, there is an endogenously determined *stigma cost*, denoted by χ. Stigma arises from learning about the bank's idiosyncratic collateral quality that affects the future likelihood of runs and then the bank's future profits. The magnitude of the stigma cost will be determined in equilibrium depending on the aggregate use of the discount window and, as we will discuss, it is critical in the implementation of opacity.[10]

3. At the end of the first period, discount window participants with successful projects repay deposits using the proceeds from the project and repurchase their collateral back from the central bank. Failing participants lose their bonds to depositors, who redeem them at the central bank. Successful banks that did not participate repay their deposits with the proceeds from the project and retain their collateral. Failing non-participants default and hand over their collateral to their depositors.

4. The central bank liquidates the collateral left in its possession (not repurchased) but imperfectly, only extracting a fraction ϕ of its value at the end of the period. The numeraire generated by liquidating such collateral plus distortionary taxes (transfers at a social cost δ per unit of numeraire) are used to redeem bonds.

In addition to a new player—the central bank—we have added three additional exogenous parameters in this section: the leakage probability, ε, the inefficiency of public liquidation, ϕ, and the social cost of distortionary taxation, δ. The leakage probability just avoids discontinuous changes in discount window participation and better highlights the forces behind opacity. Inefficiency of public liquidation and distortionary taxation costs are simply introduced to avoid the trivial result that the central bank should always lend at no discount.

We have also added the concept of stigma cost, χ, which is endogenous and plays a more fundamental role. Banks participating in lending facilities will be those with worse collateral in expectation. As banks operate in subsequent periods, revealing participation (and then revealing that they have worse collateral) exposes them to future runs, even when the economy returns to normal times.

Our focus is on the interplay between socially optimal disclosure (optimal for a planner that maximizes aggregate consumption, present and future, net of intervention distortions) and individually optimal disclosure (optimal for an individual bank that maximizes its own profits, present and future). We will show that in our model these two are aligned: when the planner wants transparency, banks also have incentives to privately disclose participation, and when the planner wants opacity, the *threat of a run* discourages banks that do not participate and *stigma* discourages banks that do participate to reveal their statuses, implementing the socially optimal allocation as an equilibrium outcome.

6.5   The Role of Opacity and Stigma in Fighting Crises

In this section we solve the central bank's problem in two steps. First, we compute the equilibrium and welfare in the economy under *opacity* (Op) and then under *transparency* (Tr), as a function of the bonds B that the central bank exchanges per unit of collateral through the discount window. Then we obtain the optimal B^* that maximizes welfare in each case and allows the central bank to choose the best disclosure policy, $\{Op, Tr\}$. We will discuss policy in terms of the central bank's discount. Define

$$B \equiv \widetilde{p}C,$$

such that the central bank choosing $\widetilde{p}$ implicitly chooses how many bonds B to offer per unit of collateral. Then the *discount* for a bank with collateral of expected quality $E(p)$ is given by $(E(p) - \widetilde{p})C$. For convenience, and based on this one-to-one mapping between $\widetilde{p}$ and B, we will discuss comparative statics in terms of $\widetilde{p}$.[11]

In announcing its policy the central bank cannot force banks to participate in the discount window, or force depositors to not examine collateral and maintain deposits in banks. Most importantly, the central bank cannot force banks to follow its desired disclosure policy and keep secret their own participation (or lack thereof).

As such, in computing welfare, the central bank has to take into account two equilibrium objects, the fraction of banks participating in the discount window, $y(\widetilde{p}|\{Op, Tr\})$, and the probability of runs, $\sigma(\widetilde{p}|\{Op, Tr\})$. After we obtain these equilibrium objects, we compute the incentives of banks to deviate and individually report their participation status, potentially making the announced disclosure policy unsustainable.

6.5.1   *Ending a Crisis with Opacity*

By intervening, the central bank cannot force depositors to maintain their funds in a bank or force banks to participate. The central bank can, however, choose the right discount to steer those decisions. Now we solve for how agents react to the discount rate when participation is maintained in secret.

6.5.1.1 BANK RUNS WITH AN OPAQUE DISCOUNT WINDOW.   When a depositor chooses whether to examine the bank's collateral (run) or not, he takes the fraction of banks participating in the discount window, y, as fixed (this is, of course, an equilibrium object that we endogenize in the next section). As there is no information about participation, the expected value of (any) bank's portfolio is $yB + (1 - y)E^{nw}(p)C$, where

$E^{nw}(p)$ is the expected collateral quality of banks that do not participate (also an equilibrium object). Given this expectation, depositors are indifferent between withdrawing or not at the beginning of a period when $D = qR_{nr}^{R} + (1-q)R_{nr}^{D}$, where R_{nr}^{D} is now given by the expected return in case the bank defaults, $R_{nr}^{D} = D - K_{nr} + x_{nr}[yB + (1-y)E^{nw}(p)C]$.

In equilibrium any bank will promise in expectation the same in case of repayment or default (for the same truth-telling reasons as in the previous section), so $D = R_{nr}^{R} = R_{nr}^{D}$. We can then obtain the fraction of collateral in the portfolio that is promised to depositors in case of default,

$$x_{nr} = \min\left\{\frac{K_{nr}}{yB + (1-y)E^{nw}(p)C}, 1\right\}.$$

Now we can compute the incentive of a depositor to privately acquire information about the portfolio of the bank. At a cost γ the depositor can privately learn whether the bank has bonds or private collateral in its portfolio and, in the case where the bank has private collateral, its type. The benefits of acquiring information are as follows: with probability y the bank has bonds and the depositor that examines the portfolio does not withdraw, getting a payoff of $qR_{nr}^{R} + (1-q)[D - K_{nr} + x_{nr}B] - \gamma$. With probability $(1-y)(1-E^{nw}(p))$ the bank has bad private collateral and the depositor withdraws at the beginning of the period, getting a payoff of $D - \gamma$. Finally, with probability $(1-y)E^{nw}(p)$ the bank has good private collateral, and the depositor keeps his deposits in the bank, getting a payoff of $qR_{nr}^{R} + (1-q)[D - K_{nr} + x_{nr}C] - \gamma$.

Adding the previous payoffs weighted by the respective probabilities, considering that $R_{nr}^{R} = D$ and $x_{nr}(yB + (1-y)E^{nw}(p)C) = K_{nr}$, there is no examination as long as

$$K_{nr}(E^{nw}(p)) \le \frac{\gamma}{(1-q)(1-y)(1-E^{nw}(p))}, \quad (6.8)$$

and we can define $\sigma(\widetilde{p})$ (making explicit that it depends in equilibrium on the discount offered by the central bank), the probability of a run, as

$$\sigma(\widetilde{p}) = \begin{cases} 0 & \text{if } K < \frac{\gamma}{(1-q)(1-y(\widetilde{p}))(1-E^{nw}(p|\widetilde{p}))} \\ [0,1] & \text{if } K = \frac{\gamma}{(1-q)(1-y(\widetilde{p}))(1-E^{nw}(p|\widetilde{p}))} \\ 1 & \text{if } K > \frac{\gamma}{(1-q)(1-y(\widetilde{p}))(1-E^{nw}(p|\widetilde{p}))}. \end{cases} \quad (6.9)$$

The next proposition is trivial and it comes from comparing the condition for no information acquisition in the absence of intervention (equation 6.4) and in the presence of intervention (equation 6.8).

Proposition 18 (Runs with Interventions).   Runs are less likely with intervention when there are many banks participating at the discount window (i.e., high y).

6.5.1.2 PARTICIPATION IN OPAQUE DISCOUNT WINDOWS.   We have solved for the depositors' incentives to examine a bank's portfolio conditional on the fraction of banks participating at the discount window, y. Now we show, in four stages, that this fraction y is in equilibrium a function of $\widetilde{p}$. First, define

$$L(p,\widetilde{p}) \equiv pK^*(qA-1) - \frac{p}{E^{nw}(p|\widetilde{p})}\gamma + pC$$

as the "(L)ow" bank's expected payoffs when the bank faces a run given that it did not participate in the discount window (as in equation 6.2). Second, define

$$H(K(\widetilde{p})) \equiv K(\widetilde{p})(qA-1) + p_L C$$

as the "(H)igher" bank's expected payoffs when the bank does not face a run and is able to invest $K(\widetilde{p})$ (as in equation 6.6).[12] Finally, define

$$d(\widetilde{p}) \equiv (p_L - \widetilde{p})C$$

as the bank's discount when borrowing from the discount window.

Having defined all these elements, we can compute the gains of a bank p from participating at the discount window. If the discount is determined by $\widetilde{p}$, the expected payoffs of a bank p of no participation are

$$E_{nw}(\pi|p,\widetilde{p}) = \sigma(\widetilde{p})L(p,\widetilde{p}) + (1-\sigma(\widetilde{p}))[(1-\varepsilon)H(K) + \varepsilon L(p,\widetilde{p})], \quad (6.10)$$

while the expected payoffs of participation are

$$E_w(\pi|p,\widetilde{p}) = \sigma(\widetilde{p})[H(K) - d(\widetilde{p}) - \chi(p,\widetilde{p})] + (1-\sigma(\widetilde{p}))[H(K) - d(\widetilde{p})]. \quad (6.11)$$

As can be seen, these payoffs depend both on the quality of the bank's collateral, p, and on the discount from participating in the discount window, $\widetilde{p}$.

6.5.1.3 OPACITY EQUILIBRIUM.   Since both the probability of runs and participation depend on each other and both depend on the discount $\widetilde{p}$, the next four lemmas characterize the equilibrium depositors' run (examination) strategies and banks' participation strategies, which can be divided into four ranges of $\widetilde{p}$, under opacity.

Lemma 4.   *Very low discount region.*
There exists a cutoff $\widetilde{p}_h < p_L + \overline{\eta}$ such that, for all $\widetilde{p} \in [\widetilde{p}_h, p_L + \overline{\eta})$ ("very low discount region"), no depositor runs (that is, $\sigma(\widetilde{p}) = 0$) and all banks borrow from the discount window (that is, $y(\widetilde{p}) = 1$). There is no stigma in equilibrium (that is, $\chi(p,\widetilde{p}) = 0$ for all p).

This lemma shows that there are always levels of discount low enough ($\widetilde{p}$ large enough) to induce all banks to participate at the discount window and, based on this outcome, no depositor examines any bank's portfolio, keeping their deposits available for investment. Further, as all banks participate, there is no stigma if participation is revealed.

Lemma 5. *Low discount region.*

There exists a cutoff $\widetilde{p}_m < \widetilde{p}_h$ such that, for all $\widetilde{p} \in [\widetilde{p}_m, \widetilde{p}_h)$ ("low discount region"), no depositor runs (that is, $\sigma(\widetilde{p}) = 0$), not all banks participate (this is, $y(\widetilde{p}) < 1$), and participation declines with the level of discount (that is, $y(\widetilde{p})$ increases with $\widetilde{p}$). Stigma is positive and increases in expectation with the level of discount (that is, $\chi(p, \widetilde{p})$ increases with $\widetilde{p}$).

Intuitively, when the discount is low ($\widetilde{p}$ is large), many banks choose to borrow at the discount window because the cost in terms of exchanging private collateral for bonds at a low discount more than compensates for the risk of a run and information about the private collateral being revealed. Given high participation, depositors do not have incentives to run and examine any bank's portfolio.

In this region, banks that choose not to participate are those with high collateral quality, and then participation reveals relative low collateral quality, creating a stigma cost in case participation is revealed. However, even though stigma is positive in case of participation, in equilibrium there is no examination that reveals participation, so in equilibrium no bank faces a stigma cost. This is relevant later when studying private incentives to disclose participation, as stigma is an off-equilibrium threat that does not arise in equilibrium but would arise with voluntary disclosure.[13]

Lemma 6. *Intermediate discount region.*

There exists a cutoff $\widetilde{p}_l < \widetilde{p}_m$ such that, for all $\widetilde{p} \in [\widetilde{p}_l, \widetilde{p}_m)$ ("intermediate discount region"), depositors run with positive probability but not always (that is, $\sigma(\widetilde{p}) \in (0, 1)$) and a constant fraction $\overline{y}$ of banks goes to the discount window (that is, $y(\widetilde{p}) = \overline{y}(\widetilde{p}_m) > 0$).

In the intermediate discount range the equilibrium cannot involve pure run strategies by depositors. Since participation when depositors do not run is low, depositors have incentives to run. In contrast, if depositors run, banks have more incentives to participate, discouraging runs. Then, depositors have to be indifferent between running or not. As the discount increases in this range, banks' lower incentives to participate have to be compensated for by a larger probability of runs that increases the costs of no participation. As there are runs on the equilibrium path, stigma costs are realized.

Lemma 7. *High discount region.*

There exists a cutoff $\widetilde{p}_l > 0$ such that, for all $\widetilde{p} \in (0, \widetilde{p}_l]$ ("high discount region"), banks do not borrow from the discount window (that is $y(\widetilde{p}) = 0$) and depositors always run (that is, $\sigma(\widetilde{p}) = 1$). There is no stigma in equilibrium (that is, $\chi(p, \widetilde{p}) = 0$ for all p).

Intuitively, when the discount is high enough ($\widetilde{p}$ is low), no bank chooses to borrow from the discount window, even if depositors run. Given this reaction, depositors always

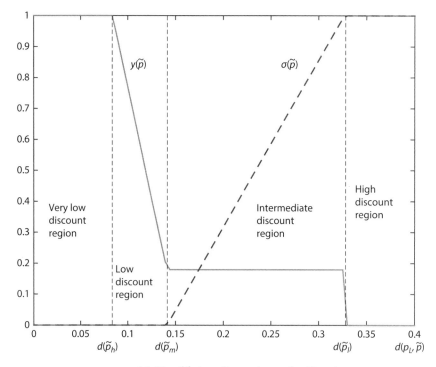

FIGURE 6.1. Equilibrium Strategies under Opacity

run. The economy generates the same consumption as in the case of a crisis without intervention. As there is no participation, stigma is based on off-equilibrium beliefs, which, however, cannot overturn this result. If beliefs are such that (off-equilibrium) participating banks have collateral with above-average quality, then there is no gain in the second period beyond what is achievable with average quality. If, on the other hand, beliefs are such that (off-equilibrium) participating banks have collateral with below-average quality, then there is a stigma cost and banks are even more discouraged to participate.

The equilibrium strategies derived in Lemmas 4–7 are illustrated in Figure 6.1. On the horizontal axis we show the average discount $d(p_L, \widetilde{p})$, the solid line function shows the fraction of depositors who run, $\sigma(\widetilde{p})$, and the dashed line function shows the fraction of banks that participate in the discount window, $y(\widetilde{p})$. We use the average discount instead of $\widetilde{p}$ as it is more intuitive to think of the discount as the cost of participation. The strategies in the "very low discount region" $[0, d(p_L, \widetilde{p}_h)]$ are shown in Lemma 4, in the "low discount region" $[d(p_L, \widetilde{p}_h), d(p_L, \widetilde{p}_m)]$ are shown in Lemma 5, in the "intermediate discount region" $[d(p_L, \widetilde{p}_m), d(p_L, \widetilde{p}_l)]$ in Lemma 6, and in the "high discount region" $[d(p_L, \widetilde{p}_l), C]$ in Lemma 7.

6.5.2 The Role of Stigma in Sustaining Opacity

The previous analysis is based on the presumption that the central bank announces and commits to a policy of not disclosing participation. But this policy of opacity unravels if banks choose to individually reveal their participation status. There are two possible deviations. Banks that participated hold bonds and may want to disclose it to avoid runs. Banks that did not participate may want to announce that they did not need to participate. An opaque policy cannot be implemented if any of these deviations happens. Once banks disclose participation, no disclosure is a signal of no participation, and vice versa. Considering these deviations is particularly relevant in our framework, since the gains from opacity come from sustaining the functioning of credit for all banks, but without lending to all banks, just a fraction of them. Here we study the incentives of banks to deviate from public opacity, and then the implementability of secrecy as a way to combat crises.

What prevents participants from disclosing their participation? The answer is stigma: as participants in equilibrium are those with the lowest-quality collateral, and the idiosyncratic component is persistent, disclosure would put those banks in a weak position to prevent runs in the second, normal, period. But then what prevents non-participants (with higher-quality collateral) from disclosing their participation? The answer is a run: non-participants are subject to a run when it becomes known with certainty that they do not hold bonds in the first, crisis, period.

To show this, consider an opaque intervention with intermediate discount (say, $\widetilde{p} = \widetilde{p}_m$) such that there is no run in equilibrium and just a fraction of banks participates. Take a participating bank that does not disclose its participation. The first-period profit is $H(K^*) - d(p, \widetilde{p})$ and the second-period profit is $H(K^*)$ (recall the second period's aggregate component of collateral is $\bar{p}_{t=2} = p_H > p^H$, such that the average bank does not suffer a run in the second period). Revealing participation does not increase the first-period outcome, as the bank would still not be examined, would still obtain the optimal loan size, and would still pay the discount. The second-period profit, however, can be smaller if the revised belief about the bank's collateral is such that it triggers a future run, a *stigma cost*.

Stigma, $\chi(p, \widetilde{p})$, is the cost in terms of a higher probability of a run in the second period coming from information that the bank participated at the discount window in the first period. Intuitively, since banks participate when their collateral quality is lower than average (specifically, $p < p_w^*$), revelation of participation would make those banks more prone to be examined in the second period. Formally, *in the second period*, the bank suffers a run (obtaining $H(K^*)$ only with probability p and loses the cost of information γ) if equation (6.4) is not fulfilled at the optimal scale K^*, that is, if

$$K^* > \frac{\gamma}{(1-q)(1 - E^w(p|\widetilde{p}, \bar{p}_{t=2}))} \quad \Longrightarrow \quad p_H + E^w(\eta|\widetilde{p}) < 1 - \frac{(1-q)K^*}{\gamma},$$

where $E^w(\eta|\widetilde{p})$ is the expectation of the idiosyncratic component of collateral, conditional on participation, in which case the bank would lose on net $(1-p)K^*(qA-1) + \gamma$. This implies that stigma is given by

$$\chi(p, \widetilde{p}) = \begin{cases} 0 & \text{if} \quad E^w(\eta|\widetilde{p}) \geq 1 - p_H - \frac{(1-q)K^*}{\gamma} \\ (1-p)K^*(qA-1) + \gamma & \text{if} \quad E^w(\eta|\widetilde{p}) < 1 - p_H - \frac{(1-q)K^*}{\gamma}. \end{cases} \quad (6.12)$$

Notice the stigma cost is more likely to be positive the lower the aggregate component of collateral (i.e., the weaker the recovery from the crisis). Intuitively, a weak recovery makes beliefs about the idiosyncratic component more relevant to avoid runs. Similarly, the stigma cost is more likely the higher the discount $d(\widetilde{p})$ and the smaller the participation (i.e., the lower the $E^w(\eta|\widetilde{p})$). Intuitively, when participation is low, participation is a very bad signal about quality. These considerations are summarized in the following proposition, which comes trivially from equation (6.12).

Proposition 19 (Stigma).   Stigma costs are more likely when the second period's collateral is weaker (lower $\bar{p}_{t=2}$) and when the discount is larger (smaller $\widetilde{p}$ such that participation is lower).

That participating banks do not want to disclose their participation is just one side of the coin. How about non-participating banks? If disclosing participation is costly, isn't it profitable to disclose non-participation? Take a non-participating bank that does not disclose its lack of participation. The first-period profit is $(1 - \varepsilon)H(K^*) + \varepsilon L(p, \widetilde{p})$ and the second-period profit is $H(K^*)$. Revealing no participation is costly as it would trigger a run on the bank. Why? Because if, by disclosing no participation, a bank could avoid a run every bank would do it instead of paying a discount, and that would not be an equilibrium. Revealing no participation, however, sends a signal that the bank has better-than-average collateral. This potential benefit is only useful if in the second period the average quality of collateral also triggers a crisis, not otherwise. If the average quality of collateral is such that in the second period there is no run (as we have assumed), with and without signaling the bank would still obtain $H(K^*)$.

In short, participating banks do not obtain any additional gain during the crisis but lose in expectation in future normal periods. In contrast, non-participating banks may lose from disclosure during the crisis, while not gaining anything in future normal times. The two necessary conditions that generate the implementability of secrecy are: (1) there is a single signal (participation or not) that is informative about two variables (the portfolio composition today *and* the collateral quality tomorrow) and (2) good and bad news map asymmetrically into payoffs.

To be more precise, denote by $s \in \{s_A, s_B\}$ a binary signal, when s_A implies good news (g) about a first information dimension and bad news (b) about a second, while s_B implies the opposite. Denote the payoff from each information dimension by $z \in \{z_1, z_2\}$. An agent does not want to disclose either signal, neither s_A nor s_B, then opacity is sustainable, if and only if

$$\bar{z}_1 + \bar{z}_2 > z_1(g) + z_2(b) \qquad \text{and} \qquad \bar{z}_1 + \bar{z}_2 > z_1(b) + z_2(g),$$

where $\bar{z}$ represents the "status quo," non-disclosure payoffs.

In our setting, s_A is participation, s_B is no participation, the first information dimension is the portfolio composition after a crisis intervention, and the second information dimension is the idiosyncratic collateral quality. The first condition (no disclosing participation) is satisfied because, under a successful intervention, $z_1(g) = \bar{z}_1$ and because of stigma

$z_2(b) < \bar{z}_2$. The second condition (no disclosing non-participation) is satisfied because $z_2(g) = \bar{z}_2$ and because runs to non-participants during crises, $z_1(b) < \bar{z}_1$.

Notice that there are several applications, beyond banking, which can accommodate these payoff properties and allow for secrecy as an equilibrium outcome. Take, for instance, local and state restaurant inspections. Assume restaurants' payoffs increase in today's average perceived food quality (z_1) and decrease in tomorrow's variance of perceived food quality $(-z_2)$. Assume also that an inspection sends a very bad signal about today's food quality (if inspection is triggered by regulators' concerns about today's food quality), and non-inspection sends a very bad signal about tomorrow's expected variance (if inspection today puts restrictions on food quality tomorrow). Under these assumptions, an inspected restaurant would not report inspection, as it may lose many clients who expect low food quality today, while not being compensated with a significant reduction in tomorrow's variance. A non-inspected restaurant, on the other hand, may not gain much from reporting not being inspected in terms of expecting more clients today but would potentially generate many doubts among clients about tomorrow's food quality.[14]

The next corollary summarizes this insight in our banking application.

Corollary 5. Under a successful opaque intervention policy that bypasses a crisis, stigma discourages participating banks from revealing participation and runs discourage non-participating banks from revealing non-participation. There are no deviations in equilibrium and the policy of opacity can be successfully implemented.

6.5.3   Ending a Crisis with Transparency

When the central bank discloses the identity of banks participating at the discount window, the information-acquisition strategy of depositors is conditional on this information. More specifically, when depositors know a bank has borrowed from the discount window, they never run on it, as they know the bank uses government bonds as collateral, and there is nothing to learn about. Then $\sigma(\tilde{p}) = 0$ for all $\tilde{p}$, conditional on participation, and $E^w(\pi) = H(K^*) - d(p,\tilde{p}) - \chi(p,\tilde{p})$. In contrast, when depositors know a bank has not participated, they always run on it, as they know the bank has a private asset in its portfolio. Then $\sigma(\tilde{p}) = 1$ for all $\tilde{p}$, conditional on no participation, and $E_{nw}(\pi \,|\, p,\tilde{p}) = L(p,\tilde{p})$.[15] The next lemma characterizes this equilibrium.

Lemma 8. *In the equilibrium under transparency, all banks borrow from the discount window* $y(\tilde{p}) = 1$ *for* $\tilde{p} \in [\tilde{p}_T, \bar{p} + \bar{\eta}]$ *such that* $\tilde{p}_T < \tilde{p}_h$. *For* $\tilde{p} < \tilde{p}_T$ *is* $y(\tilde{p}) = Pr(p < p^*_{wT})$ *where* p^*_{wT} *is given by*

$$L(p^*_{wT}, \tilde{p}) + d(p^*_{wT}, \tilde{p}) + \chi(p^*_{wT}, \tilde{p}) = H(K^*).$$

Intuitively, when banks receive bonds they can invest at optimal scale, at the cost of paying a discount and stigma (only positive in case $y(\tilde{p}) < 1$). When the discount is not that large all banks choose to participate. In this case, the alternative of not participating is suffering a run for sure. This is in stark contrast to a policy of opacity in which, if all banks participate, a non-participating bank is only examined in case of a leakage. Hence full participation with opacity collapses at lower discount levels.[16]

6.5.4   Opacity or Transparency?

Given the equilibrium strategies for each $\widetilde{p}$ under both opacity and transparency, we can compute the total production (or welfare in our setting) for each $\widetilde{p}$ under each disclosure policy.

Since the unconstrained welfare is $2H$ in both periods, a non-treated crisis costs

$$Cost\ Crisis = H - L \equiv (1 - p_L)K^*(qA - 1) + \gamma. \tag{6.13}$$

As banks keep the net gains from production, welfare is an aggregation of the payoffs of all banks with different quality p, given by

$$W(\widetilde{p}) = \int_p [\mathbb{I}_w[H + B - pC] + (1 - \mathbb{I}_w)[\sigma L(p) + (1 - \sigma)((1 - \varepsilon)H + \varepsilon L(p))]]\, dF(p)$$

$$+ \int_p \mathbb{I}_w[q(pC - B) + (1 - q)(\phi pC - B)]dF(p)$$

$$+ \int_p [\mathbb{I}_w[q(H - \sigma\chi(p)) - (1 - q)\delta(1 - \phi)pC] + (1 - \mathbb{I}_w)H]\, dF(p),$$

where $\mathbb{I}_w$ is an indicator function that takes the value 1 if the bank participates at the discount window and 0 otherwise.

Taking integrals and rewriting the expression,

$$W(\widetilde{p}) = y(H + B - E^w(p)C) + (1 - y)[\sigma\widehat{L} + (1 - \sigma)((1 - \varepsilon)H + \varepsilon\widehat{L})]$$

$$+ y[q(E^w(p)C - B) + (1 - q)(\phi E^w(p)C - B)]$$

$$+ y[q(H - \sigma\widehat{\chi}) - (1 - q)\delta(1 - \phi)E^w(p)C] + (1 - y)H,$$

where $H \equiv H(K^*)$, $\widehat{L} \equiv \int_{p|nw} L(p, \widetilde{p})dp$ and $\widehat{\chi} \equiv \int_p \chi(p, \widetilde{p})dp$.

The first two terms (the first line) represent the welfare of banks in the crisis period. A fraction y of banks borrows from the discount window, leading to a production of H and exchanging private collateral for bonds at an average discount of $B - E^w(p)C$. A fraction $1 - y$ of banks does not participate and their investments lead to a production level that depends on whether they suffered a run or if there was an informational leak. This first line of the welfare function can be rewritten as

$$H - y(E^w(p)C - B) - (1 - y)(\varepsilon + \sigma(1 - \varepsilon))(H - \widehat{L}).$$

The third term (the second line) represents the welfare for the government. From the fraction y of banks borrowing from the discount window, a fraction q has their private collateral seized, which delivers $E^w(p)C$ in expectation, while a fraction $1 - q$ defaults and the private collateral has to be liquidated, recovering just $\phi E^w(p)C$. Still, in both cases the government has to repay B for the bonds. This second line of the welfare function can be rewritten as

$$y(E^w(p)C - B) - y(1 - q)(1 - \phi)E^w(p)C.$$

The last term (the third line) captures investments in the second period (no discount). The banks that did not borrow from the discount window and those that did without their participation being revealed can borrow without triggering a run in the second period (then leading to production level H). Those banks that participated and their participation was revealed (because they were examined) can potentially suffer a run in the second period because of stigma (captured by L). Finally, the government has to repay (facing inefficiency costs $1 - \phi$ and distortionary taxation costs δ) the bonds that could not be covered by liquidating private assets in the previous period. The third line can then be rewritten as

$$H - y[q\sigma\widehat{\chi} + (1 - q)\delta(1 - \phi)E^w(p)C].$$

Adding (and canceling) terms, total welfare is

$$W(\widetilde{p}) = 2H - (1 - y)(\varepsilon + \sigma(1 - \varepsilon))(H - \widehat{L})$$
$$- y[(1 - q)(1 + \delta)(1 - \phi)E^w(p)C - q\sigma\widehat{\chi}].$$

Since the unconstrained welfare is $2H$ in both periods, we can denote the distortion from fighting a crisis as:

$$Dist(\widetilde{p}) = (1 - y)(\varepsilon + \sigma(1 - \varepsilon))(H - \widehat{L}) + y[(1 - q)(1 + \delta)(1 - \phi)E^w(p)C] + yq\sigma\widehat{\chi}, \tag{6.14}$$

where $\widehat{L} \equiv \int_{p|nw} L(p, \widetilde{p})dp$ and $\widehat{\chi} \equiv \int_{p|w} \chi(p, \widetilde{p})dp$ are the losses from runs and stigma among non-participants and participants, respectively. The fraction of participants y, the fraction of runs σ, and the level of stigma χ depend on both the disclosure policy and the lending discount $\widetilde{p}$. Intuitively, the first component shows the distortion that comes from the lower output of non-participant banks, either due to information leaks or because runs. The second component shows the costs of the distortionary taxation needed to cover deposits from defaulting participating banks and that cannot be covered by liquidating their private collateral. Finally, the third component shows the lower production in the second period from the stigma costs of participating banks that are examined. Notice that in the computation of distortions the level of discount is irrelevant, as it just represents a non-distortionary transfer of resources from banks to the central bank (and ultimately households).

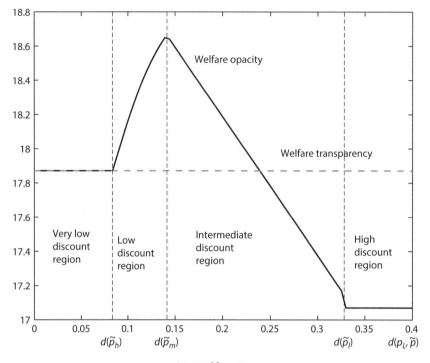

FIGURE 6.2. Welfare Comparison

The next proposition characterizes the condition under which intervention under transparency is socially preferred to no intervention.

Proposition 20 (Transparent Intervention).   Intervention under transparency is preferred to no intervention only when the distortionary costs of taxation $(1 + \delta)$ and public liquidation $(1 - \phi)$ of private assets are small relative to the gains of intervention, that is,

$$(1 + \delta)(1 - \phi) < \frac{(1 - p_L)K^*(qA - 1) + \gamma}{(1 - q)p_L C}.$$

The condition in the proposition just comes from equation (6.13) being smaller than equation (6.14) evaluated at $y = 1$ and $\sigma = 0$ (and then $E^w(p) = p_L$).[17]

With opacity, welfare depends less trivially on the discount. Figure 6.2 shows welfare graphically, under both disclosure policies (dashed line for transparency and solid line for opacity) for all discount rates.[18] Notice that the welfare implemented with a transparent intervention is the same for all discounts in the range of this illustration. Under opacity, however, welfare depends on the discount as characterized by Lemmas 4 to 7.

As can be seen, in the very low discount region, all banks participate and there are no runs, so welfare is the same as that obtained under transparency. This implies that there is always a (low enough) discount rate that replicates with opacity the welfare implementable with transparency. This is summarized in the next corollary.

Corollary 6.   There is always a low enough discount rate that replicates with opacity the welfare obtained with transparency.

In the low discount region, some banks prefer to take advantage of pooling and do not participate. If the leakage probability is not very large relative to the cost of distortions, welfare increases with the discount. More specifically, as in this region $\sigma = 0$, welfare increases with lower participation (lower y) when $\varepsilon(H - \widehat{L}) < (1 - q)(1 + \delta)$ $(1 - \phi)E^w(p)C$. Since $y < 1$, $H - L > H - \widehat{L}$, and $E^w(p) < p_L$, a sufficient condition for distortions to decrease (or welfare to increase) in this region is

$$\frac{(1 + \delta)(1 - \phi)}{\varepsilon} > \frac{H - L}{(1 - q)p_L C}. \tag{6.15}$$

In the intermediate discount region, only a fraction $\bar{y}$ of banks borrows from the discount window but more and more depositors run as the discount increases, hence more and more banks are forced to produce less in expectation in the first period and suffer from stigma in the second. This reduces welfare. In this region, once the discount level is so large that the "stigma" effect dominates the "less distortion" effect, welfare under opacity is indeed lower than welfare under transparency. Finally, in the high discount region, the level of the discount is so high that there is no participation in equilibrium under opacity, with welfare reaching a no intervention level.

Putting these regions together, it is clear that the policy that maximizes welfare under the sufficient condition (6.15) is charging a discount $d(\widetilde{p}_m)$ under secrecy about the banks participating in the discount window. At this discount, and without disclosure, the distortionary cost of participation is minimized, still not triggering any runs. Proposition 21 characterizes this optimal policy.

Proposition 21 (Opaque Intervention).   When the distortionary costs are large relative to leakage probabilities, a discount rate of $\widetilde{p}_m$ under opacity strictly dominates transparency. A sufficient condition for this result is given by equation (6.15).

When welfare decreases in the low discount region (leakage probabilities are large compared to distortionary costs) it is better to have all banks participating, and then setting the discount window lower than $d(\widetilde{p}_h)$ and operating under opacity generates the same welfare as operating under transparency. Combining Corollary 6 and Proposition 21, we obtain the next corollary, about the optimality of opacity. More details of design are in the appendix of Gorton and Ordoñez (2020a).

Corollary 7.   If intervention is beneficial, there is always a discount level that turns opaque interventions (at least weakly) preferable to transparent interventions.

Relation with Literature on Optimal Disclosure.   Our work is related to the recent discussion on the optimal disclosure of information about financial variables by governments and regulators. A clear example is the literature that studies stress tests (which we discuss next) and focuses on the possible impact of information disclosure about a bank's portfolio on funding (Alvarez and Barlevy 2015), on runs (Bouvard, Chaigneau, and De Motta 2015; Faria-e Castro, Martinez, and Philippon 2017), and on risk sharing (Goldstein and Leitner 2018). (For a survey, see Goldstein and Sapra 2013.) Our work differs from this literature in several ways. First, stress tests are primarily about preventing crises, not fixing them. Second, the disclosure of stress test results is the revelation of a state/type, while the disclosure of lending facilities' participation is the revelation of a choice. Finally, the stress test literature focuses on solving a planning problem, whereas we are interested in not only the optimality of the policy but also its sustainability as an equilibrium outcome, in particular the role of discount rates to pin down the stigma cost that discourages banks from deviating from the central bank's intended disclosure plan. Among the scholarship on stress tests, Alvarez and Barlevy (2015) may be the closest to our setting in terms of focusing on the disclosure choice of banks. They study disclosure of stress tests by interconnected banks. During crises, when contagion is strong, the planner may need to force disclosure because banks would individually prefer opacity. In our case the planner wants opacity but banks may prefer disclosure, potentially making the intended plan non-sustainable. While in principle it is easy to force disclosure of hard information, preventing it may prove more challenging. Alvarez and Barlevy show the former may be necessary; we show that the latter is feasible because of endogenous stigma on the design of lending facilities.

6.5.5   Additional Remarks

Remarks on Implications for Stress Tests.   Stress tests are simulations based on a bank's balance sheet to assess how the bank would fare against different systemic distress scenarios. Even though introduced formally by Basel in 1996, they were mostly performed internally by banks until recent financial crises.[19] Should individual stress test results be disclosed? When should stress tests be performed? Before or during crises? Even though disclosure about stress tests (information about the portfolio quality) and disclosure about participation in lending facilities capture very different forces, our model sheds light on some of these issues.

If by performing stress tests regulators learn each bank's collateral quality, p, they can strategically choose how and when to disclose it. Regulators could disclose which banks have a p below a threshold, preventing runs for the rest of banks with higher p. In this sense early disclosure can be relevant from a precautionary perspective, *to prevent a crisis from happening*. Revealing p *conditional on a crisis happening*, however, can be detrimental for the implementation and efficacy of opacity on the use of lending facilities. If banks understand their p will be disclosed after the crisis, participating banks are not concerned about the stigma from revealing their participation since their low-quality collateral will be revealed anyway. In short, when stress test disclosure eliminates stigma considerations, banks want to individually reveal their participation status, potentially jeopardizing the implementation of opaque lending facilities.

This last point suggests a complementarity between the opacity of stress tests and the opacity of intervention policies. By preventing too much revelation of stress tests it is easier to sustain the role of stigma on sustaining the social advantage of opacity on lending facilities to fight crises. This consideration is absent in the literature about stress test disclosure, which is silent about the interaction with intervention policies and about the individual incentives to disclose participation, potentially in opposition to a planner's optimal disclosure choice.

Remarks on Comparisons with Bagehot's Rule.   The classic rule for a central bank to follow in a crisis was provided by Walter Bagehot in 1873: central banks should lend freely, at a high rate, and on good collateral. In the recent financial crisis, Ben Bernanke, Mervyn King, and Mario Draghi, the respective heads of the Federal Reserve System, the Bank of England, and the European Central Bank, reported that they followed Bagehot's advice (see Bernanke 2014b, 2014a; King 2010; and Draghi 2013). But, in fact, there was more to their responses to the crisis. All three central banks also engaged in anonymous or secret lending to banks.

Capie noticed the omission of secrecy by Bagehot: "a key feature of the British [banking] system, its in-built protective device for anonymity was overlooked [by Bagehot]" (2007, 313). Capie also proposes a reason for this omission, explaining that if a country bank in England needed money during a crisis it could borrow from its discount house, which in turn might borrow from the Bank of England. In this way, the identities of the actual end borrowers were not publicly known.[20]

Remarks on Securitization and Deposit Insurance.   In our setting, if banks were able to sign contracts that eliminate the idiosyncratic risk of individual portfolios then no depositor would have an incentive to acquire information about a bank's asset. In other words, if idiosyncratic risk were eliminated by pooling all collateral in the economy, there would be no runs, no crisis, and no role for intervention. Even though we have assumed that banks cannot diversify their individual portfolio risk, there could be in principle two institutions that allow for such diversification: *securitization* (sustained by private contracts) and *deposit insurance* (imposed by public regulation).

In the case of securitization, a bank can sign a contract at the beginning of the period, selling shares of its own asset and buying shares of the assets of other banks, eliminating the idiosyncratic risk as the value of its portfolio would be deterministic and equal to $p_L C$. This contract discourages depositors in the bank from acquiring information about its individual portfolio, which is now irrelevant for the probabilities of recovering the deposit. There are no runs and no crisis. These private contracts are difficult to sustain, however. Banks with high η subsidize banks with low η and may not have incentives to enter into these contracts, as a way to signal a high η. Studying the sustainability of these contracts is interesting to understand the effects of securitization as a stabilizing innovation, but it is outside the scope of this work.

If securitization is not feasible, the government may have incentives to impose diversification in the form of deposit insurance. In the standard view of bank runs, under which they are triggered by a collective action problem, deposit insurance prevents panics on path and then it is not used in equilibrium. In our setting, a run is not driven by lack of coordination among depositors but instead by individual incentives to investigate the bank's portfolio, withdrawing funds backed by a low-value portfolio. The government can prevent the examination of a bank's portfolio by forcing banks to pay a premium, ex post, in case their assets are good and to receive insurance in case their assets are bad. As this cross-subsidization can be financed within the system, no taxation is used in equilibrium either.

One interpretation of what happened during the recent financial crisis is that some banks (commercial) were under deposit insurance (and nothing happened to them). Some others (shadow) used securitization, a fragile contract when adverse selection concerns become prevalent among participating banks that may want to cancel the contracts. (For a model of endogenous regulatory arbitrage that changes the composition of banks between commercial and shadow, see Ordoñez 2018b.) Again, this is a subject that requires more research.

6.6   Summary

A financial crisis occurs when some public information causes depositors to worry about the collateral backing their deposits such that they want to produce information about the bank's portfolio. This is a bank run, as it triggers withdrawal from banks that are revealed to have bad assets. Re-creating confidence means re-creating the opacity of the banking system. This is done by raising the perceived average value of collateral in the economy so that it is not profitable to produce information about any bank. The government can achieve this goal by exchanging bonds (or cash) for lower-quality assets, and the cheaper and less distortionary way to achieve this is by replacing only some bad assets in the economy, not all. But for this informational externality to operate, the identity of borrowers should be kept secret. This is accomplished by stigma.

This logic was highlighted by Bernanke: "Releasing the names of [the borrowing] institutions in real-time, in the midst of the financial crisis, would have undermined the effectiveness of the emergency lending and the confidence of investors and borrowers" (2009, 1). Opacity was indeed adopted not only by several governments to deal with recent crises but also by private bank clearinghouses in the United States prior to the Federal Reserve System. Even though the quick reading of opacity suggests that it is introduced so that participating banks do not suffer from stigma, we show that the causality may reverse: stigma is what allows the implementation of optimal secrecy. It is needed because here banks can potentially disclose their participation (or lack thereof) individually. Opacity does not try to avoid stigma but stigma is crucial to avoid transparency. The tool used by the central bank to fine-tune the participation of banks, such that not all participate but enough do to avoid runs on all, is the discount at which lending facilities operate. By restricting participation, the discount also determines the strength of stigma, and then the implementability of opacity.

7

Final Thoughts

7.1 Where We Stand

Our goal in this book has been to take a step toward building *macroeconomics with financial crises*. The financial crisis itself and the forces leading up to it are not well understood and are not present in current macro models. In fact, these forces cannot be generated by current models and it is not useful to simply try to patch them up, adding shocks that change fundamental conditions or sunspots that change equilibria. We found that a positive technology shock can lead to a credit boom fueled by optimally information-insensitive short-term debt. As the credit boom advances there is an endogenous depreciation of information and an endogenous reduction of productivity of financed projects.

A crisis occurs when short-term debt turns information sensitive: debt holders suddenly want to produce information about the backing collateral and stop lending when the collateral is perceived to be of low quality. The debt was information insensitive but becomes information sensitive. That is the crisis, a sudden burst of information production. In short, there is an endogenous increase in systemic risk and when the crisis happens, it is a larger crisis the longer the preceding credit boom. In our credit models there is always symmetric information. Either no one knows anything or everyone knows everything. There is never adverse selection. Note also that our fragility comes from informational frictions, not coordination failures, and so the logic applies to both old (demand deposits) and modern (repo) banking systems.

Information dynamics are key to linking macro and financial dynamics, which at the time influence information dynamics. The amount of information in the economy changes endogenously because of the interplay between the evolution of credit, technology, and incentives to generate information. The amount of information also changes endogenously because of the interplay between opaque, information-concealing credit markets and transparent, information-revealing stock markets. Crises are not necessarily the result of exogenous macro states changing because of "shocks" or "sunspots."

Short-term credit markets perform better when information about collateral is *not* produced. But short-term debt is paradoxical. Opacity is what makes short-term debt useful, but that is also what makes it vulnerable to runs. This conundrum is inherent to market economies. Privately produced safe debt is needed in every market economy because there

145

are never enough government securities to satisfy the demand for safe debt. Thus, a central problem for the economy is the scarcity of collateral. Even though in most of the book the amount of good collateral and the amount of bad collateral were taken as fixed, we have also discussed how more "good collateral" could be produced by pooling and tranching bad and good existing collateral. But this manufactured collateral is fragile. More generally one can imagine a dynamic economy that runs out of collateral as the credit boom continues, before a financial crisis occurs. Might an economy find a way to privately produce more collateral? Yes, for example, securitization is a process to produce collateral using bank loans as the input. Securitization can use many different types of loans. Some examples include, of course, residential mortgages and commercial mortgages. Other asset classes include car loans, student debt, and credit card receivables.

In our narrative, technological change cannot be separated from macroeconomic and financial (credit and crises) dynamics. This has implications for growth accounting and how it should incorporate financial elements. In Chapter 4, for instance, we show how growth accounting in our economy incorporates the diffusion of technology, not only directly as it is standard in growth models but also endogenously by the evolution of a credit boom.

We also highlight that technology not only is both exogenous and endogenous to the financial sector components but also has different components that affect dynamics differentially. Contrary to the large majority of macroeconomic models, we have used as a benchmark a production function that allows for the possibility that the project fails and that the firm defaults on its debt. Conditional on success, the parameter A determines how much is produced. But this only happens with a probability q. With the complementary probability the project is a complete failure and nothing can be recovered, a total loss. As a result, technological change can happen in two ways: it can make the likelihood of project success increase or it can improve the level of productivity conditional on success. Improvement in either q or A can cause growth in the economy, and both act in increasing measured productivity. Confusing these two elements in the measure of the Solow residual is not irrelevant in a model that has both stock and credit markets. While changes in q operate mostly by affecting credit (debt) markets, changes in A operate mostly by affecting stock (equity) markets. In the book we have shown that these two markets are connected by information dynamics and then the different sources of measured productivity changes will have dramatically different implications in the evolution of economic variables.

7.2   Where to Go

Our work points toward the need to improve the empirical and theoretical underpinnings of macroeconomic fluctuations. Empirically, the literature needs new methods to distinguish the sources of measured productivity changes (A and q above). Theoretically, the literature needs to move toward a completely new paradigm in modeling macroeconomics that encompasses the standard tools of real business cycles, which had made big steps in taking models to data, and our new proposed model of financial markets and information.

The main challenges are clearly how to measure information dynamics and how to model the production function of financial intermediaries (how banks use collateral and information to produce short-term debt) in a way that is open to calibrations.

We have not produced such a complete macro model that can be realistically calibrated, and we left out important aspects of a macro-economy. But theoretical clarity was our goal in this book. Hopefully clarity comes from how our work differs from standard macro-economics. In what follows we highlight elements that are critical in future endeavors to close the gap between such theoretical clarity and full quantitative blending with more standard macroeconomic models.

Abandoning Shocks and Sunspots.   In order to discipline models, we believe that it is important to push for research that does not need to rely on "shocks" to induce fluctuations. All economies suffer regular fluctuations, and just assuming that those come from particular shock processes is to abandon ambitions to understand their fundamental source. We have shown a setting in which fluctuations in the economy come from endogenous sources, not *necessarily* from shocks. In our model such a force is information production. We see this as an advantage that should be embraced. Standard macroeconomics relies heavily on "shocks," random exogenous things that happen. More and more "shocks" have been added to models in an attempt to capture realistic elements of macro dynamics. Even though these efforts have allowed us to understand how macro variables react in different states, "shocks" are free parameters, and they are not well understood. What lies behind their existence may change the predictions of the models. It's a bit like pre-Copernican astronomy, when Ptolemy added epicycles whenever some pattern of the stars couldn't be explained.

Should "shocks" be abandoned? Probably not, but certainly the concept of business cycles as deviations from an exogenous trend due to "shocks" must be revised, extended, and improved upon. The most notable and apparent problem with that conception of the business cycle is that it is forced to think of a financial crisis as a "big shock" that happens contemporaneously. But the notion of a "big shock" cannot be an explanation of a financial crisis without giving up on understanding forces that clearly repeat over time and across countries. Further, it has to be a big negative shock. Well, what is it? Without "shocks" moving the economy away from the "trend," how can macro models without perturbations around this trend be built?

An alternative explanation explored by the literature has resorted to "sunspots" instead of large shocks. This is the idea that a small shock can induce a dramatic change in equilibrium. This is also problematic, both from a scientific point of view (how to discipline sunspots?) and from an empirical standpoint (how to identify sunspots, which agents can understand to coordinate but econometricians cannot?). As a response there exists a literature based on global games techniques that refines models with multiple equilibrium with dispersed information and has the potential to generate large changes in response to small shocks (see, for instance, the application of Ordonez 2013a and 2018a). The challenge of this literature is to capture the slow recovery that happens after crises and the strong relation of crises with prior credit boom events.

Some macro models have been built so fluctuations come from "news shocks" (see Krusell and McKay 2010 and Barsky and Sims 2011) or "uncertainty shocks" (see the literature following Bloom 2009). These alternative sources of macroeconomic dynamics are usually taken as exogenous. News comes from public sources that exogenously affect the expected distribution of fundamentals that agents face, operating mostly through the first moment. Uncertainty shocks are also exogenous and come from time-varying second moments on the distribution of fundamentals, for instance, the cross-sectional dispersion of productivity. In our models news and uncertainty are endogenous objects and arise as the result of information dynamics determined by the information-insensitive nature of debt and the information-sensitive nature of equity. This endogeneity of information affects the observed dispersion in production and productivity across firms generated by an endogenous dispersion of credit availability.

More recently, Baker and colleagues (2016) have developed an index of economic policy uncertainty from newspaper coverage. Using firm-level data, they show the index is associated with greater stock price volatility (what we called fragility) and at the macro level foreshadows declines in investment, output, and employment. In this book we show that time-series volatility of stock markets affects the cross-sectional dispersion of stocks through information acquisition, which affects credit and foreshadows crises. This suggests that the predictability component of the uncertainty index that Baker and colleagues uncover may operate via information and credit for recessions accompanied with crises.

Monetary and Fiscal Policies.   The second line of research that seems fruitful is the addition of the government into the picture. What is the role of government bonds? If it was known which collateral consisted of government bonds, then those firms could always get credit (as we discussed in Chapter 6, government bonds are not of uncertain quality and then not subject to information-production incentives) and our story would simply start later, after all available government bonds were used up as collateral.[1] It is unrealistic to assume that there are so many government bonds that private collateral is not needed. The private sector will always be creating collateral from existing assets. We basically started from that point in this book, but the question of the optimal supply of government bonds remains.

Certainly this question also has implications for the conduct of monetary policy. Central banks operate by exchanging money for government bonds and vice versa (conventional monetary policy). And they engage in strategies of buying up safe debt, "quantitative easing" (unconventional monetary policy). Cash and government bonds are two different forms of money. Government bonds are money-like in that they can store value through time and guarantee being paid off at maturity with a high probability. Government bonds are the best collateral. But, cash and government bonds are not substitutes. Simply put, you cannot buy lunch with a U.S. Treasury bond. But for an institutional investor, a government bond is like cash. This can create difficulties for the central bank because financial stability erodes to the extent that there is more private collateral relative to government bonds. Private collateral can become information sensitive, unlike government bonds (though there are plenty of examples where government bonds have also become information sensitive).

We have explored some of these issues in Gorton and Ordoñez (2022), Infante and Ordoñez (2020), and Gorton and He (2020), where we show that there can be a contradiction between what is optimal for financial stability and what is optimal otherwise (i.e., to fight inflation). In Gorton and Ordoñez (2022) we show, for instance, that the central bank needs an additional tool to address the problem that both cash and government bonds are money. The central bank needs a permanent facility where agents can exchange a private bond for a government bond. This has some similarity to the Federal Reserve's Reverse Repo Program, which appears to essentially be the current operating procedure. But these issues still need further exploration.

Asset Pricing.   Our analysis also points to implications for asset pricing. The agents in this book are risk neutral and are only uncertain about the quality of collateral and the productivity of each firm. These are idiosyncratic to collateral and firms. Agents understand when a crisis is coming, but since we study an overlapping generations setting, agents don't care about what happens more than a period ahead. In other words, agents in period t do not react to potential crises in periods $t + 2$ and further. As a result, there are no risk premia imputed in prices except the period right before the crisis happens. But one can imagine a setting where some variable is not known with certainty, such that it is not clear when the crisis will occur exactly. If the date of the crisis cannot be predicted for certain, and agents were risk averse, then risk premia would arise. Moreover, these risk premia would change through time if agents are increasingly certain that a crisis might occur. In fact, our setting displays an endogenous evolution of systemic risk. In a bad boom, as more and more firms become active, the likelihood of a crisis increases. And so would the risk premium.

Note that systematic risk and idiosyncratic risk are not easily separated in our model. There is no clear distinction because idiosyncratic risk evolves into systematic risk. And if the stock market produces enough information, then the systematic risk recedes and there is only idiosyncratic risk. The properties of such risk premia definitely bear further investigation.

Financial Intermediaries.   In most of the book financial intermediation has been implicit (except Chapter 6), even when at the core of financial and credit markets. The main reason was that we focused on information properties of the contracts and instruments that financial intermediaries intermediate. We have focused on what is traded in financial markets (short-term debt), not who trades them. However, there are many important lessons to learn from introducing banks, their regulation, and their interaction explicitly in a full macroeconomic model.

It is optimal for banks, for instance, like the collateral in this book, to be opaque, something we explored in Dang et al. (2017). Banking opacity as an optimal outcome is counterintitive for many, but it has the same seeds of information insensitivity that we explain in this book. The bank is an institution in charge of maintaining secrets, and acts as a designer of a portfolio that allows for secrets, a bit like the design of collateral that we described in Chapter 2.

This informational custodian role view of banks justifies deposit insurance differently than commonly believed, to avoid coordination failure runs. From an informational perspective, deposit insurance guarantees that no agent has an incentive to produce information about banks that issue demand deposits. That is left to the regulators, but their bank examination reports are kept confidential. Optimal opacity of banks should inform bank regulation. Once we explicitly add banks into the models, there are important observations about the intricacies of interbank markets and financial networks, and in particular their interaction with regulatory efforts and informational properties, as in Allen and Gale (2000), Erol and Ordoñez (2017), and Anderson, Erol, and Ordoñez (2020).

There are also implications for the regulation of stock market participants. We identified a new role played by stock markets, to differentiate between firms when agents find that profitable. But, as mentioned above, there is a delicate tension. Information revealed in the stock market can prevent crises, but too much information reduces output and consumption. The social planner would want to avoid crises but also would want the credit boom to continue, using bad collateral. Regulatory policies with regard to the stock market are not motivated by this tension. So far, getting the right balance is a matter of luck. Take laws against insider trading, for example. Such laws may inhibit the stock market from revealing too much information, but this was not the motivation for the laws. Perhaps empirical work on emerging markets where stock markets are growing can lead to insights on this question.

Measurement. The Great Depression motivated the founding of macroeconomics as a discipline. A large part of the achievement was the construction of a system of national accounts to measure macroeconomic aggregates and keep track of the economy's evolution. The National Income and Product Accounts, where GDP is measured, among many other variables, was the main result of those achievements and for which Kuznets was awarded the Nobel Prize. (See Coyle 2015 and Fogel, Fogel, and Guglielmo 2013). Macroeconomics would have not been possible (and not even interesting) without the accomplishment of National Income Accounting measures and Bureau of Labor Statistics measures of employment. This large innovation to measure aggregates was later standardized across countries, allowing for serious international comparisons.

The potential of macroeconomics is limited by the available data. To paraphrase Einstein: Theory determines what is measured. And so, based on the models in this book, we went further in using stock price–based measures of information and economy-wide distance-to-default. These stock price–based measures of information and fragility are new to macroeconomics and they are important because we showed how information plays a crucial role in the macroeconomic dynamics. But we need other measures, new measures, better measures, of information and how it relates to aggregates. Some have been proposed by Brunnermeier and colleagues (2012). Their measures are essentially measures of risk in the economy, more precise but more difficult to generate cross country for long periods than the ones used in this book.

Specifically, Brunnermeier and colleagues proposed requiring banks and other financial firms to report a large number of option deltas. Answers to questions like: By how much (in terms of dollars) would your firm's value change if the dollar/yen exchange rate appreciated by 5 percent, including derivative positions? Imagine asking questions like that with respect to, say, 100 variables, quarterly, for ten years. Such a panel data set would more precisely allow us to understand risk in the economy. Macroeconomics would change dramatically! At one time, before Dodd-Frank was passed, it seemed as if the one thing we might get out of the experience of the Great Recession was a new measurement system. But this did not happen.

The Great Depression motivated a new comprehensive system of national accounts. The Great Recession showed the importance of constructing a similar system that relates financial and real variables in the aggregate. The flow of funds that the Federal Reserve Bank provides is definitely a step in such a direction but should aim to construct and measure how information flows within the financial sector. Our work shows that such measures would uncover new links between financial markets and the macroeconomy.

7.3   Final Remarks

It will take time to develop a new macroeconomics with financial crises, perhaps a generation. It was the physicist Max Planck (1968) who wrote that science advances one funeral at a time. And there is evidence that this is true (see Azoulay, Fons-Rosen, and Zivin 2019). Over the last three decades or so, the macroeconomics that involves fluctuations has been about monetary theory and about business cycles without financial intermediaries. In the same period, finance has been dominated by the analysis of stock markets, without much focus on the role of financial markets and without intermediation. These economists have not died, but the financial crisis has revealed many weaknesses and gaps in their ideas and concepts, a kind of funeral. Information and credit was a missing link that connects macroeconomics and finance. We cannot understand macro fluctuations without understanding the fluctuations of credit in an economy. Similarly, we cannot understand the fluctuation, of credit without understanding the fluctuations of the macroeconomy. The recent financial crisis was a wake-up call for younger generations to recognize this.

APPENDIX A

Proofs

A.1 Proof of Proposition 3

Assume a negative aggregate shock of size η after t periods without an aggregate shock. Aggregate consumption before the shock is given by equation (2.15) when $\hat{p} > p^H$ and the average collateral does not induce information. In contrast, aggregate consumption after the shock is:

$$W_{t|\eta} = \bar{K} + \left[\lambda^t \hat{p} K(\eta) + (1 - \lambda^t) K(\eta \hat{p}) \right] (qA - 1).$$

Defining the reduction in aggregate consumption as $\Delta(t|\eta) = W_t - W_{t|\eta}$,

$$\Delta(t|\eta) = [\lambda^t \hat{p} [K(1) - K(\eta)] + (1 - \lambda^t)[K(\hat{p}) - K(\eta \hat{p})]](qA - 1).$$

That $\Delta(t|\eta)$ is non-decreasing in η is straightforward. That $\Delta(t|\eta)$ is non-decreasing in t follows from

$$\hat{p}[K(1) - K(\eta)] \leq [K(\hat{p}) - K(\eta \hat{p})],$$

which holds because $K(\hat{p}) = K(1)$ (by assumption $\hat{p} > p^H$) and $K(p)$ is monotonically decreasing in p.

A.2 Proof of Proposition 4

If the negative shock happens in period t, the belief distribution is $f(\eta) = \lambda^t \hat{p}, f(\eta \hat{p}) = (1 - \lambda^t)$ and $f(0) = \lambda^t (1 - \hat{p})$.

In period $t + 1$, if information is acquired (IS case), after idiosyncratic shocks are realized, the belief distribution is $f_{IS}(1) = \lambda \eta \hat{p}(1 - \lambda^t), f_{IS}(\eta) = \lambda^{t+1} \hat{p}, f_{IS}(\hat{p}) = (1 - \lambda)$, $f_{IS}(0) = \lambda[(1 - \lambda^t \hat{p}) - \eta \hat{p}(1 - \lambda^t)]$. Hence, aggregate consumption at $t + 1$ in the IS scenario is

$$W_{t+1}^{IS} = \overline{K} + [\lambda \eta \hat{p}(1 - \lambda^t)K^* + \lambda^{t+1} \hat{p} K(\eta) + (1 - \lambda)K(\hat{p})](qA - 1). \quad \text{(A.1)}$$

In period $t + 1$, if information is not acquired (II case), after idiosyncratic shocks are realized, the belief distribution is $f_{II}(\eta) = \lambda^{t+1} \hat{p}, f_{II}(\hat{p}) = (1 - \lambda), f_{II}(\eta \hat{p}) = \lambda(1 - \lambda^t)$,

$f_{II}(0) = \lambda^{t+1}(1 - \hat{p})$. Hence, aggregate consumption at $t + 1$ in the II scenario is

$$W_{t+1}^{II} = \overline{K} + [\lambda^{t+1}\hat{p}K(\eta) + \lambda(1 - \lambda^t)K(\eta\hat{p}) + (1 - \lambda)K(\hat{p})](qA - 1). \qquad (A.2)$$

Taking the difference between aggregate consumption at $t + 1$ between the two regimes,

$$W_{t+1}^{IS} - W_{t+1}^{II} = \lambda(1 - \lambda^t)(qA - 1)[\eta\hat{p}K^* - K(\eta\hat{p})]. \qquad (A.3)$$

This expression is non-negative for all $\eta\hat{p}K^* \geq K(\eta\hat{p})$, or alternatively, for all $\eta\hat{p} < \overline{\eta\hat{p}} \equiv \frac{1}{2} + \sqrt{\frac{1}{4} - \frac{\gamma}{K^*(1-q)}}$. From threshold p^{Ch}, $p^{Ch} < \overline{\eta\hat{p}} < p^H$.

A.3   Proof of Proposition 6

Assume a shock η at period t that triggers information acquisition about collateral with belief $\eta\hat{p}$. If the shock is "*small*" ($\eta > p^{Ch}$), there is no information acquisition about collateral *known to be good before the shock*. If the shock is "*large*" ($\eta < p^{Ch}$), there is information acquisition about collateral *known to be good before the shock*. Now we study these two cases when the shock arises after a credit boom of length t.

1. $\eta > p^{Ch}$. The distribution of beliefs in case information is generated is given by $f(0) = \lambda^t(1 - \hat{p}) + (1 - \lambda^t)(1 - \eta\hat{p})$, $f(\eta) = \lambda^t\hat{p}$ and $f(1) = (1 - \lambda^t)\eta\hat{p}$. Then, at period t the variance of beliefs with information production is

$$Var_t(p|IS) = \lambda^t\hat{p}(1 - \hat{p})\eta^2 + (1 - \lambda^t)\eta\hat{p}(1 - \eta\hat{p}).$$

Then

$$Var_t(p|IS) - Var_t(p|II) = (1 - \lambda^t)\eta\hat{p}(1 - \eta\hat{p}) - \lambda^t\hat{p}(1 - \hat{p})(1 - \eta^2),$$

increasing in the length of the boom t.

2. $\eta < p^{Ch}$. The distribution of beliefs in case information is produced is given by $f(0) = \lambda^t(1 - \hat{p}) + (1 - \lambda^t(1 - \hat{p}))(1 - \eta\hat{p})$, and $f(1) = (1 - \lambda^t(1 - \hat{p}))\eta\hat{p}$. Then, at period t the variance of beliefs with information production is

$$Var_t(p|IS) = \lambda^t\hat{p}(1 - \hat{p})\eta^2\hat{p} + (1 - \lambda^t(1 - \hat{p}))\eta\hat{p}(1 - \eta\hat{p}).$$

Then

$$Var_t(p|IS) - Var_t(p|II) = (1 - \lambda^t(1 - \hat{p}))\eta\hat{p}(1 - \eta\hat{p}) - \lambda^t\hat{p}(1 - \hat{p})(1 - \eta^2\hat{p}),$$

also increasing in the length of the boom t.

The change in the variance of beliefs also depends on the size of the shock. For very large shocks ($\eta \to 0$) the variance can decline. This decline is lower the larger t is.

A.4 Proof of Proposition 7

Denote the expected discounted consumption sustained by a unit of collateral with belief p if producing information as $V^{IS}(p)$ and if not producing information as $V^{II}(p)$. The value function from such unit of land is then $V(p) = \max\{V^{IS}(p), V^{II}(p)\}$.

If acquiring information, expected discounted consumption is

$$V^{IS}(p) = pK^*(qA - 1) - \gamma + \beta[\lambda(pV(1) + (1-p)V(0)) + (1-\lambda)V(\hat{p})] + pC.$$

Since we know that for $p = 0$ and $p = 1$ there is no information acquisition, $(V(1) = V^{II}(1)$ and $V(0) = V^{II}(0))$, we can compute

$$V(1) = K^*(qA - 1) + \beta[\lambda V(1) + (1-\lambda)V(\hat{p})] + pC,$$

and

$$V(0) = 0 + \beta[\lambda V(0) + (1-\lambda)V(\hat{p})] + pC.$$

Taking expectations

$$pV(1) + (1-p)V(0) = \frac{pK^*(qA - 1)}{1 - \beta\lambda} + \frac{\beta(1-\lambda)}{1 - \beta\lambda}V(\hat{p}) + \frac{pC}{1 - \beta\lambda},$$

and solving for $V^{IS}(p)$, we get

$$V^{IS}(p) = \frac{pK^*(qA - 1)}{1 - \beta\lambda} - \gamma + Z(p, \hat{p}), \qquad (A.4)$$

where

$$Z(p, \hat{p}) = \frac{\beta(1-\lambda)}{1 - \beta\lambda}V(\hat{p}) + \frac{pC}{1 - \beta\lambda}.$$

If *not* acquiring information, expected discounted consumption is

$$V^{II}(p) = K(p|II)(qA - 1) + \beta[\lambda V(p) + (1-\lambda)V(\hat{p})] + pC.$$

Assume $V(p) = V^{II}(p)$, then

$$V^{II}(p) = \frac{K(p|II)(qA - 1)}{1 - \beta\lambda} + Z(p, \hat{p}), \qquad (A.5)$$

and $V(p)$ is indeed information insensitive if $V^{II}(p) > V^{IS}(p)$

$$(1 - \beta\lambda)\frac{\gamma}{qA - 1} > pK^* - K(p|II).$$

Similarly, assume $V(p) = V^{IS}(p)$. We denote as $V^{II}(p|Dev)$ the expected discounted consumption from deviating and not producing information only for one period. Then

$$V^{II}(p|Dev) = K(p|II)(qA-1) + \beta[\lambda V^{IS}(p) + (1-\lambda)V(\hat{p})] + pC$$

replaces equation (A.4),

$$V^{II}(p|Dev) = K(p|II)(qA-1) + \beta\left[\lambda\left(\frac{pK^*(qA-1)}{1-\beta\lambda} - \gamma + Z(p,\hat{p})\right)\right.$$
$$\left. + (1-\lambda)V(\hat{p})\right] + pC,$$

and plugging in $Z(p,\hat{p})$ and rearranging, obtain

$$V^{II}(p|Dev) = \left[K(p|II) + \frac{\beta\lambda pK^*}{1-\beta\lambda}\right](qA-1) - \beta\lambda\gamma + Z(p,\hat{p}).$$

$V(p)$ is indeed information sensitive if $V^{II}(p|Dev) < V^{IS}(p)$, which is again

$$(1-\beta\lambda)\frac{\gamma}{qA-1} < pK^* - K(p|II).$$

This result effectively means that the decision rule for the planner is the same as the decision rule for decentralized agents, but with $\beta > 0$ for the planner and $\beta = 0$ for the agents.

This result allows us to characterize value functions in equilibrium generally as

$$V(p) = \frac{\widetilde{\pi}(p)}{1-\beta\lambda} + Z(p,\hat{p}), \tag{A.6}$$

where $\widetilde{\pi}(p) = \widetilde{K}(p)(qA-1)$ and $\widetilde{K}(p) = \max\left\{K(p|II), pK^* - \frac{\gamma(1-\beta\lambda)}{qA-1}\right\}$, which is the same as array (2.14), but with new cutoffs given by lower effective costs of information $\gamma(1-\beta\lambda)$.

A.5   Proof of Proposition 8

Without loss of generality we assume the negative shock η can happen only once. Until the shock occurs, its ex ante probability is μ per period, turning to 0 after the shock is realized. This assumption just simplifies the analysis because, conditional on a shock, we can impose the results obtained previously without aggregate shocks. Furthermore, we do not need to keep track of all the possible paths of shocks and beliefs. Generalizing this result just requires more algebra but hides the main forces at work behind the results.

Denote by $\widehat{V}(p)$ the expected discounted consumption sustained by a unit of collateral with belief p prior to the realization of the shock. As in Proposition 7, denote by $V(p)$ the expected discounted consumption sustained by a unit of collateral with belief p after the shock is realized, hence in the absence of possible future shocks. This is convenient because we can replace value functions after the shock with the results from Proposition 7 and because we do not need to keep track of different paths of beliefs.

The value of producing information (IS) in periods preceding potential shocks is

$$\widehat{V}^{IS}(p) = pK^*(qA - 1) - \gamma + \beta(1 - \mu)\lambda[p\widehat{V}(1) + (1 - p)\widehat{V}(0)]$$
$$+ \beta(1 - \mu)(1 - \lambda)\widehat{V}(\hat{p}) + \beta\mu\lambda[pV(\eta) + (1 - p)V(0)]$$
$$+ \beta\mu(1 - \lambda)V(\eta\hat{p}) + pC.$$

Again we know that for $p = 0$ and $p = 1$ there is no information acquisition, $(\widetilde{V}(1) = \widetilde{V}^{II}(1)$ and $\widetilde{V}(0) = \widetilde{V}^{II}(0))$, and we can compute

$$p\widehat{V}(1) + (1 - p)\widehat{V}(0) = \frac{1}{1 - \beta\lambda(1 - \mu)}\left[pK^*(qA - 1) + \beta(1 - \mu)(1 - \lambda)\widehat{V}(\hat{p}) + pC\right]$$
$$+ \frac{1}{1 - \beta\lambda(1 - \mu)}\left[\beta\mu\lambda(pV(\eta) + (1 - p)V(0))\right.$$
$$\left. + \beta\mu(1 - \lambda)V(\eta\hat{p})\right].$$

Also, using value functions in the absence of shocks, $V(p)$, from equation (A.6).

$$pV(\eta) + (1 - p)V(0) = \frac{p\widetilde{K}(\eta)(qA - 1)}{1 - \beta\lambda} + Z(p, \hat{p}).$$

Plugging these results in $\widehat{V}^{IS}(p)$ and rearranging we obtain:

$$\widehat{V}^{IS}(p) = \frac{pK^*(qA - 1)}{1 - \beta\lambda(1 - \mu)} - \gamma + \frac{\beta\lambda\mu}{1 - \beta\lambda(1 - \mu)}\left[\frac{p\widetilde{K}(\eta)(qA - 1)}{1 - \beta\lambda} + Z(p, \hat{p})\right]$$
$$+ \widehat{Z}(p, \hat{p}, \eta, \mu), \tag{A.7}$$

where

$$\widehat{Z}(p, \hat{p}, \eta, \mu) = \frac{\beta(1 - \lambda)[(1 - \mu)\widehat{V}(\hat{p}) + \mu\widehat{V}(\eta\hat{p})] + pC}{1 - \beta\lambda(1 - \mu)}.$$

The value of *not* producing information (II) in periods preceding potential shocks,

$$\widehat{V}^{II}(p) = K(p|II)(qA - 1) + \beta(1 - \mu)\lambda\widehat{V}(p) + \beta(1 - \mu)(1 - \lambda)\widehat{V}(\hat{p})$$
$$+ \beta\mu\lambda V(\eta p) + \beta\mu(1 - \lambda)V(\eta\hat{p}) + pC.$$

Assuming $\widehat{V}(p) = \widehat{V}^{II}(p)$,

$$\widehat{V}^{II}(p) = \frac{K(p|II)(qA-1)}{1-\beta\lambda(1-\mu)} + \frac{\beta\lambda\mu}{1-\beta\lambda(1-\mu)}\left[\frac{\widetilde{K}(\eta p)(qA-1)}{1-\beta\lambda} + Z(p,\hat{p})\right]$$
$$+ \widehat{Z}(p,\hat{p},\eta,\mu), \tag{A.8}$$

and $\widehat{V}(p)$ is indeed information insensitive if $\widehat{V}^{II}(p) > \widehat{V}^{IS}(p)$, which happens if

$$\frac{\gamma}{qA-1}(1-\beta\lambda) < \frac{(1-\beta\lambda)}{(1-\beta\lambda+\beta\lambda\mu)}[pK^* - K(p|II)]$$
$$+ \frac{\beta\lambda\mu}{(1-\beta\lambda+\beta\lambda\mu)}[p\widehat{K}(\eta) - \widehat{K}(\eta p)].$$

Assuming $\widehat{V}(p) = \widehat{V}^{IS}(p)$, the question is if the planner gains anything by deviating and not producing information for one period. We denote this possibility as $\widehat{V}(p|Dev)$:

$$\widehat{V}^{II}(p|Dev) = K(p|II)(qA-1) + \beta\lambda(1-\mu)\left[\frac{pK^*(qA-1)}{1-\beta\lambda(1-\mu)} - \gamma\right] + \widehat{Z}(p,\hat{p},\eta,\mu)$$
$$+ \frac{\beta\lambda\mu}{1-\beta\lambda(1-\mu)}\left[\frac{\widetilde{K}(\eta p)(qA-1)}{1-\beta\lambda} + Z(p,\hat{p}) + \beta\lambda(1-\mu)\frac{\widetilde{K}(\eta p)(qA-1)}{1-\beta\lambda}\right].$$

$\widehat{V}(p)$ is indeed information insensitive if $\widehat{V}^{II}(p|Dev) > \widehat{V}^{IS}(p)$, which happens if

$$\frac{\gamma}{qA-1}(1-\beta\lambda) < \frac{(1-\beta\lambda)}{(1-\beta\lambda+\beta\lambda\mu)}[pK^* - K(p|II)]$$
$$+ \frac{\beta\lambda\mu}{(1-\beta\lambda+\beta\lambda\mu)}[p\widehat{K}(\eta) - \widehat{K}(\eta p)],$$

which is the same condition obtained before. Based on this condition, the following lemmas are self-evident.

Lemma 9. *Incentives to acquire information are larger in the presence of future shocks if $pK^* - K(p|II) < p\widetilde{K}(\eta) - \widetilde{K}(\eta p)$, and smaller otherwise. Hence, whether there are more or less incentives to acquire information in the presence of shocks just depends on their size η, and not on their probability μ.*

Lemma 10. *If in the presence of aggregate shocks there are more incentives to acquire information, these are larger the larger the difference between $pK^* - K(p|II)$ and $p\widetilde{K}(\eta) - \widetilde{K}(\eta p)$ and the larger μ.*

Proof. The first part of the lemma is trivial. The second arises from noting the weight assigned to $p\widetilde{K}(\eta) - \widetilde{K}(\eta p)$ increases with μ. □

These two lemmas, together with the condition for information acquisition we derived, provide a complete characterization of the *IS* and *II* ranges of beliefs under the possibility of a future aggregate shock η that occurs with probability μ, and that is summarized in the proposition.

A.6   Proof of Proposition 17

We first characterize p^H. The maximum profits that a bank with the highest-quality collateral $\bar{p} + \bar{\eta}$ expects when inducing a run, conditional on no other bank facing a run (that is, when $E^r(p) = \bar{p} + \bar{\eta}$), are

$$E_r(\pi \,|\, \bar{p} + \bar{\eta}, \bar{p} + \bar{\eta}) = (\bar{p} + \bar{\eta})K^*(qA - 1) - \gamma.$$

The expected profits when not inducing a run, conditional on no other bank facing a run, are

$$E_{nr}(\pi \,|\, \bar{p}) = K_{nr}(\bar{p})(qA - 1),$$

where, from equation (6.5),

$$K_{nr}(\bar{p}) = \min \left\{ K^*, \frac{\gamma}{(1 - q)(1 - \bar{p})}, \bar{p}C \right\}.$$

There is always a $\bar{p}$ large enough such that $K^* < \frac{\gamma}{(1-q)(1-\bar{p})}$ and $K^* < \bar{p}C$ such that $K_{nr}(\bar{p}) = K^*$. Then no bank would rather face a run and have a positive probability of not being able to invest, given that it can invest at optimal scale without examination. For all $\bar{p} > p^H$, all banks invest without runs, where p^H is defined by $E_r(\pi \,|\, p^H + \bar{\eta}, p^H + \bar{\eta}) = E_{nr}(\pi \,|\, p^H)$, or

$$(p^H + \bar{\eta})K^*(qA - 1) - \gamma = \frac{\gamma}{(1 - q)(1 - p^H)}(qA - 1).$$

In this region, $p^* = \bar{p} + \bar{\eta}$, which trivially increases one for one with $\bar{p}$.

We now characterize p^L. The maximum expected profits that a bank with the lowest-quality collateral $\bar{p} - \bar{\eta}$ can obtain when avoiding a run when all other banks face runs (that is, $E^{nr}(p) = \bar{p} - \bar{\eta}$) are

$$E_{nr}(\pi \,|\, \bar{p} - \bar{\eta}) = K_{nr}(\bar{p} - \bar{\eta})(qA - 1),$$

where, from equation (6.5),

$$K_{nr}(\bar{p} - \bar{\eta}) = \min \left\{ K^*, \frac{\gamma}{(1 - q)(1 - (\bar{p} - \bar{\eta}))}, (\bar{p} - \bar{\eta})C \right\}.$$

The expected profits when the bank induces a run, conditional on all other banks inducing a run, are

$$E_r(\pi \,|\, \bar{p} - \bar{\eta}, \bar{p}) = (\bar{p} - \bar{\eta}) \left[K^*(qA - 1) - \frac{\gamma}{\bar{p}} \right].$$

Defining p^L by the point at which $E_r(\pi\,|p^L - \bar{\eta}, p^L) = E_{nr}(\pi\,|p^L - \bar{\eta})$, such that

$$(p^L - \bar{\eta})\left[K^*(qA - 1) - \frac{\gamma}{p^L}\right] > \frac{\gamma}{(1 - q)(1 - (p^L - \bar{\eta}))}(qA - 1),$$

then when $\bar{p} < p_L$ all banks invest such that there is examination of their collaterals. In this region, $p^* = \bar{p} - \bar{\eta}$, which also trivially increases one for one with $\bar{p}$.

In the best equilibrium and by monotonicity, in the intermediate region of $\bar{p}$ the threshold p^* also increases with $\bar{p}$.

A.7   Proof of Proposition 18

Follows from comparing the condition for no information acquisition in the absence of intervention (equation 6.4) and in the presence of intervention (equation 6.8), and on the comparative statics in equation (6.8) with respect to y.

A.8   Proof of Lemma 4

Assume first that the central bank chooses $\widetilde{p} = p_L + \bar{\eta}$, and then no discount even for the bank holding the highest-quality collateral, this is $d(p_L + \bar{\eta}, \widetilde{p}) = 0$. Compare equations (6.10) and (6.11) for $p = p_L + \bar{\eta}$. It is optimal for such a bank to participate, but if this is the only bank participating, then stigma is positive in the sense that participation reveals the highest possible idiosyncratic component. Then, participating is also the optimal strategy for all other banks, which implies that there is no learning from participation and no stigma (i.e., $\chi = 0$), confirming that this is indeed the best sustainable equilibrium.[1] Hence, for $\widetilde{p} \geq p_L + \bar{\eta}$, a fraction $y(\widetilde{p}) = 1$ of banks participates, from equation $(A.9)$ $\sigma(\widetilde{p}) = 0$ and from equation (6.8) $K(\widetilde{p}) = K^*$.

For lower levels of $\widetilde{p}$, this is still an equilibrium as long as the bank with the highest-quality collateral finds it optimal to participate, and then all other banks do as well. The critical level $\widetilde{p}_h$ is determined by the point at which the bank with the highest quality (evaluated at $\chi = 0$) is indifferent between participating or not,

$$H(K^*) - d(p_L + \bar{\eta}, \widetilde{p}_h) = (1 - \varepsilon)H(K^*) + \varepsilon L(p_L + \bar{\eta}, \widetilde{p}_h).$$

Using the definitions of $L(p, \widetilde{p})$, $H(K(\widetilde{p}))$ and $d(p, \widetilde{p})$,

$$\widetilde{p}_h = (p_L + \bar{\eta}) - \frac{\varepsilon}{C}\left[(1 - p_L - \bar{\eta})K^*(qA - 1) + \gamma\right].$$

A.9   Proof of Lemma 5

Assume first the extreme case in which $\widetilde{p} = \widetilde{p}_h$. From the previous proposition, $y(\widetilde{p}_h) = 1$ and $\sigma(\widetilde{p}_h) = 0$. For $\widetilde{p} = \widetilde{p}_h - \epsilon$ (from the definition of $\widetilde{p}_h$),

$$H(K^*) - d(p_L + \bar{\eta}, \widetilde{p}_h - \epsilon) < (1 - \varepsilon)H(K^*) + \varepsilon L(p_L + \bar{\eta}, \widetilde{p}_h - \epsilon),$$

and then banks with collateral quality $p_L + \bar{\eta}$ strictly prefer to not participate at the discount window. This implies that $y(\widetilde{p}_h - \epsilon) \equiv Pr(p < p_w^*(\widetilde{p}_h - \epsilon)) < 1$, where $p_w^*(\widetilde{p}_h - \epsilon)$ is given by the indifference condition

$$H(K^*) - d(p_w^*, \widetilde{p}_h - \epsilon) = (1 - \epsilon)H(K^*) + \epsilon L(p_w^*, \widetilde{p}_h - \epsilon),$$

or

$$d(p_w^*, \widetilde{p}_h - \epsilon) = \epsilon[H(K^*) - L(p_w^*, \widetilde{p}_h - \epsilon)],$$

where p_w^* declines monotonically as we reduce $\widetilde{p}$. Notice that this construction relies on the conjecture that $\sigma(\widetilde{p}_h - \epsilon) = 0$, but for relatively low ϵ this is the case as long as $y(\widetilde{p}_h - \epsilon)$ and $E^{nw}(p|\widetilde{p}_h - \epsilon)$ are such that

$$K^* < \frac{\gamma}{(1-q)(1-y)(1-E^{nw}(p))}.$$

Define by $\bar{p}_w^*$ the threshold such that $\bar{y}(\bar{p}_w^*)$ is the fraction of banks borrowing from the discount window and $\bar{E}^{nw}(p|\bar{p}_w^*)$ is the expected quality of the non-participating banks' collateral, such that depositors are indifferent between running or not when the bank invests K^*, that is,

$$K^* = \frac{\gamma}{(1-q)(1-\bar{y})(1-\bar{E}^{nw}(p))}.$$

The bank with the marginal-quality collateral $\bar{p}_w^*(\widetilde{p}_m)$ is determined by

$$H(K^*) - d(\bar{p}_w^*, \widetilde{p}_m) = (1 - \epsilon)H(K^*) + \epsilon L(\bar{p}_w^*, \widetilde{p}_m),$$

such that

$$\bar{y} = Pr(p < \bar{p}_w^*(\widetilde{p}_m)) \qquad \text{and} \qquad \bar{E}^{nw}(p) = E(p|p > \bar{p}_w^*(\widetilde{p}_m)).$$

Finally, the threshold $\bar{p}_w^*$ is well-defined, as both y and $E^{nw}(p)$ monotonically increase in p_w^*, which monotonically decreases in $\widetilde{p}$.

Even when there is no examination and then stigma on the equilibrium path, there would be stigma in case participation is leaked or voluntarily disclosed. Stigma, $\chi(p, \widetilde{p})$, is the cost in terms of a higher probability of a run in the second period coming from information that the bank participated at the discount window in the first period. Intuitively, since banks participate when their collateral quality is lower than average (specifically $p < p_w^*$), revelation of participation would make those banks more prone to be examined in the second period. Formally, *in the second period*, the bank will suffer a run and obtain $H(K^*)$ only with probability p and lose the cost of information γ if equation (6.4) is not fulfilled at optimal scale K^*, this is if

$$K^* > \frac{\gamma}{(1-q)(1-E^w(p|\widetilde{p}, \bar{p}_{t=2}))} \qquad \text{or} \qquad E^w(p|\widetilde{p}, \bar{p}_{t=2}) < 1 - \frac{(1-q)K^*}{\gamma},$$

where $E^w(p|\widetilde{p}, \bar{p}_{t=2})$ is the expectation of p in the second period, conditional on having participated in the discount window in the first period and conditional on the second period displaying an aggregate component $\bar{p}_{t=2}$. Since we have assumed that $\bar{p}_{t=2} = p_H > p^H$ we can rewrite this expectation as

$$E^w(p|\widetilde{p}_m, \bar{p}_{t=2}) = p_H + E^w(\eta|\widetilde{p}),$$

in which case the bank would lose in net $(1-p)K^*(qA-1) + \gamma$.

This implies that stigma is given by

$$\chi(p,\widetilde{p}) = \begin{cases} 0 & \text{if} \quad E^w(\eta|\widetilde{p}) \geq 1 - p_H - \frac{(1-q)K^*}{\gamma} \\ (1-p)K^*(qA-1) + \gamma & \text{if} \quad E^w(\eta|\widetilde{p}) < 1 - p_H - \frac{(1-q)K^*}{\gamma}. \end{cases}$$

A.10   Proof of Lemma 6

Assume first the extreme case where $\widetilde{p} = \widetilde{p}_m$. From the previous lemma, $y(\widetilde{p}_m) = \bar{y}$ and $\sigma(\widetilde{p}_h) = 0$. For $\widetilde{p} = \widetilde{p}_m - \epsilon$, the bank that is indifferent about borrowing from the discount window has slightly lower quality, $p_w^*(\widetilde{p}_m - \epsilon) < p_w^*(\widetilde{p}_m)$. Then $y(\widetilde{p}_m - \epsilon) < \bar{y}$ and $E^{nw}(p|\widetilde{p}_m - \epsilon) < \bar{E}^{nw}(p)$, and there are incentives to run if investment is K^*, as there are relatively few participants at the discount window (low y) and the collateral of those not participating at the discount windows is worse in expectation (low $E^{nw}(p)$). Formally,

$$K^* > \frac{\gamma}{(1-q)(1 - y(\widetilde{p}_m - \epsilon))(1 - E^{nw}(p|\widetilde{p}_m - \epsilon))}.$$

One possibility for banks to prevent runs, $\sigma(\widetilde{p}) = 0$, is to scale back the investment in the project to $K(p_w^*) < K^*$, to avoid information acquisition. The size of the investment K, however, also determines y, as $p_w^*(\widetilde{p}_m - \epsilon)$ is pinned down by the condition

$$d(p_w^*, \widetilde{p}_m - \epsilon) = \epsilon[H(K(p_w^*)) - L(p_w^*, \widetilde{p}_m - \epsilon)].$$

A lower K relaxes the constraint and reduces the incentive to run, but at the same time reduces p_w^* for a given $\widetilde{p}$, increasing the incentive to run. Intuitively, for a given discount, a reduction in the gains of borrowing from the discount window (from lower $H(K)$) reduces the quality of the marginal bank, which is indifferent between borrowing or not, that is, reducing p_w^* further.

If $H(K(p_w^*))$ declines faster than $L(p_w^*)$, then no participant will go to the discount window if, at the lowest possible p, which is $p_L - \bar{\eta}$,

$$H(K(p_L - \bar{\eta})) - L(p_L - \bar{\eta}, p_L) < 0,$$

which we have assumed in the definition of a crisis (p_L is low enough such that all banks would rather face examination than restricting their investments to avoid runs). In words, it is not in the best interests of banks to discourage runs by reducing the size of their investments in the project, which is in contrast to what happens in the absence of intervention. Our result here comes from the endogenous participation of banks at the discount window. By reducing K, the effect of a lower y in inducing information acquisition is stronger than the effect of a lower K in discouraging information acquisition, thus increasing on net the incentives for depositors to examine a bank's collateral as K declines.

Under these conditions, the equilibrium should involve either the discount window sustaining an investment of K^* (when a fraction $\bar{y}$ of banks borrows from the discount window) or no participation in the discount window at all, which replicates the allocation without intervention. To maintain the fraction $\bar{y}$ constant in this region as $\widetilde{p}$ declines, the marginal bank with collateral quality $p_w^*(\widetilde{p}_m)$ should be indifferent between borrowing from the discount window or not. This is achievable only if depositors choose to run with some probability and examine the portfolio of banks as $\widetilde{p}$ declines, as this increases the incentives to have bonds in the portfolio.

As the fraction of banks participating at the discount windows is constant at $\bar{y}$, depositors are indeed indifferent between running or not, and $\sigma(\widetilde{p}) > 0$ is an equilibrium. To determine $\sigma(\widetilde{p})$ in equilibrium we next discuss the determination of endogenous stigma.

With positive information acquisition ($\sigma(\widetilde{p}) > 0$) there is stigma when the depositor discovers a bank's participation at the discount window. The reason there is stigma is that the banks borrowing from the discount window are the ones with relatively low collateral quality (relatively low η_i). Once a bank is stigmatized, it may face withdrawals during normal times in the second period. To be more precise about the endogeneity of stigma, once back in normal times, the bank will face a run when investing at the optimal scale of production if

$$K^* > \frac{\gamma}{(1-q)(1-E^w(p))},$$

and the bank will not suffer a run in the second period based on an indifference condition that pins down p_2^* in the second period where

$$E_r(\pi \,|\, p_2^*, E^r(p|p < p_w^*)) = E_r(\pi \,|\, E^{nr}(p|p < p_w^*)).$$

We denote by $K^w(p, \widetilde{p})$ the investment size that a bank with a collateral of quality p can obtain in the second period conditional on it having been revealed that the bank borrowed from the discount window in the first period.

Then, stigma is given by

$$\chi(p, \widetilde{p}) = [K^* - K^w(p, \widetilde{p})](qA - 1),$$

where χ is an increasing function of the discount (a decreasing function of $\widetilde{p}$). As the discount increases, p_w^* decreases, $y(p_w^*)$ decreases, and $E^w(p)$ decreases. This leads to a decline in K^w and then an increase in stigma from going to the discount window.

Given $\bar{y}$, to maintain the investment size K^* without triggering information, the indifference of the marginal bank $\bar{p}_w^*$ pins down the probability the depositor runs. This is $E^{nw}(\pi | p_w^*) = E^w(\pi | p_w^*)$, which implies

$$\sigma L(\bar{p}_w^*, \tilde{p}) + (1 - \sigma)[(1 - \varepsilon)H(K^*) + \varepsilon L(\bar{p}_w^*, \tilde{p})] = [H(K^*) - d(\bar{p}_w^*, \tilde{p})] - \sigma \chi(\bar{p}_w^*, \tilde{p})$$

and then

$$\sigma(\tilde{p}) = \frac{d(\bar{p}_w^*, \tilde{p}) - \varepsilon[H(K^*) - L(\bar{p}_w^*, \tilde{p})]}{(1 - \varepsilon)[H(K^*) - L(\bar{p}_w^*, \tilde{p})] - \chi(\bar{p}_w^*, \tilde{p})}. \tag{A.9}$$

Finally, depositors randomize between running and not running given that the bank is investing K^* in the project, and a bank with collateral quality $\bar{p}_w^*$ is indifferent between borrowing from the discount window or not.

A.11 Proof of Lemma 7

From equation (A.9), $\sigma(p_w^*) = 1$ for $d(\bar{p}_w^*, \tilde{p}) \geq H(K^*) - L(\bar{p}_w^*, \tilde{p}) - \chi(\bar{p}_w^*, \tilde{p})$. Define $\tilde{p}_l$ to be the discount that solves this condition with equality. Evaluating $E_{nw}(\pi)$ and $E_{(\pi)}$ at $\sigma(\tilde{p}) = 1$ given a project of size K^* and at the threshold $\bar{p}_w^*$ a bank with collateral p_w^* goes to the discount window whenever

$$H(K^*) - d(\bar{p}_w^*, \tilde{p}) - \chi(\bar{p}_w^*, \tilde{p}) > L(\bar{p}_w^*, \tilde{p}),$$

which is never the case in this region by the previous condition. Then $y(\tilde{p}) = 0$ and then it is indeed optimal for depositors to run, that is $\sigma(\tilde{p}) = 1$.

A.12 Proof of Lemma 8

Define $\tilde{p}_T$ by

$$H(K^*) - d(p_L + \bar{\eta}, \tilde{p}_T) = L(p_L + \bar{\eta}, \tilde{p}_T).$$

For all $\tilde{p} > \tilde{p}_T$

$$H(K^*) - d(p_L + \bar{\eta}, \tilde{p}) > L(p_L + \bar{\eta}, \tilde{p})$$

and the bank with collateral of quality $p_L + \bar{\eta}$ strictly prefers to borrow from the discount window. Notice that as all banks participate, $\chi(p, \tilde{p}_T) = 0$ for all p.

For all $\tilde{p} < \tilde{p}_T$, the fraction of participating banks y_T in a transparent window is given by the threshold p_{wT}^* such that $H(K^*) - d(p_{wT}^*, \tilde{p}) - \chi(p_{wT}^*, \tilde{p}) = L(p_{wT}^*, \tilde{p})$ and $y_T = Pr(p < p_{wT}^*)$.

Recall the condition that pins down $\tilde{p}_h$ in Lemma 4 is

$$H(K^*) - d(p_L + \bar{\eta}, \tilde{p}_h) = (1 - \varepsilon)H(K^*) + \varepsilon L(p_L + \bar{\eta}, \tilde{p}_h).$$

Then, as the right-hand side is larger than in the condition above that pins down $\tilde{p}_T$, the discount has to be smaller and $\tilde{p}_T < \tilde{p}_h$.

A.13   Proof of Proposition 21

Here we compare the distortions for different levels of discount $\widetilde{p}$ (in the different regions that we characterized in the previous section) for different disclosure policies.

We consider first the parametric case for which $\widetilde{p}_T < \widetilde{p}_l$. Under transparency, all banks participate when $\widetilde{p} \geq \widetilde{p}_T$. This implies that $y = 1$, $\chi = 0$, and $E^w(p) = p_L$. Distortions in this range are then

$$Dist(\widetilde{p} \mid Tr) = (1 + \delta)(1 - q)(1 - \phi)p_L C.$$

In contrast, for all $\widetilde{p} < \widetilde{p}_T$, the discount window is not sustainable and distortions are the same as without intervention, $H - L \equiv (1 - p_L)K^*(qA - 1) + \gamma$.

Under opacity, distortions also depend on the equilibrium regions. In the "very low" discount region all banks participate, then $y = 1$ and $\chi = 0$, and distortions are the same as under transparency (in the region $\widetilde{p} \geq \widetilde{p}_T$ above).

In the "low" discount region, $y < 1$ but $\sigma = 0$, then from equation (6.14)

$$Dist(\widetilde{p} \mid Op) = (1 - y)(H - \widehat{L})\varepsilon + y(1 + \delta)(1 - q)(1 - \phi)E^w(p \mid Op)C.$$

Since $yE^w(p \mid Op) < p_L$ and $H - L > H - \widehat{L}$, the sufficient condition under which the opacity distortion is lower than the transparency distortion is

$$(1 + \delta)(1 - q)(1 - \phi)p_L C > \varepsilon(H - L).$$

In the "intermediate" discount region, $y = \bar{y}$, but $\sigma > 0$ and increases with the discount. From equation (6.14) it is clear that in this region the distortion increases with σ and then with the discount. While the fraction of banks participating is fixed, there are more runs and then more banks not participating end up producing less, in both the first period (less deposits) and the second period (more stigma).

Finally, in the "high" discount region, the discount window is not sustainable under opacity, so distortions are the same as without intervention, $H - L$.

Summarizing, as the discount increases, distortions under opacity are fixed in the very low discount region, decrease in the low discount region, increase in the intermediate discount region, and reach the maximum in the high discount region. In contrast, distortions under transparency are fixed whenever the discount window is sustainable, as either all banks participate or neither does. This implies the optimal discount is $\widetilde{p}_m$ under opacity.

Consider finally the parametric case for which $\widetilde{p}_T \geq \widetilde{p}_l$. In this case the discount window under opacity collapses at lower discount levels than under transparency. Still the optimal policy is a discount of $\widetilde{p}_m$ under opacity because $\widetilde{p}_T < \widetilde{p}_h$, as shown in Lemma 8.

Additional Tables and Figures

Our analysis uses data on the countries listed in Table B.1 and the variables defined in Table B.2. For each country we use time-series data from 1960 to 2010. Table B.1 also shows the number of booms, number of bad booms, the frequency of boom periods, and the average time between booms for each country in our sample. If there was only one boom, then the average time between booms is not available (NA). Otherwise it is computed as the average number of years from a boom end to the subsequent boom start.

Table B.3 and Figure B.1 show our classification of the booms.

Table B.1. Frequency of Booms

Country	Booms	Bad Booms	Frequency of Boom Periods	Average Time between Booms
US	1	1	0.52	NA
UK	3	1	0.58	7.00
Austria	1	0	0.68	NA
Belgium	3	1	0.68	9.00
Denmark	2	1	0.30	14.00
France	2	1	0.68	13.00
Netherlands	1	1	1.00	NA
Sweden	3	2	0.62	10.00
Japan	3	1	0.48	8.50
Finland	2	1	0.40	10.00
Greece	2	1	0.62	14.00
Ireland	2	1	0.50	11.00
Portugal	3	1	0.76	6.00
Spain	3	2	0.72	8.00
Turkey	4	2	0.40	10.00
Australia	2	0	0.76	10.00
New Zealand	3	0	0.70	3.00
Argentina	4	2	0.34	8.67
Brazil	3	1	0.38	13.50
Chile	2	1	0.52	11.00
Colombia	4	2	0.38	9.33
Costa Rica	2	0	0.32	31.00
Ecuador	4	2	0.58	6.33
Mexico	3	1	0.36	14.50
Peru	4	1	0.48	6.00
Uruguay	3	2	0.42	11.00
Israel	3	1	0.64	5.50
Egypt	2	0	0.44	7.00
India	2	0	0.78	12.00
Korea	4	0	0.52	7.00
Malaysia	2	1	0.62	8.00
Pakistan	1	0	0.18	NA
Philippines	3	2	0.60	4.50
Thailand	1	1	0.62	NA

Table B.2. Data Definitions

Variable	Definition	Source
A. Macroeconomic data		
Domestic credit to private sector	Domestic credit to private sector refers to financial resources provided to the private sector by financial corporations, such as through loans, purchases of nonequity securities, and trade credits and other accounts receivable, that establish a claim for repayment. For some countries these claims include credit to public enterprises.	IMF-IFS, World Bank, and OECD GDP estimates
Total factor productivity	Total factor productivity calculated using the PWT6.2	Kose, Prasad, and Terrones 2008
Real GDP	Total PPP Converted GDP, G-K method, at current prices, PWT 7.1	Penn World Tables 7.1
Per capita investment	Per capita investment, PWT 7.0	Penn World Tables 7.0
Labor productivity	Labor productivity per hour worked in 2014 US$ (converted to 2014 price level with updated 2011 PPPs)	The Conference Board Total Economy Database
Equity premium	Excess stock returns computed as the difference of country equity total return indices and country risk free rates	Global Financial Data
Patents Granted	Counts are based on the grant date	WIPO Statistics Database, December 2011
Patent applications	Counts are based on the filing date	WIPO Statistics Database, December 2011
Distance to Insolvency	The measure is computed as 1/Vol. Vol is the median annual firm level volatility computed using daily stock return data	Thomson Reuters DataStream

Continued on next page

Table B.2. (*continued*)

Variable	Definition	Source
B. Financial Crises and Credit Booms		
Financial Crises	A systemic banking crisis occurs if (1) there are significant signs of financial distress in the banking system (as indicated by significant bank runs, losses in the banking system, and/or bank liquidations), and (2) if there are significant banking policy intervention measures in response to significant losses in the banking system.	Laeven and Valencia (2012)
Credit Boom	A credit boom begins whenever a country experiences three consecutive years of positive credit growth that average more than 5%, and it ends whenever a country experiences at least two years of credit growth not higher than zero	Gorton and Ordonez
Good Boom	A credit boom that does not end with a financial crisis	Gorton and Ordonez
Bad Boom	A credit boom that ends with a financial crisis occurring within a window of $(t-3, t+3)$, where t is the end of the boom	Gorton and Ordonez

Table B.3. Booms in the Sample

	Country	Years	Classification
1	US	1985–2010	crisis
2	UK	1970–1974	no crisis
3	UK	1979–1990	no crisis
4	UK	1999–2010	crisis
5	Austria	1964–1997	no crisis
6	Belgium	1961–1981	no crisis
7	Belgium	1986–1992	no crisis
8	Belgium	2005–2010	crisis
9	Denmark	1983–1986	no crisis
10	Denmark	2000–2010	crisis
11	France	1965–1992	no crisis
12	France	2005–2010	crisis
13	Netherlands	1961–2010	crisis
14	Sweden	1962–1973	no crisis
15	Sweden	1984–1992	crisis
16	Sweden	2001–2010	crisis
17	Japan	1961–1966	no crisis
18	Japan	1970–1972	no crisis
19	Japan	1985–1999	crisis
20	Finland	1982–1991	crisis
21	Finland	2001–2010	no crisis
22	Greece	1967–1981	no crisis
23	Greece	1995–2010	crisis
24	Ireland	1976–1983	no crisis
25	Ireland	1994–2010	crisis
26	Portugal	1963–1975	no crisis
27	Portugal	1979–1983	no crisis
28	Portugal	1991–2010	crisis
29	Spain	1961–1976	crisis
30	Spain	1987–1991	no crisis
31	Spain	1996–2010	crisis
32	Turkey	1964–1969	no crisis
33	Turkey	1981–1983	crisis
34	Turkey	1995–1997	crisis
35	Turkey	2003–2010	no crisis
36	Australia	1964–1973	no crisis
37	Australia	1983–2010	no crisis
38	New Zealand	1972–1974	no crisis
39	New Zealand	1977–2000	no crisis
40	New Zealand	2003–2010	no crisis
41	Argentina	1968–1971	no crisis
42	Argentina	1977–1982	crisis
43	Argentina	1996–1999	crisis
44	Argentina	2005–2007	no crisis

Continued on next page

Table B.3. *(continued)*

	Country	Years	Classification
45	Brazil	1967–1975	no crisis
46	Brazil	1991–1993	crisis
47	Brazil	2004–2010	no crisis
48	Chile	1975–1984	crisis
49	Chile	1995–2010	no crisis
50	Colombia	1967–1970	no crisis
51	Colombia	1980–1984	crisis
52	Colombia	1995–1997	crisis
53	Colombia	2004–2010	no crisis
54	Costa Rica	1963–1965	no crisis
55	Costa Rica	1996–2008	no crisis
56	Ecuador	1966–1968	no crisis
57	Ecuador	1975–1984	crisis
58	Ecuador	1992–2000	crisis
59	Ecuador	2004–2010	no crisis
60	Mexico	1966–1971	no crisis
61	Mexico	1989–1994	crisis
62	Mexico	2005–2010	no crisis
63	Peru	1961–1967	no crisis
64	Peru	1971–1975	no crisis
65	Peru	1980–1983	crisis
66	Peru	1992–1999	no crisis
67	Uruguay	1962–1964	no crisis
68	Uruguay	1970–1982	crisis
69	Uruguay	1998–2002	crisis
70	Israel	1962–1979	crisis
71	Israel	1982–1984	no crisis
72	Israel	1992–2002	no crisis
73	Egypt	1974–1986	no crisis
74	Egypt	1993–2001	no crisis
75	India	1961–1986	no crisis
76	India	1998–2010	no crisis
77	Korea	1965–1974	no crisis
78	Korea	1978–1982	no crisis
79	Korea	1996–2002	no crisis
80	Korea	2005–2008	no crisis
81	Malaysia	1961–1986	no crisis
82	Malaysia	1994–1998	crisis
83	Pakistan	1961–1969	no crisis
84	Philippines	1961–1967	no crisis
85	Philippines	1972–1983	crisis
86	Philippines	1987–1997	crisis
87	Thailand	1967–1997	crisis

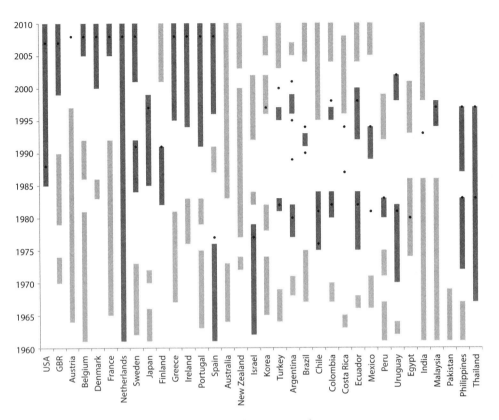

FIGURE B.1. Credit Booms and Crises

Table B.4. BIS Data Description

Country	Credit	Corporate Credit	Household Credit
United States	1960	1960	1960
United Kingdom	1960	1976	1966
Austria	1960	1995	1995
Belgium	1960	1980	1980
Denmark	1960	1994	1994
France	1960	1977	1977
Netherlands	1960	1990	1990
Sweden	1960	1980	1980
Japan	1960	1964	1964
Finland	1960	1970	1970
Greece	1960	1994	1994
Ireland	1960	NA	NA
Portugal	1960	1979	1979
Spain	1960	1980	1980
Turkey	1960	1986	1986
Australia	1960	1977	1977
New Zealand	1960	1998	1990
Argentina	1960	1994	1994
Brazil	1960	1995	1995
Chile	1960	NA	NA
Colombia	1960	NA	NA
Costa Rica	1960	NA	NA
Ecuador	1960	NA	NA
Mexico	1960	1994	1994
Peru	1960	NA	NA
Uruguay	1960	NA	NA
Israel	1960	1992	1992
Egypt	1965	NA	NA
India	1960	NA	NA
Korea	1960	1962	1962
Malaysia	1960	NA	NA
Pakistan	1960	NA	NA
Philippines	1960	NA	NA
Thailand	1960	1991	1991

Table B.5. Number of Firms per Year for the Countries with Available Daily Firm-Level Data

Country	1965	1966	1967	1968	1969	1970	1971	1972	1973	1974	1975	1976	1977	1978	1979	1980	1981	1982	1983	1984	1985	1986	1987
Argentina																							
Australia									78	78	80	83	84	84	85	86	88	89	94	104	107	115	140
Austria									24	23	17	13	16	20	18	17	21	19	21	20	29	34	37
Belgium									36	40	40	40	41	41	41	41	42	41	44	48	50	88	93
Brazil																							
Chile																							
Colombia																							
Denmark									31	31	32	31	25	30	30	33	33	37	39	40	44	45	45
Ecuador																							
Egypt																							
Finland																							
France									67	71	84	88	88	90	90	94	99	101	101	105	108	112	134
Greece																							
India	26	23	28	29	34	29	36	40															
Ireland									46	46	46	46	45	47	45	42	45	44	41	44	41	43	56
Israel																						165	182
Japan									753	763	770	779	793	793	825	831	844	860	885	905	908	910	1036
Malaysia																						199	213
Mexico																							
Netherlands									97	103	104	103	104	108	108	108	108	113	113	118	124	140	154
New Zealand																							17
Pakistan																							
Peru																							
Philippines																							16
Portugal																							
South Korea																				293	308	335	374
Spain																							46
Sweden																		34	40	48	53	61	69
Thailand																							97
Turkey																							
United Kingdom	570	583	592	610	1227	1247	1324	1417	1460	1461	1458	1456	1481	1505	1517	1542	1577	1571	1585	1624	1633	1663	1679
United States									731	737	802	803	808	816	822	867	916	947	1054	1102	1188	1357	1495

Table B.6. Number of Firms per Year for the Countries with Available Daily Firm-Level Data

Country	1988	1989	1990	1991	1992	1993	1994	1995	1996	1997	1998	1999	2000	2001	2002	2003	2004	2005	2006	2007	2008	2009	2010
Argentina	16	16	18	20	30	84	92	88	91	89	84	81	80	72	76	79	79	78	75	82	81	74	79
Australia	269	387	429	455	476	521	611	648	944	999	1021	1069	1185	1260	1278	1316	1415	1520	1690	1866	1874	1832	1854
Austria	31	54	68	72	83	87	90	99	98	106	104	109	126	122	106	108	99	97	102	111	115	105	108
Belgium	96	98	107	110	111	115	137	135	152	182	214	229	232	221	214	201	205	211	223	237	244	237	234
Brazil			20	43	51	64	83	79	106	113	135	166	165	147	146	167	180	179	193	270	265	256	266
Chile		111	130	144	154	171	181	183	190	194	195	187	177	174	169	170	169	174	188	174	172	172	168
Colombia					48	48	81	86	77	79	73	54	52	58	52	56	59	69	62	68	52	50	54
Denmark	172	180	192	217	235	240	242	245	259	265	267	256	248	234	204	197	190	183	197	217	221	211	207
Ecuador						7	13	14	13	17	16	17	17	9	10	13	14	19	19	16	21	16	25
Egypt							8	9	61	64	74	110	110	112	129	167	173	152	145	139	141	144	141
Finland	35	48	58	60	63	68	110	118	132	144	159	179	186	177	171	167	160	154	160	159	151	145	142
France	194	476	578	594	609	627	701	740	908	1008	1128	1013	1074	1060	1027	964	926	920	953	997	978	928	899
Greece	89	93	131	152	158	170	214	230	252	254	274	309	343	355	354	349	351	344	321	310	302	291	277
India		904	904	1014	1164	1552	2028	2994	3067	3066	2728	2696	2719	2394	2194	2201	2203	2671	2710	2962	3086	3121	3331
Ireland	60	67	68	65	65	62	58	57	58	59	62	66	62	63	61	57	54	56	64	68	67	62	56
Israel	184	191	199	200	260	451	540	554	565	569	600	644	678	658	632	582	572	586	604	647	628	610	602
Japan	1618	1949	2226	2459	2514	2618	2797	2986	3148	3288	3359	3431	3590	3690	3758	3765	3849	3914	4030	4060	4010	3913	3787
Malaysia	221	236	272	317	362	405	471	526	619	707	733	738	771	774	832	887	943	1013	1037	1043	1000	972	971
Mexico	63	71	84	112	158	211	229	204	201	205	184	188	158	150	132	123	131	130	125	126	117	115	124
Netherlands	159	167	170	174	177	180	185	194	205	219	244	253	250	221	198	184	170	161	166	167	164	151	141
New Zealand	56	59	64	69	79	95	110	114	121	120	119	120	129	131	131	141	163	164	158	155	149	137	132
Pakistan				25	135	163	194	201	221	261	301	379	393	373	361	358	366	328	305	290	273	266	256
Peru				24	52	76	102	107	119	108	111	116	120	126	137	131	139	135	146	149	149	141	128
Philippines	16	65	96	123	123	147	180	215	231	240	226	223	226	217	215	210	219	229	229	238	226	230	233
Portugal	86	104	114	121	133	138	139	142	141	140	142	123	116	95	87	79	73	70	70	67	61	62	62
South Korea	479	590	633	651	660	670	700	726	945	1062	1048	1193	1406	1475	1582	1616	1646	1692	1715	1800	1851	1897	1908
Spain	55	88	101	108	114	123	124	122	131	147	176	187	190	190	193	174	159	154	163	173	167	163	164
Sweden	108	169	192	196	202	218	250	271	303	373	407	457	481	456	425	400	408	428	477	519	542	532	537
Thailand	133	165	206	266	302	349	398	428	468	468	431	382	355	347	364	396	446	487	505	520	528	540	547
Turkey	59	64	96	123	133	149	171	200	224	252	271	272	302	292	293	288	294	299	313	317	313	311	335
United Kingdom	1658	1629	1572	1468	1405	1403	1409	1434	1532	1599	1599	1539	1616	1581	1627	1609	1803	2065	2228	2214	2144	1918	1797
United States	1553	1596	1634	1741	1915	2144	2406	2655	2937	3176	3047	2997	2794	2583	2581	2640	2764	2889	3037	3222	3296	3346	3479

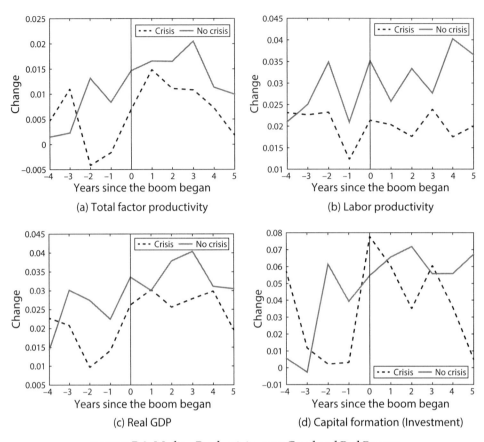

FIGURE B.2. Median Productivity over Good and Bad Booms

Table B.7. Median Productivity Growth by Country

Country	TFP	LP	TFP	LP	TFP		LP	
	Booms		No Booms		Bad B.	Good B.	Bad B.	Good B.
United States	0.90%	2.11%	0.24%	1.47%	1.16%	0.73%	1.92%	2.93%
United Kingdom	1.11%	2.61%	−0.79%	2.43%	1.07%	1.76%	2.49%	4.19%
Austria	1.12%	2.93%			1.12%		2.93%	
Belgium	0.90%	2.98%	−0.94%	1.14%	0.80%	1.07%	0.92%	3.66%
Denmark	0.84%	2.11%	0.42%	2.44%	0.84%	0.63%	0.96%	2.95%
France	0.79%	2.80%	−0.30%	2.06%	0.04%	1.24%	1.15%	3.86%
Netherlands	0.93%	1.98%	0.77%	2.28%	0.80%	1.66%	1.43%	4.23%
Sweden	0.81%	2.58%	−0.15%	1.96%	0.81%		2.58%	
Japan	0.51%	3.02%	0.33%	2.33%		0.51%		3.02%
Finland	1.46%	3.20%	2.95%	3.52%	1.53%	0.17%	3.39%	2.18%
Greece	1.01%	3.36%	−2.72%	−2.70%	0.93%	1.55%	2.94%	3.41%
Ireland	2.85%	4.63%	−0.40%	3.78%	1.98%	3.24%	4.63%	5.24%
Portugal	0.90%	2.90%	2.40%	4.65%	0.70%	3.34%	1.73%	7.58%
Spain	−0.55%	0.86%	−1.20%	4.85%	−1.12%	0.96%	0.83%	1.42%
Turkey	2.66%	4.76%	−1.49%	1.25%	1.96%	2.69%	4.08%	4.99%
Australia	0.73%	2.08%	−0.93%	1.22%		0.73%		2.08%
New Zealand	0.68%	1.49%	1.09%	3.42%		0.68%		1.49%
Argentina	2.69%	2.75%	−3.33%	−1.14%	2.33%	2.69%	3.16%	0.50%
Brazil	1.05%	3.12%	−1.49%	0.75%	0.52%	1.32%	3.70%	2.71%
Chile	2.14%	2.81%	0.47%	0.63%	2.07%	2.21%	2.22%	3.16%
Colombia	0.48%	1.35%	0.08%	1.07%	−0.05%	0.84%	0.72%	1.97%
Costa Rica	−0.24%	1.37%	0.06%	0.83%		−0.24%		1.37%
Ecuador	2.05%	4.03%	−0.63%	0.59%	2.15%	2.05%		4.03%
Mexico	−0.03%	1.55%	1.03%	0.18%	−0.38%	0.03%	0.08%	2.50%
Peru	2.17%	2.40%	−1.04%	−1.04%	−0.19%	2.34%	1.07%	3.08%
Uruguay	2.27%	0.22%	0.21%	4.63%	2.23%	3.16%	−0.20%	1.61%
Israel	0.85%	0.77%				0.85%		0.77%
Egypt	0.79%		1.97%		1.34%	0.61%		
India	2.04%		0.50%			2.04%		
Korea	1.86%	5.59%	0.24%	4.29%		1.86%		5.59%
Malaysia	1.86%	4.06%	2.13%	3.07%	2.20%	0.59%	4.15%	−0.13%
Pakistan	2.77%		0.29%			2.77%		
Philippines	0.01%		0.96%		0.01%	0.35%		
Thailand	2.61%	3.76%	0.81%	1.60%	2.64%	2.56%	3.73%	3.79%

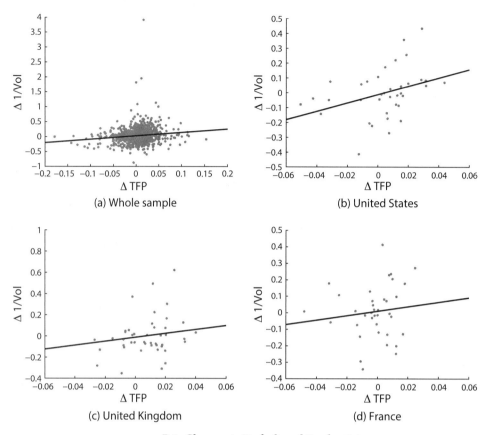

FIGURE B.3. Changes in Default and Productivity

NOTES

Chapter 1. Crises, Credit, and Macro Facts

1. Later, we also use the Bank for International Settlements (BIS) "Total Credit Statistics." The BIS provides data on credit to households and credit to corporations. As we discuss later, however, this panel data is not as complete as the World Bank series on credit.

2. For example, Jorda, Schularick, and Taylor (2011) study 14 developed countries over 140 years (1870–2008) and conclude that "credit growth emerges as the single best predictor of financial instability." Laeven and Valencia (2012) study 42 systemic crises in 37 countries over the period 1970 to 2007 and conclude, "Banking crises are . . . often preceded by credit booms, with pre-crisis rapid credit growth in about 30 percent of crises." Desmirguc-Kunt and Detragiache (1998) obtain the same result using a multivariate logit model in a panel of 45–65 countries (depending on the specification) over the period 1980–1994. Other examples include Gourinchas and Obstfeld (2012), Claessens, Kose, and Terrones (2011), Schularick and Taylor (2012), Reinhart and Rogoff (2009), Borio and Drehmann (2009), Gourinchas, Valdes, and Landerretche (2001), Kaminsky and Reinhart (1999), Hardy and Pazarbasioglu (1991), and Goldfajn and Valdez (1997).

3. As the HP filter is forward looking, for example, it does not consider the initial and the final phases of a credit expansion as part of a boom, potentially missing related changes in other macro variables during those phases.

4. The subsamples for crisis and non-crisis booms are small, as shown in Table 1.2, so there may be concerns about the power of the test. Resampling by randomly selecting pairs (a bootstrap) and repeating the test shows that the null is rejected with more confidence, confirming that the differences in the data do indeed exist.

5. The variable "Pt Gnt'd" refers to patents granted from the World Intellectual Property Organization (http://www.wipo.int/en/statistics/patents/).

6. As we run the regressions conditional on being in a boom, positive changes in productivity should predict good booms, and the coefficient should be the same but with the opposite sign.

7. Since introducing fixed effects into a logit model has well-known problems, such as the incidental parameter problem (see Arellano and Hahn 2007 and Greene 2004), we also run a linear probability model (LPM) to assess the relevance of country fixed effects.

8. The marginal effects are the average change in the conditional expectation function implied by the model. See the discussion in Angrist and Pischke (2009).

9. We show here the logit specification, but the same holds for LPM regressions.

10. The models presented in the next chapters do not depend on what kind of credit is being produced during the boom. For example, it could be mortgages.

Chapter 2. Collateral and Information

1. In this chapter, to keep things manageable, we study a single-sided information problem (only lenders have the chance to acquire information about the collateral). In the next chapter we will extend the model

to allow both borrowers and lenders to be able to acquire information about collateral. At that time we will discuss what changes this brings to the model and why they are important.

2. The positive root for the solution of $pC = \gamma/(1-p)(1-q)$ is irrelevant since it is greater than p^H, and then firms are not credit, but technologically, constrained, just borrowing K^*.

3. See the description of subprime mortgage-backed securities in Gorton (2010).

Chapter 3. Credit Booms and Financial Crises

1. Still, our results are robust since the information dynamics that we focus on remain an important force in the other equilibria we ruled out, as long as the price of land increases with p. In the appendix of Gorton and Ordoñez (2014), we discuss the multiplicity of land prices.

2. In the appendix of Gorton and Ordoñez (2014), we can characterize the competitive environment to sustain this assumption on the bargaining power and trading protocol of land.

3. To guarantee that all land is traded, households should have enough resources to buy good land, $\overline{K} > C$, and they should be willing to pay C for good land even when facing the probability that it may become bad next period, with probability $(1-\lambda)$. Since this fear is the strongest for good land, the sufficient condition is enough persistence of collateral, $\lambda(K^*(qA-1)+C) > C$.

Chapter 4. Technology and Financial Crises

1. The assumption that active firms are those for whom $p > 0$ is just imposed for simplicity and is clearly not restrictive. If we add a fixed cost of operation, then it would be necessary to have a minimum amount of funding to operate, and firms having collateral with small but strictly positive beliefs p would not be active either.

2. If $\gamma_b p(qA-1) > \gamma_l$ (as it was in the case in Chapter 3), in Figure 2.1, with $\gamma_b = \infty$, the figure is identical but the dotted line intercepts the horizontal axis at $p > 0$.

3. The positive root for the solution of $pC = \gamma/(1-p)(1-q)$ is irrelevant since it is greater than p^H, and then it is not binding given all firms with collateral that is good with probability $p > p^H$ can borrow the optimal level of capital K^* without triggering information acquisition.

4. Chapter 2 showed the alternative in which $\gamma_l < \gamma_b p(qA-1)$, where we assumed $\gamma_b = \infty$.

5. We have assumed a particular process for idiosyncratic shocks that generates a three-point belief distribution, but endogenous cycles exist as long as there is mean reversion in any such process. As soon as there is mean reversion and information is not acquired, beliefs will tend to concentrate around the average quality of land, $\widehat{p}$, regardless of the specific process of idiosyncratic shocks. As soon as the threshold p^* crosses $\widehat{p}$ a positive measure of land will be affected, creating a crisis-like event. The longer the economy is in a boom without information acquisition the larger will be the affected measure of land.

6. Ordoñez and colleagues (2018) study how an economy that becomes more volatile hinders the use of collateral to signal the quality of borrowers, hence magnifying the importance of endogenizing economic volatility in relation to the use of collateral. In their work the friction is not about information about collateral but instead information about the borrower.

7. The impact of these technologies has been studied by economic historians and growth economists. See, e.g., Kendrick (1961), Abramovitz (1956), Gordon (2010), and Shackleton (2013). These high-impact technologies have been formalized as General Purpose Technologies (GPTs), whose introduction affects the entire economy. There is now a large literature on GPTs. See, e.g., Helpman (1998), David (1990), and Bresnahan and Trajtenberg (1995). The eleven-year average length of credit booms is roughly consistent with the diffusion of GPTs.

8. Asset-backed commercial paper is short-term debt issued by an asset-backed commercial paper conduit, which is a managed special purpose vehicle that holds asset-backed securities.

9. See Bernanke et al. (2011) and Bertaut et al. (2012).

10. See Gourinchas and Jeanne (2012), chapter 3 of IMF (2012), and Caballero, Farhi, and Gourinchas (2017).

11. A "dealer bank" is authorized to buy and sell government securities. Here it refers to what were called the investment banks prior to the crisis. During the crisis, they became commercial banks.

12. This view is consistent with Eichengreen and Michener (2003).

13. Atkeson and colleagues (2013) define the distance-to-insolvency in period t by $DI_t = \left(\frac{V_{At} - V_{Bt}}{V_{At}} \right) \frac{1}{\sigma_{At}}$, where V_{At} and V_{Bt} are the market value of the assets and liabilities future cash flows, respectively, while σ_{At} is the standard deviation of innovations to V_{At}. They also define the distance-to-default by $DD_t = \left(\frac{V_{At} - V_A^*}{V_{At}} \right) \frac{1}{\sigma_{At}}$, where V_A^* is the threshold asset value below which the firm defaults. As these components are difficult to measure in the data, they use a structural model of cash flows and show that the inverse of equity volatility is between these two measures, $DI_t \leq \frac{1}{\sigma_{Et}} \leq DD_t$, and that when creditors are quick in forcing an insolvent firm into default, DI and DD are close to each other and $\frac{1}{\sigma_{Et}}$ is a good proxy of the firm's financial distress.

Chapter 5. The Crisis Prevention Role of Stock Markets

1. The role of having the endowment of numeraire arriving at the end of the period for middle-aged agents, instead of at the beginning of the period as for young agents, is just to assign the role of lenders only to young agents and the role of land buyers only to middle-aged, so not to confuse who does what.

2. This variable is related to the cross section of firms' stock return volatility: *CsVol*, and are highly correlated, 0.96. Hence, we will restrict attention to *CsAvg* in the remainder of the book.

3. Fragility is essentially a measure of economy-wide bankruptcy risk. There is a history of research that shows that firms are increasingly prone to bankruptcy leading up to a recession. Burns and Mitchell (1946) show that the liabilities of failed non-financial firms is a leading indicator of recession. Also see Zarnowitz and Lerner (1961). As mentioned above, Gorton (1988) shows that when the unexpected component of this variable spiked there was a banking panic during the U.S. National Banking Era, 1863–1914. There was never a panic without the threshold being exceeded; and the threshold was never exceeded without a panic. See the discussion in Gorton (2012), 75–77.

4. Vassalou and Xing (2004) use the Merton (1975) model measure of default risk to show that default risk is a systematic risk and that the Fama-French asset pricing factors partially reflect default risk.

5. We drop stock price data when there are less than 100 listed stocks.

6. There are recession episodes that include both crises and no-crises episodes.

7. Recall that the economy is more fragile when *Vol* increases, and so 1/*Vol* decreases.

Chapter 6. The Crisis-Fighting Role of Central Banks

1. "[Because of] the competitive format of the auctions, the TAF [Term Auction Facility] has not suffered the stigma of the conventional discount window" (Bernanke 2010, 2).

2. See Bank for International Settlements (BIS) Committee on the Global Financial System, Report 31, "Central bank operations in response to the financial turmoil," July 2008.

3. *Bloomberg L.P. v. Board of Governors of the Federal Reserve System*, 649 Supp 2d 263; *Fox News Network v. Board of Governors of the Federal Reserve System*, 639 F. Supp 2d 388. See Karlson (2010).

4. See http://www.jec.senate.gov/public/index.cfm/2009/3/03.1.09.

5. An example of collateral in our setting is the construction of a building, financed by the banker's own funds and then sold to a property manager in charge of selling the units and dealing with tenants. The quality of the construction depends on both aggregate components (i.e., an aggregate TFP shock) and idiosyncratic components (i.e., the expertise of the banker to monitor the contractor).

6. Assuming that banks can also learn the bank's collateral type does not modify the main insights, as we discussed in Chapter 5.

7. Even though the bank could use the proceeds of the good collateral to finance the project up to K^* this is not possible because the bank has to finance the project at the beginning of the period and the collateral proceeds happen at the end of the period.

8. The assumption of information leakages during crises becomes irrelevant when all banks are investigated, as the types of all collateral are revealed anyway.

9. Borrowing a bond corresponds to using the Fed's Term Securities Lending Facility; see Hrung and Seligman 2011. But bonds could also be thought of as cash or reserves.

10. See Hu and Zhang (2019), Anbil (2017), Armantier et al. (2015), Ennis and Weinberg (2013), and Furfine (2003) for evidence on the relevance of stigma for participation in discount windows.

11. We can also define the *haircut* by the ratio $1 - \frac{B}{E(p)C} = 1 - \frac{\tilde{p}}{E(p)}$. When we refer to discount, it can also be interpreted as the haircut of government bonds.

12. Here we focus on a situation with no bank purposefully choosing a run, and then $E(p) = p_L$.

13. Exploiting data on the use of discount windows and TAF programs during the recent financial crisis, Hu and Zhang (2019) show that (1) banks participating in discount windows were smaller and weaker and (2) among banks participating in TAF auctions, those with worse collateral bid the highest for funds. These findings are consistent with our implication that only banks under serious distress and bad collateral are willing to pay the discount, and then stigma is an endogenously determined cost.

14. We thank a referee for suggesting this example.

15. No participation should always involve a run, otherwise all banks would choose not to participate and depositors would indeed prefer to run, not an equilibrium.

16. If $\tilde{p}_T < \tilde{p}_I$, for all discount levels $\tilde{p}_T < \tilde{p} < \tilde{p}_I$, there is full participation under transparency and no participation under opacity. With opacity, if all banks were participating, depositors would not run and deviating to no participation is profitable, making this equilibrium unsustainable. In contrast, with transparency the alternative option of not participating always triggers a run, turning the deviation unprofitable.

17. Notice that it is enough to use the distortion with full participation for the comparison, as the distortion from partial participation is just a convex combination between these two equations.

18. For illustration purposes we use a set of parameters such that the discount level that prevents full participation in a transparent lending facility is greater than 0.4 (i.e., $d(p_L, \tilde{p}_I) < 0.4 < d(p_L, \tilde{p}_T)$).

19. In 2009 the U.S. authorities conducted a macro stress test under the framework of the Supervisory Capital Assessment Program (SCAP) for 19 bank holding companies (66% of total U.S. banking sector). In 2010 a stress test exercise was coordinated by the Committee of European Banking Supervisors (CEBS), the ECB, and the European Commission for 91 EU banks (65% of total U.S. banking sector). The level of disclosure of these tests was higher than that of standard supervisory tests performed afterward. See details in ECB 2010.

20. See also Capie (2002). King (1936) provides a nice discussion on the industrial organization of British banking in the nineteenth century and the complicated interactions between the Bank of England and the discount houses. Also see Pressnell (1956) and Flandreau and Ugolini (2011).

Chapter 7. Final Thoughts

1. This is certainly not the case for the sovereign bonds of countries with high sovereign risk, as discussed by Cole and colleagues (2018), among others.

Appendix A. Proofs

1. Notice that this is only one possible equilibrium. If everybody believes that some banks did not borrow from the discount window, $\chi > 0$, and it may be indeed optimal for those banks not to borrow from the window. This shows how endogenous stigma may induce equilibrium multiplicity and may generate self-confirming collapses in the use of discount windows. Here we focus on the best equilibrium based on intervention and show its limitations.

BIBLIOGRAPHY

Moses Abramovitz. Resource and output trends in the United States since 1870. NBER Occasional Paper 52, 1956.

Mark Aguiar and Gita Gopinath. Emerging market business cycles: The cycle is the trend. *Journal of Political Economy*, 115(1):69–102, 2007.

Franklin Allen and Douglas Gale. Financial contagion. *Journal of Political Economy*, 108:1015–1048, 2000.

Fernando Alvarez and Gadi Barlevy. Mandatory disclosure and financial contagion. *Journal of Economic Theory*, 194:105237, 2021.

Sriya Anbil. Managing stigma during a crisis. *Journal of Financial Economics*, 130:166–181, 2017.

Haelim Anderson, Selman Erol, and Guillermo Ordoñez. Interbank networks in the shadows of the Federal Reserve Act. NBER Working Paper 27721, 2020.

Joshua D. Angrist and Jorn-Steffen Pischke. *Mostly Harmless Econometrics*. Princeton University Press, 2009.

Manuel Arellano and Jinyoung Hahn. Understanding bias in nonlinear panel models: Some recent developments. In Richard Blundell, Whitney Newey, and Torsten Persson, editors, *Advances in Economics and Econometrics*, 3:381–409. Cambridge University Press, 2007.

Olivier Armantier, Eric Ghysels, Asani Sarkar, and Jeffrey Shrader. Discount window stigma during the 2007–2008 financial crisis. *Journal of Financial Economics*, 118:317–335, 2015.

Vladimir Asriyan, Luc Laeven, and Alberto Martin. Collateral booms and information depletion. *Review of Economic Studies*, 89:517–555, 2022.

Andrew G. Atkeson, Andrea L. Eisfeldt, and Pierre-Olivier Weill. Measuring the financial soundness of U.S. firms, 1926–2012. NBER Working Paper 19204, July 2013.

Pierre Azoulay, Christian Fons-Rosen, and Joshua Graff Zivin. Does science advance one funeral at a time? *American Economic Review*, 109:2889–2920, 2019.

Scott Baker, Nicholas Bloom, and Steven Davis. Measuring economic policy uncertainty. *Quarterly Journal of Economics*, 131:1593–1636, 2016.

Robert Barsky and Eric Sims. News shocks and business cycles. *Journal of Monetary Economics*, 58:273–289, 2011.

Paul Beaudry, Dana Galizia, and Franck Portier. Putting the cycle back into business cycle analysis. *American Economic Review*, 101:1–47, 2020.

Thorsten Beck and Ross Levine. Stock markets, banks, and growth: Panel evidence. *Journal of Banking and Finance*, 28:423–442, 2004.

Jess Benhabib and Kazuo Nishimura. Competitive equilibrium cycle. *Journal of Economic Theory*, 35:284–306, 1985.

Efraim Benmelech and Nittai Bergman. Debt, information, and illiquidity. NBER Working Paper 25054, 2018.

Ben Bernanke. The Federal Reserve's balance sheet: An update. Speech at the Federal Reserve Board Conference on Key Developments in Monetary Policy, Washington, D.C., 2009.

Ben Bernanke. Committee on Financial Services, U.S. House of Representatives. http://www.federalreserve.gov/newsevents/testimony/bernanke20100210a.pdf, February 10, 2010.

Ben Bernanke. The Federal Reserve: Looking back, looking forward. http://www.federalreserve.gov/news events/speech/bernanke20140103a.htm, January 3, 2014a.

Ben Bernanke. Central banking after the great recession: Lessons learned and challenges ahead: A discussion with Federal Reserve chairman Ben Bernanke on the Fed's 100th anniversary. Brookings Institution (January), 2014b.

Ben Bernanke, Carol Bertaut, Laurie Pounder DeMarco, and Steven Kamin. International capital flows and the returns to safe assets in the United States, 2003–2007. *Financial Stability Review*, 15:13–27, 2011.

Carol Bertaut, Laurie Pounder DeMarco, Steven Kamin, and Ralph Tyron. ABS inflows to the United States and the global financial crisis. *Journal of International Economics*, 88:219–234, 2012.

Javier Bianchi and Enrique Mendoza. Optimal time-consistent macroprudential policy. *Journal of Political Economy*, 126(2):1166–1186, 2018.

Nicholas Bloom. The impact of uncertainty shocks. *Econometrica*, 77(3):623–685, 2009.

Michele Boldrin and Michael Woodford. Equilibrium models displaying endogenous fluctuations and chaos: A survey. *Journal of Monetary Economics*, 25:189–222, 1990.

Claudio Borio and Mathias Drehmann. Assessing the risk of banking crisis—revisited. *BIS Quarterly Review*, pages 29–46, March 2009.

Matthieu Bouvard, Pierre Chaigneau, and Adolfo De Motta. Transparency in the financial system: Rollover risk and crises. *Journal of Finance*, 70:1805–1837, 2015.

John Boyd, Gianni De Nicolo, and Elena Loukoianova. Banking crises and crisis dating: Theory and evidence. IMF Working Paper, 2011.

Emanuele Brancati and Marco Macchiavelli. The information-sensitivity of debt in good times and bad times. *Journal of Financial Economics*, 133:99–122, 2019.

Timothy Breshnahan and Manuel Trajtenberg. General purpose technologies: Engines of growth? *Journal of Econometrics*, 65:83–108, 1995.

Markus Brunnermeier, Gary Gorton, and Arvind Krishnamurthy. Risk topography. *Macroeconomics Annual*, 27:149–176, 2012.

Markus Brunnermeier and Yuliy Sannikov. A macroeconomic model with a financial sector. *American Economic Review*, 104:379–421, 2014.

G. Bry and C. Boschan. Cyclical analysis of time series: Selected procedures and computer programs. NBER Technical Working Paper 20, 1971.

Francisco Buera, Joseph Kaboski, and Yongseok Shin. Finance and development: A tale of two sectors. *American Economic Review*, 101:1964–2002, 2011.

Arthur F. Burns and Wesley C. Mitchell. *Measuring Business Cycles*. National Bureau of Economic Research, Inc., 1946.

Ricardo Caballero, Emmanuel Farhi, and Pierre Olivier Gourinchas. The safe assets shortage conundrum. *Journal of Economic Perspectives*, 31(3):29–46, 2017.

Forrest Capie. The emergence of the Bank of England as a mature central bank. In Donald Winch and Patrick K. O'Brien, editors, *The Political Economy of British Historical Experience, 1688–1914*, 295–315. Oxford University Press, 2002.

Forrest Capie. The emergence of the bank of england as a mature central bank. In Forrest Capie and Geoffrey Wood, editors, *The Lender of Last Resort*. Routledge, 2007.

Youseff Cassis. *Crises and Opportunities: The Shaping of Modern Finance*. Oxford University Press, 2011.

Gilbert Cette, John Fernald, and Benoit Mojon. The pre–great recession slowdown in productivity. *European Economic Review*, 88:3–20, 2016.

In-Koo Cho and David Kreps. Signaling games and stable equilibria. *Quarterly Journal of Economics*, 102:179–222, 1987.

Stijn Claessens, M. Ayhan Kose, and Marco Terrones. Financial cycles: What? how? when? IMF Working Paper No. WP/11/76, 2011.

Harold Cole, Jeremy Greenwood, and Juan Sanchez. Why doesn't technology flow from rich to poor countries? *Econometrica*, 84(4):1477–1521, 2016.

Harold Cole, Daniel Neuhann, and Guillermo Ordoñez. A Walrasian theory of sovereign debt auctions with asymmetric information. NBER Working Paper 24890, 2018.

Daniel Covitz, Nellie Liang, and Gustavo Suarez. The evolution of a financial crisis: Collapse of the asset-backed commercial paper market. *Journal of Finance*, 68:815–848, 2013.

Diane Coyle. *GDP: A Brief but Affectionate History*. Princeton University Press, 2015.

Tri Vi Dang, Gary Gorton, and Bengt Holmström. The information view of financial crises. *Annual Review of Financial Economics*, 12:39–65, 2020.

Tri Vi Dang, Gary Gorton, Bengt Holmström, and Guillermo Ordoñez. Banks as secret keepers. *American Economic Review*, 107(4):1005–1029, 2017.

Joel David, Hugo Hopenhayn, and Venky Venkateswaran. Information, misallocation, and aggregate productivity. *Quarterly Journal of Economics*, 131(2):943–1005, 2016.

Paul David. The dynamo and the computer: An historical perspective on the modern productivity paradox. *American Economic Review, Papers and Proceedings*, 80:355–361, 1990.

Paul David and Gavin Wright. General purpose technologies and surges in productivity: Historical reflections on the future of the ICT revolution. University of Oxford, Discussion papers in Economic and Social History, No. 31, 1999.

Giovanni Dell'Ariccia, Deniz Igan, Luc Laevan, and Hi Tong. Credit booms and macrofinancial stability. *Ecconomic Policy*, 31:299–355, 2016.

Asli Desmirguc-Kunt and Enrica Detragiache. The determinants of banking crises in developing and developed countries. *IMF Staff Papers*, 45:81–109, March 1998.

Warren Devine. From shafts to wires: Historical perspectives on electrification. *Journal of Economic History*, 43:347–372, 1983.

Nicholas Dimsdale and Anthony Hotson. Financial crises and economic activity in the U.K. since 1825. In *British Financial Crises since 1825*. Oxford University Press, 2014.

James Dow, Itay Goldstein, and Alexander Guembel. Incentives for information production in markets where prices affect real investment. *Journal of the European Economic Association*, 15:877–909, 2017.

James Dow and Gary Gorton. Stock market efficiency and economic efficiency: Is there a connection? *Journal of Finance*, 52:1087–1129, 1997.

Mario Draghi. Building stability and sustained prosperity in Europe. Speech at "The Future of Europe in the Global Economy," hosted by the City of London. http://www.bis.org/review/r130524a.pdf?frames=0, May 23, 2013.

ECB, editor. Stress-testing banks in a crisis. In *Financial Stability Review*, 117–125. European Central Bank, December 2010.

Barry Eichengreen and Kris Michener. The Great Depression as a credit boom gone wrong. BIS Working Paper No. 137, 2003.

Huberto Ennis and John Weinberg. Over-the-counter loans, adverse selection, and stigma in the interbank market. *Review of Economic Dynamics*, 16:601–616, 2013.

Selman Erol and Guillermo Ordoñez. Network reactions to banking regulations. *Journal of Monetary Economics*, 89:51–67, 2017.

Pablo Fajgelbaum, Edouard Schall, and Mathieu Taschereau-Dumouchel. Uncertainty traps. *Quarterly Review of Economics*, 132:1641–1692, 2017.

Maryam Farboodi and Peter Kondor. Rational sentiments and economic cycles. Working Paper, MIT, 2019.

Miguel Faria-e Castro, Joseba Martinez, and Thomas Philippon. Runs versus lemons: Information disclosure and fiscal capacity. *Review of Economic Studies*, 84:1683–1707, 2017.

John Fernald. Productivity and potential output before, during and after the great recession. Federal Reserve Bank of San Francisco, Working Paper 2012-18, 2012.

Alexander Field. The most technologically progressive decade of the century. *American Economic Review*, 93: 1399–1413, 2003.

Alexander Field. Technological change and U.S. productivity growth in the interwar years. *Journal of Economic History*, 66:203–236, 2006.

Alexander Field. The procyclical behavior of total factor productivity, 1890–2004. *Journal of Economic History*, 70:326–350, 2010.

Marc Flandreau and Stefano Ugolini. Where it all began: Lending of last resort and the Bank of England during the Overend-Gurney Panic of 1866. Working Paper, Norges Bank, 2011-03, 2011.

Robert Fogel, Enid Fogel, and Mark Guglielmo. *Political Arithmetic: Simon Kuznets and the Empirical Tradition.* University of Chicago Press, 2013.

Craig Furfine. Standing facilities and interbank borrowing: Evidence from the Fed's new discount window. *International Finance*, 6(3):329–347, 2003.

Simon Gilchrist, Vladimir Yankov, and Egon Zakrajsek. Credit market shocks and economic fluctuations: Evidence from corporate bond and stock markets. *Journal of Monetary Economics*, 56:471–493, 2009.

Ilan Goldfajn and Rodrigo Valdez. Capital flows and the twin crises: The role of liquidity. IMF Working Paper No. WP/97/87, 1997.

Itay Goldstein and Yaron Leitner. Stress tests and information disclosure. *Journal of Economic Theory*, 177: 34–69, 2018.

Itay Goldstein and Haresh Sapra. Should banks' stress test results be disclosed? An analysis of the costs and benefits. *Foundations and Trends in Finance*, 8:1–54, 2013.

Gita Gopinath. Lending booms, sharp reversals and real exchange rate dynamics. *Journal of International Economics*, 62:1–23, 2004.

Robert A. Gordon. Cyclical experience in the interwar period: The investment boom of the twenties. In *Conference on Business Cycles*, 163–224. NBER, 1951.

Robert J. Gordon. Revisiting U.S. productivity growth over the past century with a view to the future. NBER Working Paper 15834, 2010.

Gary Gorton. Banking panics and business cycles. *Oxford Economic Papers*, 40:751–781, 1988.

Gary Gorton. *Slapped by the Invisible Hand: The Panic of 2007.* Oxford University Press, 2010.

Gary Gorton. *Misunderstanding Financial Crises: Why We Don't See Them Coming.* Oxford University Press, 2012.

Gary Gorton and Ping He. Optimal monetary policy in a collateralized economy. Working Paper, 2020.

Gary B. Gorton, Toomas Laarits, and Andrew Metrick. The run on repo and the Fed's response. *Journal of Financial Stability*, 48:100744, 2020.

Gary Gorton, Toomas Laarits, and Tyler Muir. 1930: First modern crisis. Working Paper, New York University, 2020.

Gary Gorton, Stefan Lewellen, and Andrew Metrick. The safe asset share. *American Economic Review, Papers and Proceedings*, 102:101–106, 2010.

Gary Gorton and Andrew Metrick. Securitized banking and the run on repo. *Journal of Financial Economics*, 104:425–451, 2012.

Gary Gorton, Andrew Metrick, and Chase Ross. Who ran on repo? *AEA Papers and Proceedings*, 110: 487–492, 2020.

Gary Gorton, Andrew Metrick, and Lei Xie. An econometric chronology of the financial crisis of 2007–2008. Working Paper, Yale University, 2014.

Gary Gorton and Guillermo Ordoñez. Collateral crises. *American Economic Review*, 104(2):343–378, 2014.

Gary Gorton and Guillermo Ordoñez. Fighting crises with secrecy. *American Economic Journal: Macroeconomics*, 12(4):218–245, 2020a.

Gary Gorton and Guillermo Ordoñez. Good booms, bad booms. *Journal of the European Economic Association*, 18(2):618–665, 2020b.

Gary Gorton and Guillermo Ordoñez. The supply and demand for safe assets. *Journal of Monetary Economics*, 125:132–147, 2022.

Gary Gorton and Ellis Tallman. *Fighting Financial Crises*. University of Chicago Press, 2018.

Pierre-Olivier Gourinchas and Olivier Jeanne. Global safe assets. Working Paper, University of California, Berkeley, 2012.

Pierre-Olivier Gourinchas and Maurice Obstfeld. Stories of the twentieth century for the twenty-first. *American Economic Journal: Macroeconomics*, 4(1):226–265, 2012.

Pierre-Olivier Gourinchas, Rodrigo Valdes, and Oscar Landerretche. Lending booms: Latin America and the world. *Economia*, 1(2):47–99, 2001.

Jean-Michel Grandmont. On endogenous competitive business cycle. *Econometrica*, 53:995–1045, 1985.

William Greene. The behavior of the fixed effects estimator in nonlinear models. *Econometrics Journal*, 7:98–119, 2004.

Nezih Guner, Gustavo Ventura, and Xu Yi. Macroeconomic implications of size-dependent policies. *Review of Economic Dynamics*, 11(4):721–744, 2008.

Don Harding and Adrian Pagan. Dissecting the cycle: A methodological investigation. *Journal of Monetary Economics*, 49(2):365–381, March 2002.

Daniel Hardy and Ceyla Pazarbasioglu. Leading indicators of banking crises: Was Asia different? IMF Working Paper No. WP/91/98, 1991.

Elhanan Helpman, editor. *General Purpose Technologies and Economic Growth*. MIT Press, 1998.

Helios Herrera, Guillermo Ordoñez, and Christoph Trebesch. Political booms, financial crises. *Journal of Political Economy*, 128:507–543, 2020.

John Hicks. *A Contribution to the Theory of the Trade Cycle*. Oxford University Press, 1950.

Robert J. Hodrick and Edward C. Prescott. Postwar U.S. business cycle: An empirical investigation. *Journal of Money, Credit and Banking*, 29(1):1–16, February 1997.

Hugo A. Hopenhayn and Richard Rogerson. Job turnover and policy evaluation: A general equilibrium analysis. *Journal of Political Economy*, 101(5):915–938, 1993.

Peter Hordahl and Michael King. Developments in repo markets during the financial turmoil. *Bank for International Settlements Quarterly Review*, 37–53, 2008.

Warren Hrung and Jason Seligman. Responses to the financial crisis, treasury debt, and the impact on short-term money markets. Federal Reserve Bank of New York, Staff Report No. 481, 2011.

Yunzhi Hu and Hanzhe Zhang. Overcoming borrowing stigma: The design of lending-of-last-resort policies. Working Paper, UNC Kenan-Flager Business School, 2019.

IMF. *Global Financial Stability Report: The Quest for Lasting Stability*. International Monetary Fund, Washington, D.C, 2012.

Sebastian Infante and Guillermo Ordoñez. The collateral link between volatility and risk sharing. Working Paper, University of Pennsylvania, 2020.

Hyoek Jeong and Robert Townsend. Sources of TFP growth: Occupational choice and financial deepening. *Economic Theory*, 32(1):197–221, 2007.

Oscar Jorda, Moritz Schularick, and Alan Taylor. Financial crises, credit booms, and external imbalances: 140 years of lessons. *IMF Economic Review*, 59:340–378, 2011.

Oscar Jorda, Moritz Schularick, and Alan Taylor. The great mortgaging: Housing finance, crises, and business cycles. NBER Working Paper 20501, 2014.

Oscar Jorda, Moritz Schularick, and Alan Taylor. Leveraged bubbles. *Journal of Monetary Economics*, 76: S1–S20, 2015.

James Kahn and Robert Rich. Tracking the new economy: Using growth theory to detect changes in trend productivity. *Journal of Monetary Economics*, 54:1670–1701, 2007.

Nicholas Kaldor. A model of the trade cycle. *Economic Journal*, 50:78–92, 1940.

Graciela Kaminsky and Carmen Reinhart. The twin crises: The causes of banking and balance-of-payments problems. *American Economic Review*, 89:473–500, 1999.

Kara Karlson. Checks and balances: Using the Freedom of Information Act to evaluate the Federal Reserve banks. *American University Law Review*, 60(1):article 5, 2010.

John Kendrick. *Productivity Trends in the United States*. Princeton University Press, 1961.

Charles Kindleberger. *Manias, Panics, and Crashes: A History of Financial Crises*. Basic Books, 1978.

Charles Kindleberger. *A Financial History of Western Europe*. Oxford University Press, 1993.

Mervyn King. Banking—from Bagehot to Basel, and back again. Speech at the Second Bagehot Lecture, Buttonwood Gathering, New York, October 25, 2010. http://www.bis.org/review/r101028a.pdf?frames=0.

Wilfred King. *A History of the London Discount Market*. Routledge, 1936.

Nobuhiro Kiyotaki and John Moore. Credit cycles. *Journal of Political Economy*, 105(2):211–248, 1997.

Tjalling C. Koopmans. Measurement without theory. *Review of Economics and Statistics*, 29(3):161–172, 1947.

Ayhan Kose, Edward Prasad, and Marco Terrones. "Does openness to international financial flows raise productivity growth?" NBER Working Paper 14558, 2008.

Arvind Krishnamurthy and Annette Vissing-Jorgensen. The aggregate demand for treasury debt. *Journal of Political Economy*, 120:233–267, 2012.

Per Krusell and Alisdair McKay. News shocks and business cycles. *Federal Reserve Bank of Richmond Economic Quarterly*, 96(4), 2010.

Finn E. Kydland and Edward C. Prescott. Business cycles: Real facts and a monetary myth. *Quarterly Review, Federal Reserve Bank of Minneapolis*, 14(2):3–18, 1990.

Luc Laeven and Fabian Valencia. Systemic banking crises database; an update. IMF Working Papers 12/163, International Monetary Fund, June 2012.

Edward Leamer. Housing is the business cycle. Paper delivered at the Federal Reserve Bank of Kansas City's annual Jackson Hole Symposium, 2007.

Hayne Leland. Corporate debt value, bond covenants, and optimal capital structure. *Journal of Finance*, 49: 1213–1252, 1994.

Guido Lorenzoni. Inefficient credit booms. *Review of Economic Studies*, 75(3):809–833, 2008.

Robert E. Lucas. Understanding business cycles. *Carnegie-Rochester Conference Series on Public Policy*, 5(1): 7–29, January 1977.

Alberto Martin and Jaume Ventura. Economic growth with bubbles. *American Economic Review*, 102:3033–3058, 2012.

Kiminori Matsuyama. Aggregate implications of credit market imperfections. In *NBER Macroeconomics Annual*, 2007.

Enrique Mendoza and Marco Terrones. An anatomy of credit booms: Evidence from macro aggregates and micro data. NBER Working Paper 14049, 2008.

Enrique G. Mendoza, Vincenzo Quadrini, and José-Víctor Ríos-Rull. Financial integration, financial development, and global imbalances. *Journal of Political Economy*, 117(3):371–416, 2009.

Robert Merton. On the pricing of corporate debt: The risk structure of interest rates. *Journal of Finance*, 29: 449–470, 1975.

Atif Mian and Amir Sufi. *House of Debt*. University of Chicago Press, 2014.

Atif Mian, Amir Sufi, and Emil Verner. Household debt and business cycles worldwide. University of Chicago, Working Paper, 2016.

John Mills. On credit cycles and the origin of commercial panics. *Transactions of the Manchester Statistical Society*, 8:9–40, 1868.

Wesley C. Mitchell. *Business Cycles*. University of California Press, 1913.

Wesley C. Mitchell. *Business Cycles: The Problem and Its Setting*. NBER, 1927. http://www.nber.org/books /mitc27-1.

Joel Mokyr. *Twenty-Five Centuries of Technological Change: A Historical Survey*. Harwood Academic Publishers, 1990.

Guillermo Ordoñez. Fragility of reputation and clustering in risk-taking. *Theoretical Economics*, 8(3):653–700, 2013a.

Guillermo Ordoñez. The asymmetric effects of financial frictions. *Journal of Political Economy*, 121:844–895, 2013b.

Guillermo Ordoñez. Confidence banking and strategic default. *Journal of Monetary Economics*, 100:101–113, 2018a.

Guillermo Ordoñez. Sustainable shadow banking. *AEJ: Macroeconomics*, 10(1):33–56, 2018b.

Guillermo Ordoñez, David Perez Reyna, and Motohiro Yogo. Leverage dynamics and credit quality. *Journal of Economic Theory*, 183:183–212, 2019.

Harry Oshima. The growth of U.S. factor productivity: The significance of new technologies in the early decades of the twentieth century. *Journal of Economic History*, 44:161–170, 1984.

Juan Ospina and Harald Uhlig. Mortgage-backed securities and the financial crisis of 2008: A post mortem. NBER Working Paper 24509, 2018.

Sunyoung Park. The size of the subprime shock. Working Paper, 2011.

Max Planck. *Scientific Autobiography and Other Papers*. Philosophical Library, 1968.

Ian Plenderleith. Review of the Bank of England's provision of emergency liquidity assistance in 2008–2009. Presented to the Bank of England, October 2012.

Edward Prescott. Can the cycle be reconciled with a consistent theory of expectations. Working Paper, Minneapolis Federal Reserve Bank, 1983.

Leslie Pressnell. *Country Banking in the Industrial Revolution*. Clarendon Press, 1956.

Vincenzo Quadrini. Entrepreneurship, saving and social mobility. *Review of Economic Dynamics*, 3(1):1–40, 2000.

Daniel Raff. Making cars and making money in the interwar automobile industry: Economies of scale and scope and the manufacturing behind the marketing. *Business History Review*, 65:721–753, 1991.

Romain Ranciere, Aaron Tonell, and Frank Westermann. Systemic crises and growth. *Quarterly Journal of Economics*, 123:359–406, 2008.

Carmen Reinhart and Kenneth Rogoff. *This Time Is Different: Eight Centuries of Financial Folly*. Princeton University Press, 2009.

Carmen Reinhart and Kenneth Rogoff. Banking crises: An equal opportunity menace. *Journal of Banking and Finance*, 37:4557–4573, 2013.

Björn Richter, Moritz Schularick, and Paul Wachtel. When to lean against the wind. *Journal of Money, Credit and Banking*, 53:5–39, 2021.

Moritz Schularick and Alan Taylor. Credit booms gone bust: Monetary policy, leverage cycles and financial cycles, 1870–2008. *American Economic Review*, 102(2):1029–1061, 2012.

Joseph Schumpeter. Mitchell's: Business cycles. *Quarterly Journal of Economics*, 45:150–172, 1930.

Robert Shackleton. Total factor productivity growth in historical perspective. Congressional Budget Office, Working Paper 2013-01, 2013.

Manmohan Singh and James Aitken. The (sizeable) role of rehypothecation in the shadow banking system. IMF Working Paper, WP/10/172, 2010.

Gene Smiley. *US Economy in the 1920s*. EH.net, 2008.

Robert M. Solow. *Growth Theory: An Exposition*. Clarendon Press, 1970.

George Soule. *Prosperity Decade: From War to Depression: 1917–1929*. Holt, Rinehart and Winston, 1947.

Ludwig Straub and Robert Ulbricht. Endogenous uncertainty and credit crunches. Working Paper, Harvard University, 2017.

Stijn Van Nieuwerburgh and Laura Veldkamp. Learning asymmetries in real business cycles. *Journal of Monetary Economics*, 53:753–772, 2006.

Maria Vassalou and Yuhang Xing. Default risk in equity returns. *Journal of Finance*, 59(2):831–868, 2004.

Laura Veldkamp. Slow boom, sudden crash. *Journal of Economic Theory*, 124:230–257, 2005.

Lei Xie. The seasons of money: ABS/MBS issuance and the convenience yield. Working Paper, Yale University, 2012.

Victor Zarnowitz and Lionel J. Lerner. Cyclical changes in business failures and corporate profits. In *Business Cycle Indicators*, 1:350–385. National Bureau of Economic Research, 1961.

INDEX

Asset prices, 149

Bagehot's Rule, 143
Balanced growth paths, 69
Banks, 149; comment on the absence of banks in the models, 5, 25; runs on, 124–128; and shadow banking, 75; transformation of banking system, 75–77
Beliefs: dispersion of, 44–45, 98–99, standard deviation of, 45
Business cycle: Burns and Mitchell and, 111; conceptualizations of, 111; definition of, 112–113; deviations from trend, 111; duration of cycles, 113; endogenous, 72–73, information measures over, 114–115; Robert Lucas and, 3, 111; NBER and, 111; shocks and, 112

Central banks: lending facilities during crisis, 121, 128–130; opacity and, 120; response to a crisis, 120
Collateral: choice of, 31–32; complexity of, 34; design of, 32; discussion of "land" as, 24; evolution of beliefs about, 38, 41; good and bad, 23; haircuts on, 78; information production about, 24; pooling and tranching, 32–34; pooling of good and bad, 43; positive productivity shocks and, 55; scarcity of, 119
Confidence: opacity and, 120; restoring, 120
Credit booms: compared to non-boom periods, 12–13; definition of, 11–12; detrending and, 12; dispersion of beliefs about quality, 44; lower frequency than usually studied, 20; not rare, 10; start of, 15–16; and technology shocks, 15–16; types of credit granted, 17–19; with and without crises compared, 13

Default: of firms during bad booms, 83–84, 114–115

Deposit insurance, 3, 4, 143–145, 150
Discount window. *See* Lending facilities

Financial crises: confusion due to central bank, 9; definition of, 2, 5, 9; ending with opacity or transparency, 137–142; incidence of, 8; information event, 5, intrinsic part of macroeconomic movements, 10; not rare, 8–9; practical definition, 8–9; and productivity growth, 13–16; start of, 9–10; triggered by fear of information acquisition, 5
Financial Crisis of 2007–2008, 1; case of a bad boom, 75–80; panic, 79; positive productivity shock, 77, 80; shock size, 37; start of, 79
Financial intermediaries. *See* Banks.
Firm defaults: more in bad booms, 83–84
Fragility, 43; endogeneity of tail risk, 37, measure of, 107–108, over good booms and bad booms, 84

Great Depression, 3–4; banks run on themselves, 4; big shock, 3; Robert Lucas and, 3–4; and National Income and Product Accounts, 150; Edward Prescott and, 4
Gross domestic product: grows less during bad booms, 84–85
Growth accounting, 63–66

Haircuts on repo. *See* Repo

Information: and crises, 43; depreciation of, 37–38, 98; measures over business cycles, 107–108, 114–115; opacity and transparency, 38; time-varying, 53
Information-insensitive and information-sensitive debt, 2, 26ff., 58, 60

Kiyotaki and Moore, 25

191